THE MAKING OF
ROMAN ITALY

ASPECTS OF GREEK AND ROMAN LIFE

General Editor: Professor H. H. Scullard

THE MAKING OF ROMAN ITALY

E. T. Salmon

THAMES AND HUDSON

Printed in Great Britain by The Pitman Press, Bath
Monochrome illustrations printed in Great Britain
by BAS Printers Ltd, Over Wallop, Hampshire.

CONTENTS

LIST OF ILLUSTRATIONS

Maps

Sources of Illustrations

Fototeca Unione 5, 8; A, Giuliani 4; Istituto Centrale per il catalogo e la Documentazione 35; Istituto di Topografia Antica, University of Rome 1; Professor N. Lamboglia 40; Museo Nazionale Archaeologico, Chieti 15, 34; Josephine Powell 36; Professor H. H. Scullard 3; UDF La Photothèque 2, 9, 11, 12, 14, 18, 20, 24, 25, 45, 46.
Maps drawn by Bryan Woodfield.

PREFACE

For more than a quarter of a century now the peoples of Italy that Rome brought under her influence and dominion have been steadily acquiring a new and important historical reality; and an ever-growing stream of studies on various aspects of their life and cultures has contributed markedly to the clarity and substance of our understanding of the Roman Republic. It shows no sign of drying up. As this book went to press, Pallottino's *Genti e culture dell'Italia preromana* was due to appear; and it seems certain that Caltabiano's recent monograph on the 'Hannibalic' coins of Bruttian Petelia will inspire many more definitive studies of coinage issues in non-Roman Italy.

So far, however, relatively little has been written in English on the new developments and the time seems opportune for a survey in that language of the growth of Roman preponderance in the light of its effects upon the Italian tribes and peoples down to the time of their absorption by Augustus' unified Roman state.

Dates throughout are BC unless otherwise stated and localities, so far as possible, are called by their ancient names. No general bibliography has been listed since one can be easily compiled from the works cited in the notes. The plates document non-Roman Italy, but do not illustrate the Etruscans or Italiotes, for whom material of this sort is plentifully available.

I must stress here my great indebtedness to the learned authors of the remarkable *Popoli e civiltà dell'Italia antica* and to La Regina, De Benedittis, Gabba, Bianchi-Bandinelli and a host of other scholars in Italy, to Galsterer, Zanker and their fellows in Germany, to Heurgon, Humbert and Morel in France, and to Frederiksen, Brunt and Toynbee in Great Britain.

This book owes much to discussions with other scholars. It is not possible to list them all, but I am grateful to each of them; and I am particularly obliged to Professor H. H. Scullard for his comments and suggestions. I also wish especially to thank Dr A. G. McKay in Hamilton and Dr Franco Bonacina in Rome for their friendly encouragement and practical assistance.

Greatly appreciated are the unfailing helpfulness of the librarians at the Institute for Classical Studies in London and the obliging competence and alertness of the publishing team at Thames and Hudson.

Hamilton, Canada 1981   E. T. Salmon

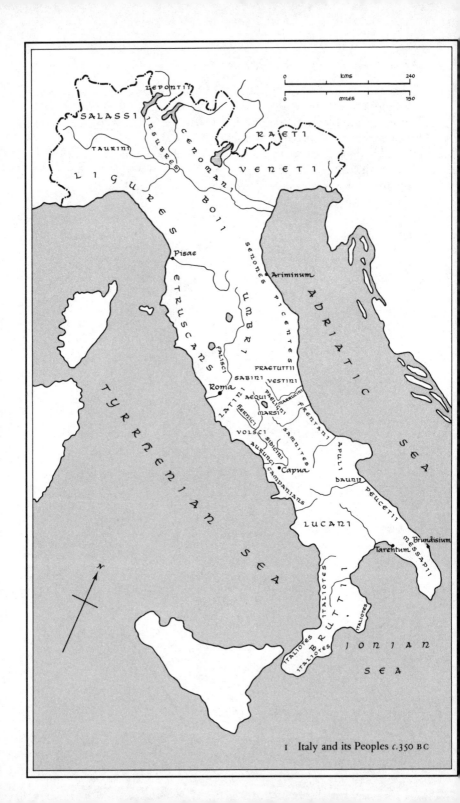

1 Italy and its Peoples *c.*350 BC

CHAPTER I

THE PEOPLES OF
ITALY *c.*350 B C[1]

The success of the Romans in inducing other peoples to adopt their language and culture is one of the momentous achievements of history. Because of it much of Europe, Africa, Asia and the New World still speaks some form of Latin, and this has important implications for patterns of thought and modes of behaviour. Yet there might have been no world-wide dissemination of Latin had it not been for the romanization in the first place of Italy, a process that was both long and difficult.[2] The Romans had to overcome large and formidable obstacles, and it is the aim of the present study to explain how and why they succeeded.

The history of Rome dates from the Iron Age, and it begins with the burgeoning of some small settlements and their amalgamation, traditionally on the Palatine Hill in the eighth century, into a single community.[3] Their language was presumably a primitive form of Latin, but even as late as 500 Latin was far from being a widely spoken tongue. It was to be heard only in Latium (=? 'the broad land'), the region that lies between the Appennine mountains and the Tyrrhenian Sea and is bounded on the north by the river Tiber and on the south by the headland of Monte Circeo.[4] Latium proper (*Latium Vetus*) was a comparatively small area, and even there the Latin-speakers' control was far from unchallenged: as late as the fourth century Aequi, Hernici, Sabini and Volsci were disputing possession of it with the Romans and Latini.

Beyond Latium there was a large number of languages and dialects, expressive of as many peoples, cultures and customs, at least one of them not even Indo-European.[5]

Yet by AD 14, when Rome's first emperor died, Italy was not only politically united, but also to a great extent culturally homogeneous; and this was true of upper Italy as well as of the peninsula proper. As the emperor Claudius noted in AD 48, Italy had been pushed forward as far as the Alps and its regions, tribes and individual inhabitants fashioned into a single nation.[6]

For this remarkable achievement, contrasting so sharply with anything that the history of the Greeks can show, many factors were responsible – geographical, military, political, economic and social. It was the peculiar virtuosity of the Romans for combining and exploiting all their opportunities that enabled them to conquer the difficulties of a rugged, mountainous country and the resistance of tough, in some cases highly cultivated peoples, and plant their Latin imprint indelibly upon the Saturnian land.

It was not until the fourth century that romanization really began to gather momentum, and by then Rome had been in existence for at least four hundred years. These were the four centuries when the Romans themselves and the various peoples that they were to encounter on their road to supremacy in Italy were in process of formation and development. Rome had used the four centuries to ensure her own survival and assert her dominance of Latium. What the other peoples had been doing, however, is very obscure. Only the colonial Greeks in the southern coastal regions have left written accounts of their activities; and even these Italiote records are late, sketchy, and at times untrustworthy.

Archaeology helps to make up for the lack of written material, but only a few legends and scattered documents survive to help elucidate it. One thing that is possible is reasonably confident identification of the different Italian peoples in the fourth century and the areas in which they lived, even though the only clues to the origins of most of them are the languages they spoke and the few traditions about them casually mentioned by ancient authors.

Information of this sort, however, even when accurate, is of only limited usefulness. Interesting though it may be to discover the ultimate provenance of a people, it would be far more edifying and significant to trace its formation. Unfortunately complete and reliable knowledge of how and why the divers peoples of Italy came to be what they were is usually beyond reach. Details of their remoter past and of their development within their historical habitats and the tale of their early dealings with one another, or even with Rome are irretrievable. Even exact and precise delimitation of their respective territories at any given period is seldom possible;[7] and the languages that they spoke are also not known in every case.

Nevertheless, the overall picture is clear of an Italy inhabited *c.*350

by a large number of tribes that differed widely in size, speech, culture and other ways; and a review of them will give some idea of the diversity that Rome ultimately fused into a unity.[8] So far as is possible they are listed in the order of their submission to her.

By 350 ROME herself had become the largest single power in Latium, but her growth had not been without its setbacks. For more than a century after the fall of the Roman Monarchy c.500, the infant Republic had difficulty in holding its own against the many threatening enemies. But in 396 the conquest and annexation of Etruscan Veii virtually doubled the power and territory of Rome at one stroke and made her mastery of Latium seem imminent. Instead it was disaster that ensued. In 386 marauding Celts captured and plundered the city;[9] and although Rome's recovery from the Gallic sack was rapid, it took some thirty years to rebuild the strength needed for a renewal of expansion.

Fusion with weaker neighbours accounts for the growth of Rome in her earliest days. The limits of the Ager Romanus, the territory over which the Roman state exercised sovereignty, were simply pushed forward and the conquered natives amalgamated with the Romans. There were, however, physical limits to unsophisticated incorporation of this sort. Once Rome had expanded beyond what came to be called the Ager Romanus Antiquus,[10] the size of a community, or its distance from Rome, or its willingness to become a dependant made such coalescing inadvisable, and from then on the standard Roman practice was to reduce conquered states to subjection by mulcting them of territory and forcing them to become 'allies'.[11]

The land Rome confiscated was usually subdivided, in whole or in part, and distributed to individual members of the Roman citizen body, mostly but not exclusively lacklands.[12] The selected beneficiaries of such viritane distributions (to individuals) were called *coloni*. After getting their plots of land these settlers were registered in the Roman rustic Tribes,[13] either in the seventeen already existing in 495 or in the new Tribes that were created in pairs from time to time (in 387 and later) to provide for Romans resident in rural Italy.

These settlers were responsible for the growth of small centres, called *fora* (market towns) or *conciliabula* (meeting-places), and there they could come together to gossip, discuss and decide matters of local interest, and no doubt learn of the doings of the Assemblies, Senate and magistrates in Rome. No *forum* or *conciliabulum* was large enough or sufficiently developed to be a self-governing corporate entity, complete with its own assembly, council and other appurtenances of autonomy; its officials, such as the *aediles* who policed the markets, were of restricted and purely parochial competence.[14]

Most of the *coloni* must have been *proletarii* (that is, paupers not allowed to serve in the Roman legions). By receiving allotments these now became *assidui* (small proprietors) and were henceforth eligible for service. They thus increased Roman military strength. But, in view of the primitive communications of those days, it was not easy to supervise and administer them on their scattered holdings or to levy and defend them. They could not participate effectively in the popular Assemblies at Rome, where attendance was normally out of the question for peasants of the periphery even when their land was no more than twenty miles away from the Capitol. Thus they tended to loosen the compact cohesiveness of the Roman body politic. But they had not much weakened its solidarity as early as the fourth century. Indeed *c.*350 the civic solidarity of the Romans was exceptionally strong, for the plebeians had recently been made eligible for the highest offices of the Roman state and their great families were about to make their remarkable contribution to Roman public life, and to its unity of purpose.

By 350, in fact, Rome was a power very much to be reckoned with in peninsular Italy, one with which the Samnite League and even an overseas power, like the great maritime state of Carthage, was willing to sign treaties of full equality, and one which now began to impinge on the consciousness of the Greeks, whose writers noted with some surprise that the strong city that had survived and swiftly recovered from its sack by the Gauls resembled one of their own city-states.[15] This was the city that was poised and ready to make itself the undisputed power in Latium.

Latium was in a very real sense the homeland of the LATINI, since it was there that they had formed themselves into a body with distinguishing characteristics of its own. But they were politically fragmented into a number of separate small communities (*populi*),[16] some of which had special identifying ethnic epithets of their own: the Latini of Lavinium were known as Laurentes and those of Ardea as Rutuli, and similarly the Romans called themselves Quirites. But every *populus Latinus* spoke Latin, even if with local peculiarities; and all Latini closely resembled Romans.[17] In fact, the Romans regarded the Latini as their own ancestors, had similar daily habits, shared their custom of usually cremating their dead, worshipped the same gods, and jointly celebrated religious festivals with them. Roman and Latin values and principles were sufficiently akin for inter-marriage, contractual dealings, intermigration and even inter-changes of citizenship to occur.[18] Political evolution had also been very similar. By 500 every *populus Latinus* had become, like the *populus Romanus*, a small republic; and although the Romans preferred praetors (later consuls) as their chief magistrates and the Latini dictators, by 350 the Romans were occasionally appointing dictators, and some Latin communities were using praetors.[19]

Physical proximity, linguistic likeness and cultural community failed to fuse Romans and Latini into a single state.[20] The sense of identity was embryonic, and political integration was slow in coming. The practices associated with the Alban Mount, Lake Nemi and the Aventine Hill and the sanctuaries at Lavinium, Gabii, Satricum and elsewhere indicate that the speakers of Latin could co-operate in sacral associations. But spiritual affinity did not bring political unity. There was no federal union. On the contrary, the ancient tradition preserves stories of constant bickering and fighting for hundreds of years, and Romans and Latini went their separate political ways.

By the fifth century, however, in an effort to promote mutual security, the Latini had organized themselves as a Latin League. The *populi Latini* composing it cannot be certainly identified; in later times they were called the Prisci Latini, a blanket term that fails to particularize. In any case by 350 the number of independent *populi* had shrunk from what it had once been, since smaller units had been consolidated into larger. The Romans had not been the only Latin *populus* to engulf smaller neighbours. Praeneste had ended the independent existence of eight and Tibur of two communities in its immediate vicinity.[21] By 350 amalgamations like these had reduced the number of sovereign *populi Latini* to something less than twenty, and these included some new communities established on territory from which non-Latini had been ejected. Presumably it was these twenty states or less that then comprised the Latin League.

As early as 493 Rome and the Latin League signed a military alliance, the Foedus Cassianum, in order to repel invaders of alien tongue who were pressing into Latium from the central Appennines. Throughout the fifth and much of the fourth century these intruding Volsci and Aequi exerted well-nigh irresistible pressure, and the

Romans and Latini needed the help of the Hernici, themselves probably an earlier wave of invaders, to contain them. It was not until c. 350 that Latium seemed reasonably secure. By then the Aequi had been driven back into the mountains from which they came and the Volsci, although not ejected, were visibly in decline.

A major factor in the success of the Latin-speakers had been their already mentioned habit of setting up new communities in areas from which the invaders had been expelled.[22] These were the so-called Latin Colonies (coloniae Latinae). After liberating a district the Romano-Latin allies peopled it with coloni who received allotments of land.[23] These coloni differed from the like-named beneficiaries of Roman viritane distributions in that from the outset they were organized as a functioning and sovereign community, with its own organs of government and magistrates and with its own urban centre (oppidum), usually located at a strategic and defensible strong-point. In all, ten or more populi Latini seem to have been created or re-created in the guise of Latin Colonies in the fifth and early fourth centuries, and their services in keeping Latium safely Latin were invaluable. As each was instituted, it joined the Latin League, which was enabled by these accretions of strength to match the growth of Rome, at least until she incorporated Veii.

The settlers in the Latin Colonies, whether originally Romans or Latini, ceased to be burgesses of their native communities, becoming instead citizens of the new city-state into which they had been recruited. The proportion of them originating from Rome evidently varied from one colonia to another, Romans preponderating in those closest to Rome, Latini in those further away. This explains what happened in 340 when the Latin states went to war with Rome. The two Latin Colonies north of Rome, Sutrium and Nepete, stood by her, whereas the two southernmost, Setia and Circeii, actually led the forces opposing her.

The Appennine mountains to the east of Latium were peopled by speakers of the so-called Osco-Umbrian languages. These are closely related Indo-European dialects, akin to Latin in structure and syntax, but differing from it in morphology and vocabulary. The dialects all derive from a common ancestor, which modern philologists usually call Italic.[24] During the Iron Age speakers of Italic had spread over the mountainous core of peninsular Italy, the ancient tradition being that they had originally been settled in an area close to where Sabine Amiternum later stood and from there had expanded over central and southern Italy by proclaiming a succession of sacred springs.[25]

The sacred spring was a religious rite that served as a safety-valve against over-population. In a given year an Italic community solemnly vowed to devote, that is to sacrifice, all its new-born creatures of the following spring to a god, almost invariably Mars; and when the spring came the fantastic sacrifice was duly carried out, except that the new-born human infants, instead of being immolated, were earmarked for emigration: on becoming adults, they had to leave their ancestral community forever and, led by an animal sacred to the god, find for themselves fresh woods and pastures new.[26] Inevitably the emigrating bands destroyed, dispossessed or fused with the natives that they settled among; and, as the experiences of the different groups varied, neither the rhythm nor the pattern of their ongoing evolution was uniform.[27] This led to their differentiation and their growth into a number of separate tribes.

Already in prehistoric times the language of the Italici had split into two main branches, Umbrian and Oscan, of which Umbrian is the more innovative and consequently the more evolved tongue. Its dialects were spoken in the more northerly and western parts of the peninsula. In the east and south dialects of the more conservative Oscan prevailed. As its speakers seem to have called themselves Safineis or something similar, a better name than Oscan for the language would be Safine.[28] The Roman name for them later was Sabelli.

By protohistoric times both Umbrian-speakers and Oscan-speakers had burgeoned into a variety of distinct and separate peoples. They all had the same linguistic background and, generally speaking, they all preferred inhumation to cremation. But they differed quite markedly in many other respects – ethnic composition, political outlook, cultural level, economic development, material well-being and martial disposition.

Speakers of Umbrian dialects pushed into Latium early, and there a group of them seem to have evolved into the HERNICI. At any rate, ancient tradition depicted the origin of the Hernici as either Sabine or Marsic, that is Umbrian, since both Sabini and Marsi were reckoned to be of Umbrian extraction; and if their name derives from *herna*, allegedly Marsic for 'stone', the tradition might be true.[29] The Hernici could then be the Umbrians of the stony country in the Appennines (? the Monti Simbruini). Proof is lacking, since they were latinized before they became literate and no specimen of their native vernacular survives.

Strabo's statement that the Hernici once lived near Lanuvium west of the Alban Hills may mean that the initial westward thrust of their Italic forbears penetrated well into Latium.[30] If so, it was repulsed, for in historical times they were settled in the eastern marches of Latium, along the upper Trerus and in the hills immediately north of that river.

Their relations with Rome were for the most part friendly. In regal times they helped the Romans defend a spur of the Esquiline Hill, which in consequence still bears the name of their chieftain, Cispius. In the fifth century, when other 'Umbrians' (Volsci and Aequi) were pressing into the western coastlands, the Hernici sought protection against them in an alliance with Rome (486).

By then long exposure to Hellenic culture had familiarized the inhabitants of Latium with the political practices of the Greek world. As a consequence the mini-state, consisting of a town-like settlement and its surrounding territory, was normal there: the Latini, as already noted, were divided into many small political organisms of this sort. Among the Hernici, too, there seem to have been a number of small urban states, the townsites of which in time came to be provided with powerful walls of massive limestone polygonals.[31] These settlements were organized in a Hernican League (? of sacral origin), which concerned itself with matters of common interest; and there are other signs of close relations, such as intermarriage and exchanges of goods. In the fourth century the League met in a *circus maritimus* on the territory of Anagnia, but information about its activities is very scanty.[32]

Another Italic group making an impression in Latium in the fifth century were the AEQUI. A surviving specimen of their language suggests that they, too, belonged to the Umbrian branch.[33] If the name of the Hernici indicates their origin among the limestone Appennines, that of the Aequi may mean that their original homeland is to be sought in the level country, that is the district immediately adjoining the northern and western fringes of the Fucine Lake.[34] Be that as it may, in the fifth century the Aequi tried to establish themselves in Latium and for a time succeeded in penetrating as far as Mount Algidus and the pass through the eastern rim of the Alban Hills. But by 430 they had shot their bolt, and the Hernici with Roman and Latin support managed to drive them back into the central Appennines. Thereafter they had their settlements in the hill country behind Tibur and Praeneste and in the upper valleys of the rivers Himella and Tolenus. They themselves came to be known as Aequicoli or Aequicolani, which may be a diminutive of contempt, signifying their inability seriously to menace Latium: it survives to this day, Cicolano being the modern name for the district in which they lived.

The toughest of the fifth-century assailants of Latium were the VOLSCI, whose name may indicate an origin in the Fucine marshlands or along the lower reaches of the river Velinus.[35] Their vernacular is demonstrably closer to Umbrian than to Oscan.[36] They were kindred of the Aequi and frequently co-operated with them; but they were a much more persistent and dangerous threat. During the fifth century they gained control of the Monti Lepini and swept on to make themselves masters of the Tyrrhenian coast from Antium to Formiae. The Latini, aided by the Romans and Hernici, ultimately managed to eject them from the Monti Lepini, to destroy some of their settlements (Pometia, Ecetra, Satricum)[37] and to contain the rest by means of powerful Latin Colonies at Cora, Signia, Norba and Setia. But a Latin Colony at Circeii c. 395 failed to break the Volscian grip on the coast of Latium and, as late as 350, Volscian settlements still existed in the interior of Latium as well, at Velitrae in the Alban Hills, at Privernum, and along the middle Liris.

By 350, however, the Volsci were definitely in decline, and already in 354 Romans and Samnites had signed a treaty, the palpable object of which was to partition Volscian territory in the valley of the river Liris. In fact, within a few years Arpinum (and also Aquinum, Atina and Casinum, if they had ever been Volscian) had passed under Samnite control and Sora under Roman. Nevertheless, Volscian towns of some consequence still remained after 350: the coast of Latium, in particular, was notorious as the domain of Volscian 'pirates'.

Like the Latini and the Hernici, the Volsci consisted of a number of self-governing republics, each with its own council (or senate) and magistrates. Local constitutions seem to have varied. Velitrae had a pair of *meddices* for its chief officials. Other communities (Arpinum, Formiae, Fundi) seem to have preferred triads of *aediles*.[38]

Among their deities the Volsci numbered Declona and Vesona, of whom the latter at least was also worshipped by other Italici. But, so far as is known, they did not organize themselves into a league, sacral or other. Each Volscian community acted independently and when one came to the aid of another it evoked comment. Such particularism, no doubt, contributed to their undoing ultimately; but throughout the fifth century the Romans found them hardy foes and evidently accorded their martial qualities high respect.[39]

In the Latium – Campania border zone that the Elder Pliny calls Latium Adjectum, the Volsci shared possession with the AUSONES, or AURUNCI as they are more commonly known.[40] These are the same people as the OSCI (or OPICI) (=? 'those who work the fields'), whose name has been given to the most widely spoken tongue in protohistoric Italy, Oscan. Oddly enough there is no proof that the Osci (Aurunci, Ausones) themselves spoke the language. It was named after them because the Romans first encountered it in the part of Italy that was traditionally territory of the Osci. In fact, by then the territory was no longer theirs: by 350 it was in the hands of the Samnites, and it was the language of this latter people that the Romans called Oscan. Modern scholars follow the Roman practice and also call the Samnite language Oscan, although Sabellian would obviously be a more appropriate name for it. What actually was the language of the Aurunci is not known: it may, or may not, have resembled Oscan.[41]

In prehistoric times the Ausones (Aurunci, Osci) occupied a much larger area of Italy: indeed for Greek poets Ausonia served as a synonym for Italia. But by 350 they had been squeezed into Latium Adjectum and had dwindled to an insignificant remnant living in three settlements (Vescia, Ausona [Aurunca], Minturnae), on or near Roccamonfina (=? Veseris) and the Mons Massicus,[42] and in Cales close to the border with Campania. Cales, at least according to Livy, was a self-governing state.

By 300 the Aurunci had ceased to be an independent people, and they were absorbed so quickly and so completely by their neighbours that virtually no trustworthy information about them has survived other than that their favourite divinity was the marine (?) goddess Marica, who was sometimes thought to be the prototype for Homer's Circe.[43]

Next to the Aurunci were the SIDICINI, a small people of whose earlier history nothing is known with certainty. As their native tongue was Oscan, it must be assumed that they were one of the peoples that formed as a result of the Iron Age diaspora of the Italici.[44] When they first emerged from the Appennines, their impetus may have carried them to the region where the rivers Liris and Trerus came together, and where the Romans later established the fortress of Fregellae.[45] If so, they failed to maintain this forward position, for by 350 they were settled more to the east on the slopes of the Roccamonfina, where their principal settlement Teanum occupied a strong and commanding position controlling the inland route between greater Latium and Campania. It was a place of consequence, later the largest town on the Via Latina, a genuine civic commonwealth comparable in size to Capua.[46] By 350 the Sidicini had completely severed their ties with the tribal Sabelli that they had left in the mountains to the east; and now *c.*350 these mountaineers threatened to repeat the earlier adventure of the Sidicini and at their expense. In alarm the Sidicini turned to Capua and to Rome for help.

The Sidicini adjoined Campania, the plain surrounding the bay of Naples, famed then as now for its beauty, its climate and its fertility. Campania was bounded by the river Savo on the north, the river Silarus on the south and the Appennine mountains on the east. To call its inhabitants Campani is to court confusion, since that Latin ethnic was usually reserved for the burgesses of Capua and its federal associates in northern Campania. To avoid ambiguity this study will use the English expression CAMPANIANS, whenever inhabitants of Campania in general are meant, and will refer to the burgesses of Capua as CAPUANI.[47]

According to the ancient tradition, Campania was inhabited in prehistoric times by the already mentioned Opici (=Osci, Ausones, Aurunci),[48] whose native tongue may possibly have been related to Oscan. Not that this means much, since the population must have been mixed then, just as it certainly was later. Campania appears to have been prosperous already in the eighth century when the Greeks founded their first authentic colony on the Italian mainland there. Cumae not only left a profound and permanent Hellenic imprint on Campania, but also made it a centre for the diffusion of greater Greek influence in many parts of Italy.[49] Greeks, however, were not the only immigrants in Campania. Etruscans were little, if at all, later in arriving, and they countered Cumae with a colony of their own at Capua. Other Greek and Etruscan settlements soon followed: Neapolis, Dicaearchia (the later Puteoli), and an Etruscan *dodecapolis*.[50] Soon, too, the Italic expansion spilled into Campania. By 500 large numbers of Oscan-speaking Sabelli from the Appennines were descending into the region. At first they spread all over Campania as farm-workers and when Etruscan power there collapsed they were able to make themselves masters of virtually all of it. Capua became Oscan-speaking, and after 423 headed a federal state that included Casilinum, Atella, Calatia and perhaps other settlements. These Campani had a common shrine at Hamae near Cumae. From 420 on Cumae, too, was under Sabellian control, as were Acerrae, Abella, Nola, Herculaneum, Pompeii, Nuceria and the towns of the Surrentine peninsula. Neapolis managed to preserve its Hellenic character; but many of even its inhabitants bore Sabellian names.[51]

The natives that the Sabelli encountered were partly exterminated, but for the most part assimilated, and the Sabelli themselves became known as Opici (Osci) after the people that formed the substratum of the population of Campania. As already pointed out, it was their language that the Romans knew as Oscan; and it now acquired an alphabet of its own, modelled closely on Etruscan writing, but making provision for Sabellian phonetic peculiarities; and this alphabet was soon taken into use by other speakers of Oscan outside Campania, such as the Sidicini, the Samnites and the Frentani.

The more developed type of civilization that the Sabelli found in Campania suffered a setback with their arrival and stagnated for a time. But they adapted to the new form of life relatively quickly, learning skills in agriculture and commerce, and accommodating themselves to urban administration and to a money economy instead of barter. Capua became the largest Oscan-speaking city anywhere, and the Campanians could fairly be regarded as the most advanced of all the Sabelli. But they had not entirely changed character. They were still very fond of gladiatorial combats (a form of entertainment that almost certainly originated amongst the Sabelli and not amongst the Etruscans, as commonly supposed). They also retained the tribal instinct for federalism. For although the Sabellian communities in Campania were city-states, like their Etruscan and Greek predecessors, they organized themselves in leagues, that of the Campani in the north headed by Capua, that of the Alfaterni in the south headed by Nuceria; while in the centre Nola and Abella collaborated for sacral purposes.[52]

In most respects, however, the Campanians had emancipated themselves completely from their more primitive ancestors to the east in the highlands of Samnium. The latter, who can henceforth be

known as Samnites, were still tough and formidable, and shortly
after 350 they became aggressive. They first threatened the Sidicini
and then Capua when it attempted to protect these. Capua appealed
to Rome for help; and although Rome had signed a treaty with the
Samnites as recently as 354 the help was forthcoming. The Romans
simply could not afford to let the Samnites get control of
Campania.[53]

Rome thus became inextricably involved with Campania and in a
struggle for supremacy with the Samnites.

The SAMNITES were the Oscan-speakers *par excellence*, so much so
indeed that all and any who had Oscan as their mother-tongue,
Sidicini, Campanians and others, were regularly called Samnites. A
better generic would be Sabelli, for by 350, thanks to many a sacred
spring, Oscan-speaking peoples dominated most of southern Italy
apart from its two extremities, and it is less confusing to reserve the
name Samnite for those of them that actually lived in Samnium, the
region bounded on the north by the river Sagrus, on the south by the
rivers Silarus and Bradanus, on the east by the Adriatic coastal zone,
and on the west by Latium and Campania.

The Samnites, as already noted, were more backward than the
Campanians. In their mountains their life was one of the hardest
simplicity. Their rugged land, although much better wooded then
than now, could not support any but a bare agrarian economy,
based largely on farming and stock-raising and featured by the use of
barter (for the Samnites did not issue coins).[54] Their shepherds
commonly practised transhumance, seeking upland pastures in the
summers and returning to the valleys in the winters.

The Samnites worshipped the great gods Jupiter and Mars and
also, as their rustic way of life demanded, rural deities such as
Mefitis, the provider of water, and Vibia, a goddess of the
underworld. But like other Italians they were affected by Greek
religious ideas, and Hellenic influences had penetrated even their
mountain fastnesses. Divine beings of Greek origin became very
popular with them, especially if they were of stalwart character, like
Hercules, Castor and Pollux. Greek influence is very obvious in the
Agnone Tablet, the most celebrated religious document from
Samnium; however, it dates from the period of Roman supremacy
(c.250).[55]

The Samnites, in general, were less accessible and more
impervious to Hellenic influences than most Italians. They did not

organize urban commonwealths, but lived in a multitude of hamlets (*vici*) and townships (*pagi*) thickly clustered in the valleys, especially those of the rivers Sagrus, Trinius and Tifernus.[56] To defend themselves and their livestock from danger they ringed many a mountain-top with massive polygonal walls. The heights selected for this purpose usually overlooked the transhumance trails and were within sight of one another for signalling. The walled enclosures could also serve as bases from which to launch counter-attacks or raids.[57]

The villages were grouped together in tribes, four of which are known. The Pentri, settled on and around the Matese massif and in the valleys of the Sagrus, Trinius and Tifernus, were the strongest. Almost equally powerful were the Hirpini, the most southerly tribe, living in the area of Beneventum. The most westerly, the Caudini, were the most affected by Hellenic influences from nearby Campania. The Carricini in northeastern Samnium were probably the smallest of the four tribes.[58] In the absence of politically self-conscious city-states, the settlements developed a strong sense of tribal solidarity.

According to the ancients, Sabellian institutions were democratic, which presumably means that the Samnites had councils (senates) and assemblies of the adult males where their leaders and other officials (*meddices*) were elected. But as only the wealthy could afford to hold office, a handful of families constituted the governing class among them, just as among the Romans.

The four tribes were loosely federated in a league, chiefly for military purposes, although presumably the league also concerned itself with other matters, such as supervision of transhumance and religious cults. According to Livy, on the eve of a crucial battle with the Romans in 293 it assembled the Samnite *corps d'élite* around a consecrated area measuring 200 feet square; and at Pietrabbondante traces have now been found of a fourth-century sacred precinct of exactly this size: a later inscription suggests that it was a shrine for all Pentri, if not for all Samnites.[59]

The military strength of the Samnite League was formidable. The hard life in Samnium produced a tough and rugged breed of men, and over-population drove them periodically into expanding. Surrounding peoples consequently found them uncouth and uncomfortable neighbours.

Bordering Campania and Samnium on the south was Lucania. It

was controlled c.350 by an Oscan-speaking population that evidently established itself there in the fifth century at the expense of natives whom the Greeks called Oenotri (=? 'wine-makers'), a name as vague as Pelasgi for the pre-Hellenic inhabitants of Greece.[60] Tradition insisted that some of these Oenotri were expelled and settled in Sicily, where they were known as Siculi, and this obviously could well have been the case. But many of them must have remained in southern Italy and fused with the Oscan-speakers to form the LUCANI.[61] Similar native admixtures must have contributed to the ethnic make-up of every Italic people, and they help to account for the differences which Strabo assures us existed amongst the various Sabellian tribes.[62]

Hellenic influences had been penetrating Lucania from early times by way of the river valleys from Magna Graecia, and the Lucani were inevitably affected. Hence, when writing their language (from right to left like other Sabelli), they employed a Greek, not the Oscan, alphabet. But apparently they were not so hellenized as to organize themselves in city-states. They constituted a federalized tribal state that issued its own coins, mostly of bronze (but some of silver), and in time of war appointed as generalissimo a 'king', that is a supreme *meddix*.[63]

At what appears to have been their principal shrine, at Rossano di Vaglio, the Lucani worshipped the very Italian Mefitis, who protected their flocks by supplying them with water.[64]

Like the kindred Samnites they were both aggressive and tough, and the Italiotes of Magna Graecia, weakened by their insensate feuding, found them difficult to repel. Velia (Elea) held out successfully, but Paestum (Poseidonia) fell shortly after 400. Belatedly the Italiotes banded together in an alliance, but in 390 the Lucani defeated the allies heavily at the river Laus, and the next year the Italiotes were again badly beaten near Caulonia by Dionysius I of Syracuse, who seems to have had an understanding with the Lucani. Thereafter the Lucani overran most of southwestern Italy, including Bruttium (the Calabria of today),[65] thus coming uncomfortably close to Syracuse itself. In 358 Dionysius' son and successor, regretting no doubt his father's shortsighted policy, had no option but to withdraw from Locri and recognize Sabellian supremacy over the entire southwest.

Almost at once, in 356 according to tradition, the Sabelli in the 'toe' broke away from their parent stock and under the name of

BRUTTII established their independence on a territory stretching from
the river Crathis on the east of the Bruttian peninsula to the river
Laus on the west.[66]

The Lucani seem to have made little effort to reincorporate the
Bruttii within their own state, possibly because they did not think it
worth while to do so. Bruttium, with its granite mountains and
dense forests, was difficult campaigning country; and its many
Greek colonies, more thickly clustered there than anywhere else in
Italy, and including such notable centres as Croton, Locri
Epizephyrii and Rhegium, rendered the maintenance of Sabellian
superiority there problematic at best. Accordingly the Lucani left the
Bruttii largely to their own devices. In fact, even though the Bruttii
managed to make themselves masters of Terina and Hipponium and
to squeeze the other Italiote settlements drastically, their Sabellian
element was never fully secure. Bruttium, significantly, was
regarded as a bilingual land, speaking Greek as well as Oscan, until
the Romans latinized it.

Like the Lucani, the Bruttii seem to have formed a federalized
tribal state: it may have consisted of twelve communities headed by
Consentia, all of them democratic in the way normal for Sabellian
entities.[67] It issued coins of gold, silver and bronze, and it probably
resembled the Lucanian tribal state in having a generalissimo in time
of war.

The Greeks that lived in and exerted so pervasive an influence on
Italy are usually known as ITALIOTES.

Greek interest in Italy was of long standing, going back to the Late
Bronze Age well before 1000. Greek tradition told of the exploits of
Achaean heroes, Heracles, Daedalus, Diomede and others, in Italy;
and archaeology has confirmed that trading-posts were established
there in Mycenaean times.[68] It is perhaps easy to over-estimate the
extent of this so-called pre-colonial Greek activity, and perhaps it
was periodically interrupted by disturbances, such as the movement
known as the Dorian Invasion of Greece. Nevertheless contact
between Greece and Italy was never entirely broken,[69] and by
protocolonial times Greek traders were probing even the most
northerly reaches of the Adriatic coast.

Colonies, however, were something more than mere trading-
posts. Whereas the latter were essentially ephemeral stop-over
points for transients in search of what was unprocurable in their
homelands, such as the metals of Etruria (and Sardinia), the colonies

were permanent settlements, each organized as a genuine city-state with its own surrounding territory capable of fully controlling its trade and commerce. Normally a colony was the result of preliminary reconnaissance and careful preparation, and was peopled with adventurous settlers under the leadership of an enterprising 'founder'. It was politically independent and sovereign from the start, but usually showed spiritual loyalty to the state (*metropolis*) from which its founder and his band had set out. It also usually preserved and paraded an account of its origin in the form of a foundation legend. Colonies began to be established in the eighth century, and the Age of Colonization lasted until *c.*600, although one or two colonies (Heraclea, Thurii) were founded as late as the fifth century. [70] Ultimately there was a large number of them dotting the coasts of southern Italy, and from the time of Timaeus on they were known, collectively, as Magna Graecia.

Already in the ninth century the sporadic Greek presence and its influence had affected many areas of Italy, and not least Etruria and Latium. But, with the development of large-scale colonization in the eighth century, relations between the native Italians and immigrant Greeks became more complex, both socially and politically, and the Greek influence grew stronger, the more so since it was so very one-sided.

The Greeks, convinced of the superiority of their own institutions and usages, scorned an environment whose vernaculars struck them as barbarous, and for long they were not greatly affected by the cultures and customs they encountered. Many of them, of course, married native women; and some of them may have found it expedient to adopt native weights and measures. [71] Nevertheless, in general, they remained immutably Hellenic, and the comparative softness of the 'barbarians' among whom they settled helped them to maintain their identity. Their colonies took root in areas where there was little skilfully organized military or political resistance and where the natives had either fled into the hinterland or were willing to accept an inferior status and ultimate hellenization. [72] Where native opposition was obstinate and determined, as in the mountains, in the Messapic region and everywhere north of Cumae, the Greeks found it impossible to found colonies.

But even those natives that preserved their independence did not reject Greek culture. They adopted and adapted it. Greek religious ideas and notions of divinity had been naturalized in the peninsula and assimilated to native beliefs even before the eighth century, and such influences gained renewed impetus when Greek city-states were brought into being on Italian soil. The oracular shrine at Cumae, for instance, came to enjoy widespread fame.

It was unquestionably the brilliance of the colonies that made the cultural hegemony possible. Throughout the seventh, sixth and fifth centuries Magna Graecia was an exceptionally advanced part of Hellas, the home of Zaleucus the law codifier, Pythagoras the mathematician and mystic, Parmenides the philosopher, Ibycus the poet, Milo the athlete, the doctors of Croton and Velia, and the engineer architects of Paestum.[73] It was the sophisticated Italiotes who introduced the alphabet and literature to Italy. Their superior and often novel techniques in a wide range of activities, from warmaking to pottery-manufacture, including commerce in its infinite variety and not least the use of coinage, were everywhere imitated and gradually came to be adopted throughout Italy.

But, like Greeks everywhere, the Italiotes could not live in peace and harmony among themselves. Class war (*stasis*) was as prevalent as in mainland Greece; and in Magna Graecia interstate rivalries were notorious. In fact, the mutual hostility of the Chalcidian, Achaean and Dorian settlements was exceptionally ferocious. In the sixth century Metapontum, Croton and Sybaris combined to wipe Siris off the map, and some years later (*c.*510) Croton meted out the same savage treatment to Sybaris. Later, in the fifth century, Thurii, created by Periclean Athens as a substitute for the destroyed Sybaris, quickly got into a furious war with Tarentum, which had sought to replace Siris with a colony at Heraclea.

Eventually the incessant quarrelling proved fatal to the Italiote city-states. It so weakened them that they became less and less able to withstand the pressure of the neighbouring 'barbarians' or the assaults of fellow-Greeks from Sicily. Their attempts to ward off the danger by combining were half-hearted and belated, and by 350 their great days were over. A few years later Tarentum was the only Italiote state capable of offering serious resistance to the rising power of Rome.[74]

Especially exposed to Greek influence, of course, was the region closest to Greece itself. This was southeastern Italy, bounded on the north by the river Fertur,[75] on the west by the Bradanus, and on the south and east by the sea. It consists of Apulia and its two appendages, Mons Garganus and the Promunturium Sallentinum (the Calabria of the Romans).

This region was already densely populated in prehistoric times by 'Oenotri' of one kind or another.[76] But even then its fertility attracted immigrants from abroad. Some of these, so it was alleged, were Achaean heroes and others were Cretans; but the overwhelming majority were evidently Iapudes (*Greek* Iapyges) from Illyria, who poured into the Sallentine peninsula in large numbers and then expanded from there to make themselves masters of the whole region.[77] As a result it became known as Iapudia (Greek Iapygia), the expression from which the Latin name Apulia probably derives, presumably by way of Oscan.

As they spread northwards towards the tableland of Apulia and the Mons Garganus, these Iapyges split into a number of separate peoples. Inscriptions from the region numbering more than three hundred[78] show that they continued to use the same common language, albeit with many local variations; but as a result of encountering various types of natives with whom they fused in widely differing proportions, they were bound to end up as a collection of distinct and divergent tribes. All alike seem to have preferred to inhume their dead.[79]

By 400 the Illyrian element seems to have been strongest in the Sallentine peninsula where three tribes emerged: the Sallentini who have given the peninsula its modern name; the Calabri who supplied the Roman name for it; and the MESSAPII who have provided modern scholars with a name for the language used by all the 'Illyrians' of southeast Italy. Messapic is an Indo-European tongue, but distinct from Greek, Oscan or Latin; it is usually assumed to be an Illyrian dialect.

The Messapian element in the tribes was less marked the further north they were. The area of the Murge, above the Tarentum–Gnathia line, was controlled as far as the river Aufidus by the PEUCETII (*Latin* Poediculi). North of the Aufidus and as far as the river Cerbalus was the country of the DAUNII.[80]

By 400, however, the great Sabellian expansion had also reached the region. Speakers of Oscan had established a bridgehead across the Fertur at Teanum Apulum and, advancing to the Cerbalus and even further south, were infiltrating the entire Tavoliere di Puglia.[81] What parts of it by 350 were Oscan and what parts Messapic cannot be determined with certainty, and doubtless bilingualism was common.[82]

Of the two generic names for the inhabitants of southeastern Italy, APULI and IAPYGES, the former seems more appropriate for the Oscan-speakers, the latter for those who spoke Messapic. The Messapic inscriptions vary in date from the late sixth to the first century, with the majority belonging to the third, and they have been found as far north as Luceria and as far west as Metapontum and even beyond. But the bulk of them come from the region below the Mons Garganus, and there no Oscan inscriptions have ever come to light. This indicates that the extreme southeast of Italy was distinctly Messapic.[83]

But it was also very hellenized. This was because of the continuous contacts with mainland Greece from prehistoric times and with the colonies of Magna Graecia in more recent days. In the region itself there were Greek trading-posts, but no formal colonies: Tarentum and Metapontum were on the outskirts of Apulia rather than actually in it, and Hydruntum, overlooking the Adriatic narrows, although very Greek in historical times, may not have begun as a true colony. Southeastern Italy was, nevertheless, saturated with Hellenic influences. Many of the towns there actually claimed an origin from Diomede or some other Achaean hero, and much Greek could probably be heard there, not presumably as a family language, but as a vehicle for culture and commerce, especially in a port like Brundisium.[84] Apulian coins, which are both many and varied, regularly bear Greek legends; and Greek certainly provided the alphabet for those with a mind to write, no matter in what language.[85] Even Latin documents, when they began, later, to appear in Apulia, sometimes contained Grecisms.[86]

The region had also learned political lessons from the Greeks. It was composed of a multiplicity of mini-states (originally petty kingdoms,[87] but by historical times mostly republics) that were constantly feuding and fighting. Some of these must have joined together in confederacies, or at least alliances, but details are lacking. Even the exact number of states is unknown. The Sallentini and the Peucetii are each credited with the usual twelve; but not even this much is recorded of the other tribes.

But, although by 350 Greek techniques and customs were influencing all aspects of life in southeastern Italy, spiritual as well as material, they had by no means effaced the Messapic culture. The *interpretatio Graeca*, so far from eliminating the indigenous gods, had merely supplied Olympian appellations for them. Thus Menzana had acquired the Greek name Zeus,[88] but he retained his native equestrian traits. Similarly in Apulia Greek heroes, stalwarts like Diomede and Calchas, seem as much Messapic as Achaean. Apulian potters, who had long kept to an independent way of shaping and decorating their vases, continued to mould many of them into big florid forms with what has been termed a peasant exuberance. Moreover, some practices that look like borrowings from the Greeks may have been nothing of the sort; Aristotle, at least, was convinced that southeastern Italy had communal meals before either Sparta or Crete.[89]

The arrival of the Sabelli reinforced the fundamentally native character of the region. By then Magna Graecia had passed its apogee and could not make so marked an effect on these sturdy newcomers. The legends on the coins of Teanum Apulum and of Daunian Ausculum, even when written in a Greek alphabet,[90] are not in a Greek dialect: they are in Oscan.

Tradition insisted that Illyrians had immigrated into other parts of Adriatic Italy besides the southeast and this is entirely plausible. Even so *c*. 350 the coast between the Mons Garganus and Picenum was regarded as Sabellian country. Immediately above the Fertur it was inhabited by a people called FRENTANI, about whom very little is recorded. Presumably they resulted from some remote sacred spring.[91] They were certainly very Oscan – in speech, in writing, in their system of weights and measures, and in their constitutional practices.[92] Admittedly those of them living between the Tifernus and the Fertur in and around Larinum, influenced no doubt by developments in neighbouring Apulia, were sufficiently un-Oscan to have set up their own independent city-state.[93] But in general the Frentani, whose territory extended almost to the mouth of the river Aternus, were like most Sabelli content with a tribal organization. No doubt *meddices* administered their *pagi* and *vici*, but the only officials epigraphically attested are *kenzsur*.[94]

Their territory was hilly, but reasonably well watered and fertile and, while they were not affluent enough to import objects of much value, not even Apulian vases, their bronze coins indicate an economy somewhat more advanced than that of their non-coining southwestern neighbours, the Samnites. This may have made them uneasy about the possibility of aggression from the latter. At any rate, the Frentani generally preferred association with the dialectically different mid-Italic tribes of central Italy than with the Samnites who spoke standard Oscan like themselves. One consequence of this was to expedite their own latinization.[95]

The nearest mid-Italic tribe to the Frentani were the MARRUCINI immediately to their north.[96] The language of this tribe was a congener of Oscan, but they used the Latin alphabet. Their name resembles, and may have some connection with that of Marsic Marruvium: despite appearances it may not derive from the god Mars.[97] Their territory hardly touched the Adriatic: they held a bare five miles of the littoral immediately south of the Aternus. But, as Strabo notes,[98] the mid-Italic tribes were essentially mountain peoples and reached the Adriatic coast only for short stretches. As if to confirm this, their principal settlement seems to have been in the hilly interior, near modern Rapino, where a shrine to their chief goddess has been identified.[99] Only later, under the Romans, did Teate, nearer the coast, become their chief town. Their small territory was subject to earthquake, but enjoyed a mild climate and was fertile and fruitful. They were a self-governing tribe whose chief officials were most probably a pair of *meddices*.[100]

Adjoining the Marrucini on the west was another mid-Italic tribe, the PAELIGNI. Their territory stretched as far north as the south-western slopes of the Gran Sasso d'Italia and the valley of the upper Aternus where they had a settlement known, under the Romans at least, as Superaequum.[101] Their principal centre, however, lay beneath the Montagna del Morrone. This was Sulmo, later the birthplace of the poet Ovid, who was himself from a prominent Paelignian family.

Festus preserves a tradition that the Paeligni were of Illyrian descent, but Ovid more plausibly claims a Sabellian derivation for them.[102] They certainly spoke a Sabellian dialect sufficiently akin to standard Oscan for it probably to be understood without undue difficulty by speakers of the latter. Like the other mid-Italic tribes, however, the Paeligni used the Latin, not the Oscan alphabet. They also resembled the other mid-Italic peoples in their frugal and hardy way of life and in their religious practices. Their political organization was evidently tribal and their chief magistrates were *meddices*.

Another mid-Italic people, the VESTINI, were neighbours to both the Marrucini and the Paeligni and spoke a similar dialect. Their outlet to the Adriatic was slim, a mere five miles of coast north of the Aternus;[103] and they can fairly be called a mountain tribe since quite literally they straddled the highest peak of the Appennines, the Gran Sasso d'Italia. Its towering mass split them into two groups: the cismontane Vestini sharing the tough climate and the bracing valley of the upper Aternus with Sabini and Paeligni, and their trans-montane kinsmen living in and around Pinna on the fertile eastern slopes of the Appennines near the Adriatic.[104] The *cismontani* gained their livelihood chiefly from transhumant shepherding,[105] and their eastern fellows from dairy-farming, their cheeses being widely renowned. Economic activity was sufficiently complex for the Vestini to issue their own bronze coins.[106]

It is doubtful whether the Vestini were named after the goddess Vesta, whom they do not seem to have known until they came under the domination of Rome. The divinities they worshipped were those that appealed to most Italic peoples: Jupiter, Mars, Hercules and countryside goddesses such as Angitia and Feronia. Their ver-nacular, a dialect of Oscan,[107] suggests that they originated from a sacred spring, about which, however, no tradition now survives.

They seem to have been organized tribally, but *meddices* are not recorded amongst them. Epigraphic evidence suggests that boards of three *aediles* superintended life in at least some of their *pagi* and *vici*.

The western neighbours of the Paeligni were yet another mid-Italic tribe, the MARSI, so-called perhaps after Mars (*Umbrian* Mavors). They lived on the Roman side of the main crest of the Appennines, the Paeligni beyond it. Thus the Marsi controlled the western end of the Forca Caruso, the principal pass over the mountains of central Italy, the Paeligni its eastern end.[108] The Marsic territory was south and east of the Fucine Lake, the northern and western sides of that marshland being occupied by the Aequi.

To judge from the scanty remnants of their vernacular, the Marsi probably belonged to the Umbrian branch of the Italici.[109] They were a pastoral people for the most part, renowned for their frugal and strait-laced daily life and above all for their courage in battle. They were also much preoccupied with charms, drugs and incantations, and seem to have been addicted to snake-charming; it is significant that the deity that chiefly excited their devotion, even though she did not belong exclusively to them, was Angitia, the healer of snake bites.

The Marsi undoubtedly had contacts with Rome c.350: indeed epigraphic evidence suggests that by then their latinization had already begun.[110]

The number of dialects amongst the mid-Italic tribes might be indicative of excessive particularism, but was more probably due to their mountainous habitat, the ranges constituting formidable obstacles to the movement of languages as well as of people. In fact, Marrucini, Marsi, Paeligni and Vestini were not particularly chauvinist. They displayed the usual Sabellian federative instincts and co-operated closely, and not only with one another. Their links with the Frentani were also intimate. These peoples had a common interest in securing orderliness and safety for their transhumant pastoralism, and there is abundant evidence of their organization in a league, if not a confederacy. The Vestini gave the others access to their harbour at the mouth of the Aternus, and the Frentani may have done likewise at the mouth of the Sagrus.[111] The first mention of the mid-Italic tribes in history is of Marsi and Paeligni acting in unison c.340. Whether or not they celebrated religious cults in common is unknown, but they certainly all worshipped the same divinities.[112] Their military co-operation against Rome may have been something less than total, yet it is significant that when they became her allies later, they signed the treaty with her simultaneously, in 304.[113] The Romans regarded them as a single group for war-making purposes and therein showed their customary acumen, for the mid-Italic tribes supplied the best soldiers in Italy and, until the Social War, they were unwavering in their loyalty. The Romans had a saying that they had never celebrated a triumph over the Marsi, or without them; the cohors Paeligna emerges in the military annals of the Roman Republic as the model allied unit; and not even Roman historians could forbear a cheer at the panache of the Frentani and their leader in the war against Pyrrhus.[114]

Sharing the valley of the upper Aternus with the cismontane Vestini and the Paeligni were the SABINI, whose lands, however, were by no means confined to this region of the high Appennines. They inhabited a comparatively narrow but long strip of territory that stretched as far as Latium and separated the mid-Italic tribes from the Umbri. Umbri and Sabini are said to have once constituted a single people and 'Sabine' and 'Umbrian' were often used as synonymous terms; but the single people split into two in some remote past when a segment of them settled beyond the river Nar and developed into the historical Sabini and potential enemies of their former kinsmen.[115]

The Sabini are credited with quite remarkable roles in the history

of Italy. Reputedly they provided the starting-point for the great
Iron Age expansion that filled the mountainous interior of the
peninsula with Italic tribes, and the tendency of these latter to
describe themselves as *Safineis* (cognate with Latin *Sabini*) lends
some plausibility to the story. The Sabini are also said to have helped
Romulus to get Rome started and even to have given the Romans the
name, Quirites (allegedly deriving from Sabine Cures), by which
they called themselves.

No matter how fanciful these stories may be,[116] the Romans in
historical times were conscious of some relationship with the Sabini,
possibly because of the strong influence that they exerted on Roman
religious beliefs and practices. Geographical proximity could, of
course, account for similarities of usage between the two peoples.
From at least the eighth century Sabini and Romans were very near
neighbours, easily accessible to one another by what was later called
the Via Salaria.[117] There must have been much intermingling with a
good deal of reciprocal influencing and borrowing, and there could
well be kernels of truth in the stories of Sabine notables like Numa
Pompilius, Atta Clausus and Appius Herdonius migrating to Rome
in early times.

Nevertheless Romans and Sabini were not in origin closely akin.
The early latinization of the Sabini keeps their non-Latin origin from
being immediately recognized; but in their preliterate days they
almost certainly spoke an Italic dialect, of which, however, no
certain specimen survives.[118] Varro, the learned contemporary of
Cicero, and himself a son of the Sabine land, preserves a number of
Sabine glosses:[119] these do not permit positive pronouncements
about the nature of the language, but they do prove that it was not
Latinian.

The Sabini lived under tribal arrangements and were proverbial
for their lack of cities and for their life in villages. It was a simple,
frugal and Spartan way of living and the Romans greatly admired it,
some of their writers even going so far as to postulate a
Lacedaemonian origin for the Sabini.[120]

During the first sixty years of the Roman Republic the Sabini,
meaning presumably the western Sabini of Eretum and Cures, were
frequently at war with Rome. But after 449 they are not reported as
giving much trouble for the next century and a half, and latinization
made rapid headway amongst them.[121] By *c.*300 the western Sabini
were probably not easily distinguishable from Romans and perhaps

not much disposed to co-operate with their more primitive highland kinsmen further to the east. It may have been this lack of cohesiveness that enabled the Romans under M'. Curius Dentatus to subjugate the Sabini swiftly in a single campaign in 290.

Across the Tiber from the Sabini lived the FALISCI. Their principal settlement was Falerii, on a powerful site in the valley of the river Treia. But what other places were Faliscan is uncertain. Their territory certainly included Mount Soracte and Fescennia, and possibly Capena and Nepete.[122] It seems to have extended from the Ciminian Mountains in the north to the territory of Veii in the south, being bounded on the east by the Tiber and on the west by lakes Ciminius and Sabatinus.

The ancients, although, of course, aware that the Falisci spoke a different language from the Etruscans,[123] usually regarded them as a branch of the latter. Falerii itself is often called Etruscan despite its Latinian speech, which seems surprisingly free from Etruscan interference and strongly resembles Latin. Capena is actually depicted as an Etruscan foundation, even though the meagre third-century vestiges of its dialect seem more Italic than Etruscan.

Whatever the origin of the Falisci, their land was physically a part of Etruria and they were exposed, inevitably, to overwhelming Etruscan influence. The Falisci, in fact, were quite dominated by the Etruscans, culturally and even politically. They shared in the material prosperity that enabled Etruria to import Greek vases and other expensive objects, and it was probably from the Etruscans that they learned the technology for improving their own pottery.[124] Their religion, basically similar to that of the Latini and Sabini, also showed a strong Etruscan flavour. Besides their native divinities Minerva and Dis Soranus with his fire-treading priests (Hirpi), the Falisci also worshipped Nortia and Vortumnus, and the most notable remains of Etruscan temple-architecture have been found precisely at Falerii.

Politically, too, the Falisci seem very Etruscan. They often allied themselves with Etruscans, especially with Veii in the fifth century and with Tarquinii in the fourth. They were still maintaining a precarious independence from Rome c.350, despite their proximity to her.

Next to the Greeks and Romans the ETRUSCANS are the most celebrated people of classical antiquity.[125] Their ultimate origin is still quite uncertain: perhaps their peculiar non-Indo-European speech, which set them apart from their fellow Italians, will provide a clue when and if ever it is fully deciphered.

Their historical homeland, the region that made them what they were and was the core of their strength, was Etruria (later Augustus' Region VII), on the Tyrrhenian side of Italy between the rivers Tiber and Arno. Its fertile fields, but above all its metalliferous hills, islands and mountains provided the Etruscans with the economic power to make their presence felt throughout Italy and the Tyrrhenian Sea.[126] By the seventh century, if not earlier, they had expanded into Campania where their settlements at Capua and elsewhere successfully blocked Italiote expansion northwards.[127] In the sixth century the Etruscans were in effective control of much of Latium, including Rome. By then, too, they had pushed across the Appennines and established Etruscan communities in upper Italy. Felsina, Spina, Parma, Ravenna and, beyond the Po, Mantua and Atria all seem to have been Etruscan for a time.[128]

Like their Greek rivals, the Etruscans were not united and their expansion no more represented systematic, national empire building than Hellenic colonization did. More probably it was a succession of uncoordinated adventures by individual Etruscan cities.[129]

If Etruscan wealth made Etruscan conquests possible, Etruscan disunity brought them to an end. Internecine dissension was an even more potent cause of decline than exhaustion of the lodes of ore or social divisions within the city-states. Etruria consisted of a large number of separate, individual states, one-time monarchies, that had evolved by the fifth century into aristocratic republics, and they showed little or no disposition to unite. The closest that Etruria got to national union was to form a religious league of twelve states, not all of them identifiable or invariably the same, that sent delegates every year to Fanum Voltumnae on the territory of Volsinii.[130] A threat to one Etruscan state left the others seemingly unmoved. Occasionally the states are described as all mobilizing simul-taneously, but in the upshot they usually failed to do so. A state sent military aid to another only if it discerned a direct and immediate threat to itself.[131] The Etruscan city-states, in fact, displayed much of the lustre of their Hellenic counterparts, but also the same obstinate and fatal particularism.

By c.500 Etruscan power in Latium had collapsed, and by three quarters of a century later Sabelli had obtained control of Campania.[132] Etruscan domination north of the Appennines lasted a little longer. But even there the fourth century brought in new masters, the Gauls. By *c*.350 there were still important Etruscan communities outside Etruria proper (Mantua is said to have been one), but effectively the Etruscans were by then confined to their historical homeland and even there their power had greatly weakened. It is significant that when the Romans began their great expansion over Italy they were able virtually to ignore the Etruscans. They needed only to sign long-term truces with the various Etruscan states while giving their real attention to the more redoubtable enemies in the south; and once they had dealt with the Samnites they were able to reduce the Etruscans to the status of dependent allies with comparatively little ado.[133]

For all their disunity the influence of the Etruscans was pervasive and lasting, especially in Latium and Rome. With their practical and innovatory systems of urban life, with their skills in building and engineering,[134] and not least with their use of writing,[135] the Etruscans helped to lead much of sixth-century Italy out of its primitive Iron Age condition of illiteracy.[136]

Few details are known about the administration of their city-states. Their leaders seem to have belonged to a mercantile and landed aristocracy, employing a large servile population. Some idea of the functions of these leaders may be obtained from inscriptions and from the procedures of the Romans, who had kept many of the concepts, methods and institutions developed during their days under Etruscan rule. Rome's chief magistrates seem to have performed functions like those of their Etruscan counterparts, and Roman symbols and trappings of office were clearly inherited from Etruria. Certain practices of Etruscan religion, especially divination and ritual (both of which played a large part in it), were similarly adopted by the Romans and continued to be used until the Late Empire.[137]

Their daring at sea, besides earning the Etruscans a reputation among their Greek rivals for piracy, took them on trading ventures throughout the Mediterranean. They were thus brought in direct contact with the Near East and above all with the Greek world, including the colonies of Magna Graecia and Sicily, and most aspects of Etruscan culture testify to the impact that Hellenic civilization made upon them. It is particularly evident in the artistic production of Etruria from early archaic times to the Hellenistic age. Naturally the Etruscans were also affected by their neighbours nearer home. Their language, for instance, was not immune to interference from Italian vernaculars.[138] Indeed by the fourth century the cultural affinities between Etruria and other parts of Italy were becoming ever more pronounced.[139]

Most of the territory east of Etruria and the river Tiber belonged to the UMBRI, sometimes regarded in antiquity as the earliest identifiable people of the peninsula. They were undoubtedly one of the largest. Their early history is unknown, but by protohistoric times their settlements stretched from Ocriculum, a bare thirty-five miles north of Rome, to the northern Adriatic coast and even to the further side of the north Appennine watershed.

How homogeneous they were it is difficult to say. Their known vernacular was closely related to Oscan, but more innovative and evolved. This is the language used for the Iguvine Tables that contain the largest body of religious ritual to survive from pre-Christian Europe.[140] The same tongue, written in an alphabet that clearly derived from Etruria, is also found on documents ranging in date from the fourth to the early first century, that turn up from time to time in widely scattered parts of western and southern Umbria. Whether it was spoken in the more northerly areas and in what the Romans called the Ager Gallicus along the north Adriatic coast is uncertain.[141] But toponymy suggests that this was the case, and Pseudo-Scylax certainly reckoned the Ager Gallicus as Umbrian *c.*350; furthermore it has been suggested that some recently found documents from there are in archaic Umbrian.[142]

Most Umbri seem to have preferred inhumation to cremation, although some of those in the south and west of their territory certainly burned their dead. Of their many gods particular mention should be made of Jupiter Grabovius, Mavors (= Mars), Hondus and the mysterious Çerfus (or Çerfi), of whom at least the two last named seem to be very Umbrian. Divine triads, even if not of the Capitoline variety, were also not unknown in pre-Roman Umbria.

Their common language and common religion must have made the Umbri well aware that they formed an ethnic group. Other Italians certainly so regarded them. Livy, for example, refers to them in the same manner as he refers to the neighbouring Etruscans, whose ethnic consciousness is, of course, beyond question: he talks about *populi Umbrorum* (or *Umbriae*). Record is also found of a *nomen Umbrum*, even as late as the reign of Constantine.[143]

Nevertheless, the Umbri were not politically united. They did, of course, sometimes co-operate with one another when imminent danger forced them to do so. But there is no evidence that in their independent days they ever formed a league, military or other, much less a federal union.[144] They appear to have been a collection of separate mini-states administered by local magistrates known as *uhtur* and *marones*.[145] Some of them were sophisticated enough to issue their own coins. Their apparent particularism may have been the result of uneven ethnic mixtures in their settlements. The proportion of Illyrian, Etruscan, Latinian or other elements in their make-up may well have varied markedly from one Umbrian community to another.

Possibly it was their reluctance to act in unison that accounts for their failure to put up a stout resistance. Whenever it was that the Adriatic coast from Ancona to Ariminum came into Umbrian possession, control of it was yielded to the Senones (the last Celtic tribe to cross the Alps, according to Livy) very quickly after 350.[146] The Umbri offered similarly weak opposition to the advance of Rome. Livy and Diodorus mention sporadic Umbrian hostility; but Camerinum and Ocriculum in the fourth century and Iguvium in the next seem to have needed little coercion to sign treaties with Rome.[147] In fact, no Umbrian people, apart from the trans-Appennine Sarsinates, put up enough of a struggle for a Roman commander to claim and be awarded a 'triumph' over them.[148] On the whole, therefore, it is not surprising that, once Rome established her hegemony over the peninsula, the Umbri, like their putative Sabine kinsmen, accepted latinization without much demur.

Picenum, the section of Adriatic Italy lying between the rivers Matrinus and Aesis, the Fifth of the Regions into which Augustus later divided Italy, was inhabited from the seventh century and even earlier by an inhuming people whose pugnacity is proved by the plethora of weapons in their graves. They were not Umbri, but more probably an amalgam of the population settled since Bronze Age times in northeastern peninsular Italy and enterprising immigrants who had been crossing into Italy from equally early times from the Illyrian side of the Adriatic.[149]

These PICENES traded extensively with other Italian peoples, especially with Umbri, Falisci and Etruscans, and are proved to have been prosperous by the wealth of gold, silver and other valuable artifacts found in their settlements. They themselves were evidently skilled metallurgists and the many products, especially those of bronze, of their artisans are often of fine quality. Their central Adriatic culture was conservative and in its relative freedom from marked Greek influence altogether exceptional.[150] And the culture of the Picenes was durable as well as distinctive: excavations at Campovalano in Campli, Loreto Aprutino, Numana and elsewhere show that it lasted well into historical times.

The Picenes, however, seem to have been much less unitary than their material culture. Inscriptions have been found in the region that date from the seventh to the fifth century. Efforts to decipher them have so far proved vain, but they clearly fall into two groups and they are written in a variety of scripts (more than one in each group), which may or may not derive from Etruscan alphabets. The north 'Picentine' documents (from Novilara, Fano and Pesaro) are the more baffling, and the languages in which they are written (if there is more than one) may well not be Indo-European. The south 'Picentine' group (from Praetuttian territory for the most part, but including some from south of the Aternus) appear more homogeneous. In 1973 three new south 'Picentine' documents were found at Penna Sant'Andrea near Teramo. They belong to the fifth century, and as they seem to refer to Safineis and contain one other expression that is almost certainly Oscan, it can be confidently assumed that their language is an archaic form of Sabellian Italic.[151] In other words, by the fifth century Italic expansion into Picenum had already taken place. Thus the ancient tradition that Italici had been led thither by a woodpecker (*picus*) after the proclamation of a sacred spring, obvious aetiological fiction though it is,[152] rests upon some basis of solid fact: evidently in historical times the population of Picenum contained a strong Sabellian element. By 350 the southern part of Picenum, from the Matrinus to the Truentus, was under the control of the PRAETUTTII, whose very name is Italic. The important centre of Asculum and the region north of the Truentus belonged to the PICENTES, as the Romans called them, and they are positively recorded as Sabellian.[153] Nothing is certainly known of the political organization of either people, but like all Sabelli they were quite capable of giving a good account of themselves in battle.[154]

The Tyrrhenian side of Italy north of Pisa was in the hands of LIGURES. They had been there for centuries and were a far-flung people, described as inhabiting not only the northwestern region of peninsular Italy, but also upper Italy, Transalpine Gaul, Corsica and, at one time, even the Iberian peninsula.[155] But they were also a very fragmented people, split up into a large number of totally disunited tribes. Cato the censor regarded them as congenital liars who had no idea of their own origin, and if they had a common name for themselves, it has probably not survived.[156] Neither has their language. Being illiterate, they have left no specimen of it, apart perhaps from a few letters scratched on an anthropomorphic stele found more than a century and a half ago at Zignago near La Spezia. Under the circumstances, it seems rash to pronounce it Latinian, and it may not even have been Indo-European.[157]

Ligures still controlled areas *c*.350 of what is today southeastern France, and in particular the hinterland of Massilia. But their principal habitat then seems to have been the mountainous country of northwestern Italy, where they occupied both sides of the north Appennine watershed and both sides of the upper Po: their eastern limits were the Trebia south of the Po and the Ticinus north of it.

The Ligures are described as short and wiry, and they often wore their dark hair long to proclaim their fiery independence. They were good guerrilla fighters, especially skilful with the slingshot, and their hill-top forts enabled them to resist the Romans long and stubbornly.[158] They lived in scattered villages, apparently under tribal arrangements, but the names and number of the tribes, and still more their limits, are far from certain. The villages were poor and primitive,[159] and the Ligures gained their livelihood more from stock-breeding than from agriculture. Hides, timber, honey and beer were among their items of trade, and they had the reputation of being keen but unscrupulous traders. Little is known of their religion.[160]

Ligures of the coastal areas were better off than their fellows in the interior. They controlled a number of ports and became skilful sailors and daring pirates. Of all the Ligurian tribes the two coastal tribes of the Apuani and Ingauni are by far the best known:[161] the former lived in the vicinity of La Spezia and the latter controlled the territory about the harbour of Genoa. Some coastal Ligures became quite wealthy, to judge from cemeteries recently excavated at Genoa and Chiavari that contained Greek red-figure vases, Etruscan bronzes and some alabaster.[162]

The Ligures were not the only long-term residents of upper Italy. VENETI had been settled in the far northeast, apparently since very

early in the first millennium. How they got there is unknown. There
is no way of proving that they were related to other widely scattered
peoples also called Veneti, and the tradition that they first came to
Italy as refugees from the Trojan War is fanciful.[163] Any deductions
based on their language are uncertain. It survives in well over two
hundred inscriptions, most of them short and fragmentary. They are
written in an Etruscan-type script (with local variations and careful
punctuation) and date from the sixth century to *c*.50. The tongue is
certainly Indo-European and shows some resemblances to both
Germanic and Gaulish, but far more to Latin. That it was, as
frequently suggested, an Illyrian dialect seems out of the question.
More probably it is to be classified as a Latinian language.[164]

The origins of the Veneti are more likely to be sought in central
Europe than in Illyria. Whether that be so or not, they must have
been a very mixed people, consisting partly of immigrants into Italy
and partly of the populations they had encountered on their arrival.
Their predecessors in northeastern Italy are described as Euganei, a
label that is meaningless although it was still given to a people living
in upper Italy in historical times and is still used for the group of
volcanic hills that lie between Verona and Padua.[165]

The Veneti lived north and east of the river Athesis, but extended
into the Alps in both directions and also at some points into the
regions west and south of the Athesis: Venetic material has been
found near the shores of Lake Garda and in considerable quantity at
Atria.[166] Their territory was extremely fertile, but frequent flooding
of its many rivers made much of it swampy and uninhabitable and
consequently kept the Venetic population relatively small. But, by
contemporary Iron Age standards, the Veneti were fully civilized,
comparing more than favourably with neighbouring peoples in both
economic development and in social organization. They were excellent farmers, capable artisans and keen traders. They were particularly renowned as horse-breeders.[167] Theirs was certainly no closed
culture: contacts with the Etruscans were very common and from
the fourth century on they were with the Gauls.

Religion played an important part in their daily life, to judge from
their many open-air sanctuaries and the quantity of their votive
offerings. But it was somewhat unusual in the prominent role that
was assigned to female divinities of chthonic aspect and often curious
names. Goddesses, in fact, were the principal objects of Venetic
devotion, the chief one apparently being Reitia, at Ateste at least: she

was a health deity who typified the primitive force of nature.[168] The dead were normally cremated and their ashes deposited in urns that were then buried.

The Venetic communities were numerous and evidently autonomous. Each had its own armed forces and was ready to defend its boundaries against any encroachments.[169] But Livy, himself of Venetic origin, clearly thought of his people as a single nation, and it certainly looks as if the Veneti as a whole signed the treaty with Rome c.225. Moreover their ability to survive powerful military and cultural pressure from the Etruscans and the Gauls also suggests that they were linked together in some sort of federal league. Down to 350 or a little later Ateste seems to have been their principal settlement; thereafter it was clearly Patavium.[170]

The Veneti, although quite capable of defending themselves, were not a pugnacious people. They preferred trade to war.[171] Staid and prudent, they contrasted sharply with their impulsive and bellicose Celtic neighbours. In fact, the rowdy recklessness of the Gauls drove the Veneti into the arms of Rome.

Upper Italy c.350, apart from its Venetic and Ligurian areas, was probably already under the control of speakers of Celtic collectively known as GAULS (from *Latin* Galli; cf. *Greek* Galatai). For the Romans indeed all of upper Italy was Gallia, and more precisely Gallia Cisalpina to distinguish it from Gallia Transalpina on the further side of the Alps.

For the most part Cisalpine Gaul is a low-lying alluvial plain, stretching from Turin in the west to Trieste in the east, virtually encircled by mountains, the snow-capped Alps on the west, north and east and the watershed of the upper Appennines on the south; and the many rivers that flow down from these ranges into the Po can waterlog large areas of the region.[172] In fact, Cisalpina in prehistoric times was a land of swamps, marshes, fogs and uncleared forests, and in those days its population of lacustrine *terramaricoli* and others could hardly have been dense. In the sixth century, probably, Etruscans arrived and began the work of drainage and reclamation. Ultimately Cisalpina was made into a wonderfully fertile land; but as late as the reign of Augustus much of it still needed to be cleared, and even today flooding is a serious problem.[173]

Indeed in the days before Etruscan engineering skill began making Cisalpina more habitable, Celtic war-bands, attracted by the prospect of plunder, adventure and excitement, had often infiltrated there. But it was in the days of the great Celtic expansion in the late fifth and early fourth centuries that the Gauls crossed the Alps with sufficient strength to make themselves masters of most of Cisalpina, even though the pass, or passes, that they used cannot be certainly identified.[174]

The important role of the Gauls in the history of Italy began *c*.400.[175] The tradition is that on the very day in 396 that the Romans stormed Veii in southern Etruria, a motley force of Gauls captured the wealthy (? Etruscan) town of Melpum in upper Italy;[176] and about five years later another group of Gauls (? Boii) took Etruscan Felsina, the settlement that controlled the northern approach to the most important pass across the Appennines. In 386 a marauding war-band pulled off the most celebrated Celtic feat of all: it struck deep into peninsular Italy and sacked Rome. This incursion caught the notice of the Greeks and was never thereafter forgotten, or forgiven, by the Romans.[177]

Polybius describes what the Gauls were like when they first seized Cisalpina. Their life was devoted mostly to warfare and agrarian activities; their villages were unwalled and their dwellings largely bare of furniture; their possessions consisted chiefly of gold and livestock; they slept on leaves and consumed vast quantities of meat and alcohol; they quarrelled incessantly and were prompt to form war-bands around swashbuckling chiefs and set out on new adventures; and in battle some of them fought naked.[178]

This picture of the Gauls is undoubtedly exaggerated. Nevertheless, from it one can reasonably conclude that the Gauls of Cisalpina were much like Celts elsewhere, not exactly savages, but also not exactly civilized. Boastful, truculent and fearless they fought with more panache than persistence. They wore metal torques around their necks and were very fond of gold, silver and jewellery. They loved the poetry and song of their native Celtic, but took no pains to preserve it in writing. They worshipped their own gods, sometimes with rituals that included human sacrifice.[179] And like Celts elsewhere they were quickly influenced by their new environment.

The Gauls did not completely celticize upper Italy by any means, and non-Celtic pockets of population continued to exist there. Mantua, north of the Po, was protected by its marshes and remained Etruscan. Similarly Ravenna and perhaps Mutina and other places south of the river seem never to have become Gallic towns.[180] In fact, in Cisalpina as elsewhere, the Celts were not really densely settled. At the same time they were very fissiparous. They were divided into a number of separate tribes, each consisting of many quarrelsome war-bands.[181]

These tribes had not crossed the Alps simultaneously, and the differences already existing between them were made more noticeable by their experiences in Italy. Each of them became an amalgam of Celtic and native Italian elements, and the mixture varied from one tribe to another.

By the late fourth century the following tribes were firmly established: they are listed in the order in which they encountered the Romans.

The SENONES were settled in the area along the Adriatic coast that the Romans later called the Ager Gallicus. This was really a part of peninsular Italy, but does not seem to have been recognized as such until much later. The Senones are said to have been the last Celts to enter Italy and had to pass through the territories taken by earlier arrivals before they could find a region for themselves.

The BOII had crossed the Alps before them and taken possession of the large area south of the Po (but north of the Appennines) that stretched as far west as the river Trebia and on the east, in the vicinity of Ravenna, joined the territory of the Lingones.[182] These latter may have been a separate Gallic tribe or possibly only a sub-tribe of the Boii, with whom they are generally mentioned. The Boii were a very powerful Celtic people, perhaps the strongest of all in Cisalpina, although that description is usually given to the Insubres.

Immediately north of the Boii and the Po, but west of the Veneti and the river Athesis, were the CENOMANI, who were traditionally the second Celtic tribe to reach upper Italy, presumably by way of the Brenner Pass whose southern approaches they subsequently controlled from their principal settlement at Brixia. Their inclination to co-operate with the Romans against their fellow Gauls suggests that the non-Celtic element in their population was substantial.[183]

To their west, beyond the river Sarius,[184] lived the INSUBRES, reputed to be the first Celtic tribe to settle in Italy. They may also have been the largest and almost certainly they were the most thoroughly Celtic.[185] They were led into Italy, perhaps by way of one of the central Alpine passes (? the Gotthard ? the Scheideck), by a certain Bellovaesus who founded their chief settlement at

Mediolanium and founded a small empire that stretched eventually as far south as the Po and as far west as the Ticinus.[186]

The Celts had brought the La Tène phase of the Iron Age with them when they irrupted into Italy. But by the time that the Romans began their expansion into upper Italy about the middle of the third century, its Gallic inhabitants, and especially those of them living south of the Po, had already been much influenced by their new environment. They had evidently found themselves a homeland and had set up their own communities. Nevertheless, even though now much more settled in their ways than formerly, they were still recognizably Celts with many Celtic characteristics: they had not lost their insatiable lust for gold and silver, their reluctance to unite, nor their grisly habit of using the severed heads of captured enemy commanders as drinking-cups.[187]

As already noted, Ligurian tribes were likely to be found in the part of northwestern Italy west of the river Ticinus. But these were intermingled with Celts, and the number of tribes and their identity and ethnic composition are alike uncertain. Many of them make a single, evanescent appearance in the pages of just one author.

Two, however, are relatively well known: the TAURINI[188] who have bequeathed their name to Turin, and the possibly related SALASSI immediately to their north who controlled the approaches to the two Saint Bernard passes. Both of these peoples seem to have been composed of Ligurian and Celtic elements, though in differing proportions.

It is tempting to conjecture that they came into existence as a result of prehistoric Celtic infiltration of the Salyes, a Ligurian people settled near, and perhaps on both sides of, the western and maritime Alps.[189] The consequence was a Celto–Ligurian amalgam that became established in Piemonte. One part of it consolidated a hold on the fertile valley of the upper Po and was known as the Taurini. Presumably this was the more powerful group, possibly because it was more celticized: the name Taurini, at any rate, seems to derive from Celtic *tor* meaning 'hill'.[190] The weaker group had to make do with the less desirable land further north in the Val d'Aosta and it was known as the Salassi: the name, virtually identical with Salyes, may indicate that in it the Ligurian element predominated.[191]

The Romans, so far as is known, did not seriously clash with either the Taurini or the Salassi until many years after their subjugation of the Celts to the east of the river Ticinus.

The Alps proper, and the passes over them, were in the hands of sixty or more mountaineer tribes about whom not much is known. Inevitably they came into conflict with Rome and ultimately, in the time of Augustus, they were included in part at least within the borders of Italy. For that reason some notice is taken of them here.

As practically all of them were illiterate, it is difficult to make certain pronouncements about them other than that ancient authors and documents preserve the names of some of them. Actually some of the names have survived to the present day, since they are borne by the valleys that the tribes inhabited.[192] Lacking other resources the tribes lived chiefly by dairy-farming, mining, brigandage and the tolls they extracted from users of the mountain passes, and they posed the same problem for the Roman Republic as the northwest frontier tribes did for the British Empire in India.[193] The Romans did manage to use, at a price,[194] the Alpine passes that chiefly interested them, but they did not attempt a thorough-going conquest of the tribes, perhaps because the effort seemed likely to be incommensurate with the result. It was not until the year 6 that the Alps could be regarded as pacified, and even as late as AD 79 there were still some unannexed mountain peoples.

In the western Alps it is probable that there were stocks of unidentifiable origin mixed up with the Celtic and Ligurian elements. In the central Alps the LEPONTII, settled in what is today the Ticino canton of Switzerland, seem to have been more prosperous and less primitive than other Alpine tribes, probably because they controlled the principal north–south traffic artery.[195] Objects of amber, coral, silver and bronze, fashioned with varying degrees of skill, have been found on their territory. Nor were they illiterate: second-century inscriptions attributed to them have been found at Ornavasso, written in a language sometimes regarded not very convincingly as a variety of Celtic.[196] The lack of weapons and armour in their necropoleis suggests that the Lepontii were more interested in trading than in fighting, and the bronze and silver coins they issued in the second century indicate the same thing.

The ancients believed that the tribes to the east of the Lepontii were basically RAETI and descended from the wild remnants of Etruscans.[197] Actually a few meagre third-century specimens of a (? non-Indo-European) language written in an Etruscan-type script and looking something like Etruscan have been found. This could be the language of the Raeti. But it is also possible that Raeti was a blanket name given for want of a better to a wide variety of Alpine peoples.[198] Even if these peoples really were Raeti, they must have been a very mixed lot. The Carni, for example, living in the modern district known as Friuli, allegedly Raetic, were heavily celticized. Similarly the Istri, living in the peninsula that preserves their name, must have contained a strong Illyrian element.

This review of fourth-century Italy and its peoples cannot help but be incomplete, since there were tribes living there then of whom no record whatever, not even their names, survives. The account is also over-simplified, for although the separation of Italy from the rest of Europe by its Alpine barrier makes it a geographical unit, its history was anything but unitary.[199] In pre-Roman Italy fragmentation was more common and divisive, and also less static, than the nomenclature so far adopted might lead one to expect. So far from there being any tendency towards overall national solidarity, there was in many areas not even a disposition towards tribal unity.

In fact, there was a continuous ebb and flow of peoples and tribes, an incessant and at times erratic mobility; and the fluid linguistic frontiers with their shifting bilingualisms, the changing economic and social relationships, the unstable military combinations, and the endemic political turbulence cannot be sorted out with confident and definite precision. The spread of Greek civilization in Italy, the swift development of Etruria and early Rome, and the consolidation of some tribal states provide outlines, but no complete or detailed picture. By the fourth century Greek influence, either directly or through Etruscan mediation, had helped to promote some uniformity of culture.[200] But the effect was uneven, depending upon the place, the time and the local reaction, and nowhere was it much more than a veneer that was far from obliterating the native cultures.

Thus, as late as 350, the heterogeneity of the Italian peoples was still quite marked. The Romans clearly felt themselves more akin to some of these peoples than to others. Their bonds with the Latini were certainly close, and they also felt some sort of affinity with the Sabini. On the other hand, they found the Etruscans strange, the Greeks foreign, and the Gauls barbarous. Nevertheless, different though their feelings towards the various peoples might be, the Romans in the three and a half centuries after 350 succeeded in welding all the disparate elements into a single, unified nation. It is this achievement that invests their history with its great significance and unending fascination.

CHAPTER II

THE CONSEQUENCES OF THE LATIN WAR

In the fifth century the so-called Cassian Treaty had brought the Romans, Latini and Hernici together in an alliance that enabled them to keep expansionist Aequi and Volsci from conquering all of Latium, and by 400 the latter peoples had clearly passed their peak. Their decline robbed the triple alliance of its purpose and not even the Gallic raid of 386, nasty though it was while it lasted, could avail to keep the three allies together.[201] In 340 the Latini became convinced that Rome was aiming at the domination of all Latium and accordingly most of them took to arms.[202]

The ensuing struggle (340–338) is called the Latin War, somewhat misleadingly, since some Latini did not enter the conflict, while not a few of the peoples that did were not Latini at all. Aurunci, Campanians, Sidicini and Volsci all opposed Rome in fear of her growing preponderance.[203] The Samnites, on the other hand, supported Rome, won over by the promise of a free hand against the Sidicini at the war's end, and with their help the Romans disposed first of the Volsci, Campanians and Aurunci, and then proceeded to deal with the main enemy, the Latini.[204] In three years it was all over, with victory securely in the hands of the Romans; and it is the peace settlement that followed that is the starting-point for the present study.

When the Latin War broke out, Rome was already the largest state in Latium; when it ended, Rome controlled not only Latium proper (Latium Vetus), but also its extension (Latium Adjectum),[205] the area stretching southeastwards from the Circeii-Setia line to the river Savo and inhabited by Volsci and Aurunci, and for good measure northern Campania (Capua, Casilinum, Atella, Calatia, Cumae, Suessula, Acerrae) and southern Etruria (as far as the Lacus Ciminius).

This large and populous area became the base from which Rome later spread her power and influence over the whole of Italy, from the Ionian Sea to the Alps; and for that reason the terms that she imposed upon it at the end of the Latin War are of uncommon interest and importance. Livy and Velleius preserve the details but are rather vague about the dates.[206] Livy implies that the entire settlement was completed in 338, except for the incorporation of Acerrae which he places in 332. Velleius more plausibly allots several years to the settlement, but precisely which years is somewhat uncertain because of the parlous state of his text. Nevertheless, the sequence of events can be divined with some confidence, and on the whole Livy's succinct and unembellished account of the settlement carries conviction.

The total lack of a bureaucracy at Rome prevented her from annexing all of the subjugated region: she would have had no way of administering it. Greater Latium had to remain a congeries of many separate communities, each of them managing its own local affairs. Rome's concern was to regulate their mutual relations in the manner most advantageous to herself.

Her first step was the traditional seizure of territory from the conquered. Antium, Capua, Praeneste, Tibur, Velitrae and other unnamed communities were all forced to cede land, much of which was then subdivided into small allotments and distributed to individual Romans, poorer plebeians for the most part.[207] The settler beneficiaries were soon afterwards registered in Roman rustic Tribes, either in the twenty-three already existing (whose *territoria* were extended to accommodate them) or in two new ones, the Maecia and the Scaptia, that were created in 332 as a sequel to the Latin War settlement.[208]

To seize land, however, was not enough. Rome also needed to eliminate any rival authority in Latium. Accordingly she disbanded the Latin League. But the removal of one problem created another. The dissolution of the League left a serious gap in the defences of the region, and Rome could not remedy the deficiency by simply keeping her own citizen army permanently under arms; that was completely out of the question.[209] Rome, therefore, decided to secure Latium, and at the same time her own supremacy there, by diversifying her relationships with its various communities. Careful appraisal of the past record and future usefulness of each community decided the role that it was henceforth to play in Latium.

In place of an alliance with the Latin states as a group, Rome

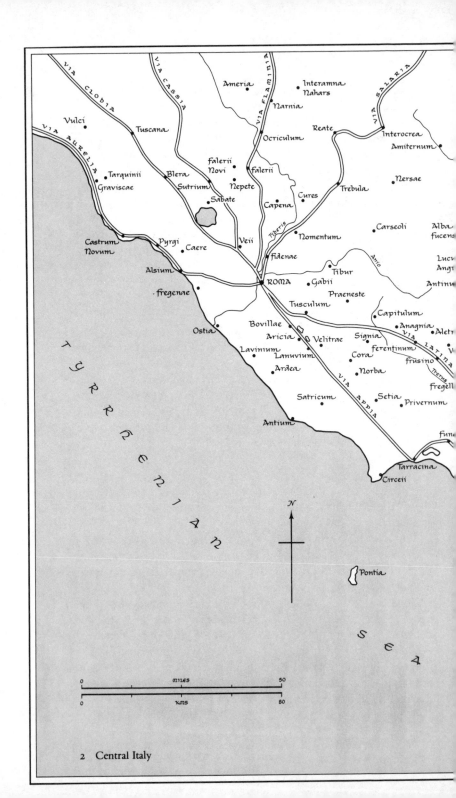

2 Central Italy

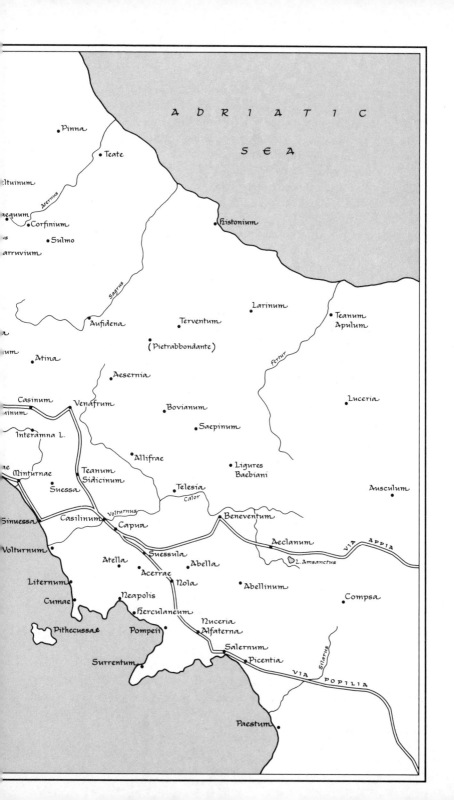

henceforth had separate alliances with some of them individually. But of far greater consequence was the use she now made of two remarkable institutions, neither of which has any exact counterpart in the modern world: the *municipium* and the *colonia*.[210]

Allusion has already been made to the autonomous urban communities called *coloniae* which Rome and the Latin League, acting jointly, had founded to safeguard Latium in the fifth and early fourth centuries. These were Latin Colonies, and presumably it was they that provided the idea for the Citizen Colonies which Rome on her own sole initiative instituted now in the latter half of the fourth century.

Two Citizen Colonies were established on land that Rome had seized on the sea-coast and they were organized from the moment of their foundation as self-administering civic units. But, as their title *coloniae civium Romanorum* suggests, settlers in them always enjoyed full Roman citizenship. Their purpose was to provide protection to the Roman coastline against hit-and-run marauders.[211] Ancient naval operations rarely took the form of huge, sea-borne invasions. But piratical attacks were only too common, and Latium lay exposed to them now that Antiate naval power had been destroyed in the Latin War. Rather than maintain a navy, the Romans preferred to defend the littoral with two watchdog Citizen Colonies, at Ostia and Antium. Neither was very large. Each seems to have consisted of only three hundred *coloni* who apparently were forbidden to absent themselves from their *colonia* and for that reason were excused from service in the legions.[212] Evidently it was felt that three hundred men, provided that they stayed at their post and were vigilant, were enough for the coastguard duties envisaged for them. Despite their small size, however, the two colonies seem to have been genuine city-states, even if not as fully developed as larger entities. A few more maritime colonies of the same kind were to be founded during the next hundred years.

Far transcending the Citizen Colony in importance was the *municipium*. It, too, was an urbanized *res publica*, but one that had grown and developed independently and did not owe its origin in any way to Rome.

Neither the *colonia* nor the *municipium*, although they were both civic organisms, conformed to Strabo's or Pausanias' stereotype of a Greek city-state with its agora, gymnasia, colonnaded streets, temples and places of assembly.[213] In Italy the city-state was basically a township, many of whose burgesses might well reside at some distance from the townsite (*oppidum*) itself. The *municipium*, moreover, differed from a Greek city-state in another and even more fundamental respect. Its burgesses, although a community by themselves, also formed part of the Roman state, physically separate though it was; and this was a condition of affairs that was unprecedented. Hitherto a man's citizenship was decided by his domicile: he was a citizen of the community in which he resided. But after 338 'soil' could be dissociated from 'state'. It was henceforth possible for a man to be born in, live in, and be a burgess of an authentic urban commonwealth (*municipium*), physically distinct and possibly distant from Rome, and yet be at the same time a citizen of the latter. This was a revolutionary idea, and it enabled Rome, a city-state republic, to incorporate and ultimately assimilate other states.

A *municipium* was thus a self-governing community, non-Roman in origin, that had been annexed by Rome and its burgesses pronounced by the Roman Assembly to be Roman Citizens.[214] But despite its loss of sovereignty, it retained its native identity and its religion, constitution, laws, language and customs, possessing a degree of local autonomy tantamount to home rule. The very essence of a *municipium* was this ability to administer itself, even though it now formed part of the Roman state.[215]

The Romans had, in effect, devised something uncommonly like dual citizenship, apparently, however, without realizing all the implications of the momentous step that they had taken. In fact, they themselves denied that dual citizenship was involved.[216] In their view the burgess of a *municipium* was a *municeps* ('assumer of functions') of his home town; he was, however, a *civis* ('citizen') of Rome.[217] To us, leaving nicety of nomenclature aside, *municipes* look like men with two citizenships; they were citizens of the city-state in which they lived and they were citizens of the state to which they owed allegiance, Rome.[218]

Although all *municipes* were *cives Romani*, they were not all of the same grade. Like the citizens who actually lived in Rome, they all enjoyed the right of appeal (*ius provocationis*) to the Roman People and were thus in theory protected against arbitrary action by magistrates; and they all apparently possessed the *ius conubii* and the *ius commercii*, the private rights that enabled Roman citizens to make valid marriages with, and to deal with, other citizens on a contractual and legal basis. But some *municipes* did not have the right to vote in the Roman Assemblies (*ius suffragii*) or to hold public office at Rome (*ius honorum*), much less to become members of the Roman Senate. They could participate fully in the public life of their own *municipium*, but at Rome theirs was only a partial citizenship (*civitas sine suffragio*) that debarred them from any kind of political activity.

The restriction did not apply to all *municipes*. Some *municipia* had been incorporated with full citizenship rights, and their burgesses were *cives optimo iure*, fully entitled to vote in the Assemblies and to seek public office in Rome. *Municipes* of this sort, like any full Roman citizens, were registered in the Roman Tribes, and this distinguished them sharply from the *cives sine suffragio*, who were not so registered, but recorded in a different fashion.

Latin Tusculum served as prototype for both varieties of *municipium*.[219] The Romans are said to have annexed it, *sine suffragio* according to Festus, in 381, presumably in order to separate the Latini of western Latium from their fellows in Tibur and Praeneste further east.[220] Livy says that the operation was not very difficult, nor even very painful, since Tusculan domestic life was but little affected: the Tusculani continued to run their own internal affairs and to present some image of an urban commonwealth with a political identity of its own. Nevertheless, they had lost the right to pursue an independent foreign policy and thus decide their own destiny. They had become a part of the Roman state and were no longer members of the Latin League. This exchange of their own citizenship for that of the Romans undoubtedly rankled. Like any people deprived of its independence, they resented their loss of liberty; and they especially disliked the duties, such as military service, that their new and unsought status imposed. Possibly it was to mollify these ruffled feelings that the Romans, some time before 340, promoted the Tusculani from the partial to the full citizenship.[221] But even this did not win them over: they joined the Latini in the war against Rome in 340.

The experiment with Tusculum demonstrated that integral annexations, although bound to be resented, were nevertheless feasible and could take place with either the partial or full citizenship. Accordingly, once the Latin War was over, the Romans decided to persevere with the municipal policy, and on a more extensive scale. They created *municipia* of both types, Latinity being the criterion to determine which communities should get the higher grade of citizenship.

Lanuvium, Aricia, Nomentum, Pedum, all of them like Tusculum Latin settlements, were constituted *municipia* with full Roman citizenship, whereas the defeated Volscian and Campanian communities chosen for incorporation received only the *civitas sine suffragio*. The earlier annexation of Tusculum was, of course, confirmed and the leaders of its rebellion executed.

The five Latin *municipia* were quickly assigned to Roman Tribes. Tusculum, Aricia and Nomentum went into Papiria, Horatia and Cornelia respectively. About Pedum there is no information, but Lanuvium was registered in Maecia, a new Tribe established in 332 on territory that Lanuvium had itself surrendered. This was an unusual arrangement since new Tribes were as a rule intended for old citizens, the Romans not relishing the idea of any Tribe being controlled by newcomers to their citizen body.

The full autonomy of the five Latin *municipia* enabled them to manage their own affairs more or less as they wished, each with its own municipal senate[222] and annually elected local magistrates of whatever kind they liked – dictators, praetors or aediles. Admittedly the competence of these magistrates was not unlimited, since the *municipes* of the five communities were now full Roman citizens and therefore subject to Roman authority and possessed of Roman rights. In particular, lawsuits might be decided in the praetor's court at Rome, and proximity doubtless ensured that this sometimes happened, especially in cases that for whatever reason were beyond the purview of the local magistrates. But the urban praetor at Rome probably had little time to spare for ordinary litigation in the *municipia*. Minor lawsuits at least were probably handled locally by the municipal magistrates themselves.[223] At the same time the *municipes* could hardly object to the jurisdictional authority of Rome's magistrates, since they themselves were eligible to wield it provided that they could win election in the City. This was not utterly impossible: L. Fulvius Curvus of Tusculum was elected consul at Rome as early as 322.[224]

The five Latin *municipia* continued, of course, to have their own cults (*sacra municipalia*), since in Italy the Romans regularly respected native religious practices. Lanuvium, it is true, was obliged to share its shrine to Juno Sospes with other Romans, but this did not mean that Rome intended otherwise to interfere with, much less to suppress it.[225]

The relatively small number of *populi Latini* absorbed into the

Roman state with full citizenship at this time was probably due to Roman caution. A greater number may have seemed unmanageable and too influential in the Assemblies. As it was, the five were assimilated without undue difficulty and, once incorporated, they never went to war against Rome again.

The Romans also displayed caution in their incorporation of the Volscian and Campanian communities. They converted these too into *municipia*, but did not confer the full citizenship upon any of them. The leaders of Velitrae were forcibly removed across the Tiber under threat of dire punishment should they return. Their landed property was confiscated and distributed to Roman *coloni*. The walls of Velitrae were dismantled and, although Livy does not actually say so, epigraphic evidence reveals that it was made a *municipium*, undoubtedly *sine suffragio* since its people spoke Volscian.[226] The *municipium*, however, included some full Roman citizens since Roman *coloni* settled on its confiscated soil were enrolled (*adscripti*) among its burgesses. Their presence and the proximity of Rome helped to romanize the native Veliterni no doubt; but the town was still Volscian-speaking and under the direction of *meddices* in the third century.[227] It was not until the second century that the chief local magistrates became *praetores*.

Antium was even more severely treated. It had repeatedly displayed hostility to Rome and for that reason was now *c.*338 reduced to impotence. Its war fleet was confiscated and even a mercantile marine was forbidden to it from now on. To replace it as guardian of the coast of Latium, as mentioned already, a Citizen Colony was established on confiscated Antiate soil. The native Volsci were pronounced Roman citizens, obviously of the partial variety, although Livy did not think it necessary to say so. Their leaders must have suffered the same fate as their Veliternan counterparts and the consequences were far more serious. For Rome's ban on maritime pursuits meant economic ruin for Antium and the disappearance of well-to-do locals capable of replacing the eliminated leaders.[228] Consequently for the next twenty years Volscian Antium was a kind of political no man's land without any regular system of administration.[229] The *colonia* of Roman citizens sharing the site presumably prevented utter lawlessness, and in 318 the patrons of the colony were instructed to regularize Antiate corporate affairs. Antium then probably became a *municipium sine suffragio*, although the possibility that it remained a *pagus* with native officials cannot be excluded.

Whatever its status, the Citizen Colony gradually absorbed it;[230] and when the Social War broke out over two hundred years later all residents of the area seem to have been full Roman citizens.

After the Volsci of Velitrae and Antium it was the turn of the northern Campanians. Capua and its confederates (Atella, Calatia and presumably Casilinum) were incorporated, Atella and Calatia at least separately, since later they are found acting independently. Cumae, Suessula and, after a few years, Acerrae were also converted into *municipia* without the right of suffrage.[231]

The Campanians escaped the harsher features of the treatment meted out to Antium and Velitrae. For this Capua could thank its local aristocrats who had prudently kept out of the fighting at a critical period in the Latin War. In appreciation the Romans honoured these *equites Campani* and neither demolished the walls nor destroyed the economic activities of their city.

After 338 it was naturally these Campanian knights who were placed in control of the *municipium* of Capua, and it is evident that they were granted the maximum of latitude by Rome. Ultimate authority, of course, did rest with her, but in general the inner life of the *municipium* was its own business, the only real limitation on its sovereignty being in the area of external policy. The same must also have been true of the other Campanian *municipia*.[232]

Thus Capua continued to have its own senate, to elect its own magistrates (*meddices*), to date the year in its own way, to collect its own taxes, to conduct its own census, to administer its own courts, to promote its own youth organization, to use its own Oscan language, and to celebrate its own cults and religious festivals (such as the one at Hamae).[233] Home rule was complete.[234] Livy's account of political life there between 338 and 216 conveys the impression of a self-governing, Greek-style city-state, that in 216 committed the fatal folly of opting for Hannibal.

No ancient writer says explicitly that the other incorporated Campanian communities enjoyed the same degree of near-sovereignty as Capua, but the fact is self-evident and is implied in any case by the devoted loyalty of Cumae and Acerrae to Rome in the Second Punic War.

The Latin War settlement obviously did not bring the separate existence of the Campanian city-states to an end. Rome's *municipes* in Capua nevertheless resented their new status, undoubtedly because their freedom of action was now no longer completely unfettered.

Capua was the principal city of Campania, a region just as large and just as populous as Latium, but in its own estimation and in reality more advanced.[235] It could, therefore, hardly relish taking orders from Rome, even if the latter was the principal city of Latium. The notorious *superbia* of the Capuani must have bridled at the thought, all the more so no doubt because the lesser cities of Campania, such as Nola and Nuceria, were still independent and, therefore, now outranked Capua. Even the Capuan aristocrats, who basked in Rome's favour, must have felt indignant when Rome made their subordinate status all too clear in 314 by naming a Roman dictator to investigate the internal situation in Capua.[236] Moreover, being only partial citizens, they could not seek balm for their wounded *dignitas* by becoming magistrates or senators at Rome. In all likelihood they would have preferred Capua to be an ally rather than a *municipium* of Rome, since an ally, even if in fact subject, was at least ostensibly sovereign.

Some years after the northern Campanian city-states, three additional Volscian communities, Privernum, Fundi and Formiae, were constituted as *municipia* of the *sine suffragio* variety. Their annexation was not, however, a direct consequence of the Latin War. In that conflict, as a matter of fact, Fundi and Formiae helped Rome by letting her troops use their territories and for that reason were honoured by her at the war's end.[237] But they soon fell out with her. In 330 Privernum sought to recover by force of arms territory that Rome had seized and was supported by Fundi and apparently also by Formiae.[238] Victory went to Rome and in 329 Privernum suffered a fate similar to that of Velitrae or Antium: its walls were razed, its leaders transported beyond the Tiber, and the community itself transformed into a *municipium* without the right of suffrage.

Fundi and Formiae were probably constituted as *municipia sine suffragio* at the same time. If they suffered less than Privernum, their previous good record was probably responsible: at any rate there is no evidence that they had to surrender territory or demolish their walls.

Partial citizenship was the bitter result of defeat in war and was, therefore, never popular. The Italians that had it imposed upon them tended to be, like the Capuani, very disgruntled: they had lost their liberty. Ancient writers regularly assume that they were ready to rebel if given the opportunity and some of them actually did so. It is significant, too, that the Hernici, when offered the choice in 306 of becoming partial citizens or staying as allies, opted for the latter alternative. At about the same time the Aequi seem to have gone to war to avoid having *civitas sine suffragio* thrust upon them.[239] What rankled with the partial citizens was their liability to the duties of Roman citizenship while being denied its highest privileges. Compulsory service in the Roman army as Roman citizens was a particular grievance. That was made clear in 216 when Hannibal only succeeded in inducing the partial citizens of Capua and some other north Campanian *municipia* to join him by promising never to conscript them.[240] Between 338 and 216 they had been called upon to fight at Rome's behest often enough, even though no details are preserved of the way that they were recruited for such service. For conducting a levy of full citizens, the Roman consuls had the tribal registers at their disposal. But partial citizens were not enrolled in the Roman Tribes and, so far as is known, lists of them were not kept at Rome until the so-called Caerite Tables were instituted, *c*.268 perhaps (see Appendix III). Probably Rome obtained soldiers from the *municipia sine suffragio* before then by simply telling the local magistrates the number of men that they had to field.

In view of the small number of Latin communities incorporated by Rome after the Latin War, it is pertinent to enquire what happened to the other *Latini*, and in particular to those *populi Latini* known as *coloniae Latinae* that had originally been established as joint foundations of Rome and the Latin League.

Two of them, Sutrium and Nepete, lay outside Latium and had not entered the Latin War. They, therefore, were left to go on functioning as before, in other words as Latin Colonies. But as they had lost their federal bond because of the dissolution of the Latin League, they now owed their allegiance exclusively to Rome. It is not likely that they objected to the change, since as controllers of the northern approaches to Rome they had probably always regarded themselves as more Roman than Latin, just as, conversely, Circeii and Setia, the sentinel colonies at the southern limit of Latium Vetus, felt themselves preponderantly Latin.

The status retained by Sutrium and Nepete set the general pattern for the treatment of the old joint foundations; and seven of them, the four just named together with Signia, Norba and Ardea, were allowed to continue as Latin Colonies, from now on, however, linked exclusively to Rome, becoming her most trustworthy allies.

So far as is known, none of them was reinforced at this juncture with a fresh infusion of settlers, as was later the regular Roman practice when confirming existing *coloniae*, but they may have undergone some unrecorded change. The orthogonal town-plan revealed by archaeology at Norba seems to date from about this time,[241] and the subsequent appearance of praetors as local magistrates at Signia may be due to Roman influence in 338.[242]

After 338 there is much evidence of the vigorous autonomy of all seven and no sign of Roman interference in their internal affairs until 204. A *colonia Latina*, in fact, was encouraged to be a self-governing *res publica*, a genuine borough, free to fashion its own civic existence and develop its own corporate personality. For good measure, its relations with Rome were close and intimate. It was not itself Roman; its burgesses possessed the citizenship of the colony, not of Rome. But, in that it used the Latin language, it resembled a *municipium optimo iure* and, in that its burgesses could not become Roman magistrates, it resembled a *municipium sine suffragio*. Its burgesses could intermarry with Romans, count on protection under Roman law, and migrate to Rome. Moreover, when only visiting there, they could participate to a limited extent in the activities of the Tribal Assembly.[243]

As if to emphasize their near identity with Rome, the Latin Colonies seem now to have lost the *ius exilii* which before 338 had served to remind them that in Roman eyes theirs was foreign territory.[244] Above all, they were now no longer members of a separate and possibly anti-Roman organization. To exist collectively as the Nomen Latinum, for that is what they constituted, was not the same thing as being enrolled in the Latin League. The Latin League had been dismantled and the direct links of the seven were now individually, and indeed for the time being exclusively, with Rome. For they were now forbidden to meet unitedly, to intermarry, or to have contractual dealings with one another. This Roman veto on their mutual activities was probably due to the leading part that Setia and Circeii had taken in planning the Latin War, and almost certainly the ban was only temporary. But while it lasted, it served to emphasize their changed relationship with Rome.

The retention of the seven communities as Latin Colonies showed that Rome had no intention of eliminating the Latin element that for centuries had played so prominent a role in Latium. On the contrary, the seven would help to propagate the Latin tradition in a wider arena, since Rome was destined to found many similar colonies at ever greater distances from Latium, an extension of the Nomen Latinum that had been foreshadowed even before 340 with the foundation of Sutrium and Nepete outside Latium in southern Etruria. The first of these new Latin Colonies was planted as early as 334, at Cales on the borders of northern Campania.

All the probabilities are that after 338 it was the Latin Colonies collectively, and (as Livy and Asconius imply)[245] the Latin Colonies alone, that composed the Nomen Latinum. In other words, from now on only the inhabitants of *coloniae Latinae* were legally Latini. To distinguish them from the Latini of old, the Latini that had peopled archaic Latium and formed the Latin League, the latter now came to be known as Prisci Latini, the label under which they appear in the Roman antiquarians Festus and Servius. It is true that, besides the *municipia* with full citizenship and the seven continuing Latin Colonies, there were other communities in Latium that for ethnic or geographic reasons could be described as Latin. But these, although Prisci Latini, were now no longer in law a part of the Nomen Latinum despite their origins and mother tongue. By contrast any *colonia Latina*, situated no matter how far away from Latium, was hence-forth Latin *de iure*, and its settlers whatever their origin were legally Latini.[246] Thus, after 338, the political status of Latini, as of Romans, was no longer linked to a specific geographical base.

Foremost among the communities of Latium that were ethnically Latin but became neither *municipia* nor *coloniae* were Tibur and Praeneste, the communities of greatest consequence after Rome. In earlier days each had successfully incorporated some weaker neigh-bours and, although neither was capable by itself of defeating Rome, each had been strong enough to trade blows with her. They were in some sense her rivals, and before 338 Rome had thought it worth her while to sign a separate treaty (*foedus*) with each of them.[247] Both had fought against Rome in the Latin War, and when it was over had to cede territory to her. But they were not now annexed as *municipia*, and they could not become *coloniae*, since they had not originated as foundations of Rome and the Latin League: in fact, they were communities as old as, if not older than, Rome herself.[248] Each had its own storied past and was very conscious of its own identity; and it may have been the tenacity with which they clung to this conviction that saved them from losing their independence in 338. The Romans may well have felt that the simultaneous integration of five separate *populi Latini* was in itself difficult enough and that the assimilation of two extra, and them the most powerful and recalcitrant, would be beyond their capacity. Accordingly in 338 Tibur and Praeneste signed separate treaties with Rome.

Bilateral treaties of alliance of this kind were no novelty for the Romans. They had been used to such instruments even in the days when kings ruled. But, as Livy points out in a celebrated passage, treaties may be 'equal' or something very different, depending on the relative strengths of the contracting parties.[249] When it suited her interests, Rome would allow another state to negotiate with her on equal terms. But this rarely happened in Italy. There only a very few states were ever granted 'equal' treaties, and neither Tibur nor Praeneste were among them. These two Latin-speaking communities were forced to accept treaties of a type that made them dependent satellites, denied them a foreign policy of their own and obliged them to support the one laid down by her, with their armed forces should she so demand. The humiliating status of Tibur is revealed by the stinging public rebuke it received from the Roman Senate in the second century.[250]

In general the rights of Tibur and Praeneste relative to Rome closely resembled those of the Nomen Latinum, so closely indeed that they are often taken to be members of that body.[251] But ancient texts indicate that officially they did not form part of the Nomen Latinum,[252] and, in fact, they differed from it in one or two particulars. The temporary ban on mutual intercourse that Rome imposed on the other Latin communities (that is, on the residual *coloniae Latinae*) did not apply to Tibur and Praeneste; then again, as noted above, after 338 members of the Nomen Latinum did not enjoy *ius exilii*, whereas Tibur and Praeneste did.[253] So far as Rome was concerned, the two towns were no longer officially and legally Latin, no matter how Latin they were ethnically, socially and geographically. They were subject allies with a status not unlike that of the Hernican communities.

Another community of Latium to obtain allied status was Cora, which may have been one of the colonies founded jointly by Rome and the Latin League in the fifth century. It is not recorded as having fought against Rome in the Latin War or as having lost territory at its end. It is not mentioned in Livy's account of the peace settlement, but epigraphy reveals that prior to the Social War (91–87) Cora was allied to and technically independent of Rome.[254] It was administered by its own *duoviri* (who sometimes bore the title of praetors), possessed its own armed forces and issued its own coins. There is no record whether, like Tibur and Praeneste, it enjoyed *ius exilii* and also no record whether it was an 'equal' ally or not.

The community of the Laurentes at Lavinium formed another allied state. Its relationship with Rome was of a very special kind. In protohistoric Latium Lavinium had been a place of some size and more consequence, and by the fourth century it was regarded as the 'metropolis' of the Latini, venerated as a cult centre and site of at least three notable sanctuaries. Long before the Latin War, so it is said, Lavinium had signed an annually renewable treaty with Rome, more religious than military in nature; and in the Latin War it had abstained just in time from taking hostile action against Rome. The Romans could thus find a reason for treating Lavinium mildly at the war's end, and, as they valued Latin religious solidarity and felt that this could best be served by keeping the Laurentes as custodians of the most celebrated Latin shrines, they had good cause to do so. Accordingly they simply renewed the old treaty with Lavinium. Annexation of Lavinium might have proved an outrageous affront and rendered any eventual genuine reconciliation with the Latini unattainable. The Laurentes were thus left nominally independent to enjoy an altogether exceptional status under their own praetors until well into the days of the Roman Empire.[255]

About two other communities, Fidenae and Gabii, both renowned in the annals of archaic Latium, the surviving account of the Latin War settlement is silent. Perhaps by 338 they had withered to such insignificance that they were no longer functioning communities and could be ignored.

It will be seen that the measures taken by Rome at the end of the Latin War to ensure her permanent control of Latium were discriminating and complex.[256] They were also successful. After 338 Rome's grip on Latium was never prized loose – not by the Samnites, Pyrrhus, Hannibal nor even by the Social War insurgents. Moreover her domination of the region did not require the maintenance of a large standing army. The ever open doors of Janus indicate that the Roman Republic always had forces in the field somewhere. But they were not needed in Latium: there Latin Colonies stood guard.

Of even more lasting consequence was the strong impetus that Rome's measures after 338 gave to the diffusion of her language. It at once began to spread further afield. Etruscan Caere has yielded the

earliest *abecedarium* for Latin and an inscription, also of the fourth
century, in barely intelligible but recognizable Latin has been found
near Lucus Angitiae in the country of the Marsi.[257] Thus Latin was
moving beyond the western Sabini and the Hernici into southern
Etruria and central Italy: the romanization of the peninsula had
started.

In fact, so successful was the Latin War settlement that it
established a pattern for ongoing Roman policy. It provided Rome
with a model for any future territorial and cultural expansion. And
this soon materialized. Shortly after 338 she was to become involved
in conflicts in other parts of Italy. But operating from her secure base
in Latium, she was able steadily to expand her supremacy and
influence; and she did so by invoking the methods and instruments
that had consolidated her position there. In less than three-quarters
of a century she had managed to systematize as her exclusive sphere
of interest all of the peninsula south of the Pisa–Ariminum line. By
268 she was a Mediterranean power of the first rank fully capable of
crossing swords with Carthage. Italy had been made ready for its
ultimate destiny.

CHAPTER III

THE ORGANIZATION OF PENINSULAR ITALY

The Romans lost no time in consolidating the region between the Ciminian mountains and Campania. In Latium Adjectum they reduced the Aurunci to utter subjection;[258] they incorporated some Volsci and made dependent allies of others; and they brought the right bank of the Liris completely under their control.[259] They strengthened communications to Campania with a Latin Colony at Cales (334) to neutralize Sabellian Teanum Sidicinum,[260] and with a Citizen Colony at Tarracina (329) to co-operate with newly annexed Privernum, Fundi and Formiae in protecting the route along the Tyrrhenian coast.

The Samnites, against whom these moves were directed, countered by ensuring their own grip on the left bank of the Liris. But for the time being the activities of a Tarentine mercenary, Alexander the Molossian, in their rear kept them from doing much more than this. When, however, the Romans crossed the Liris in 328 and founded a Latin Colony at Fregellae on its left bank, the Samnites, freed from anxiety at that very moment by the opportune death of Alexander, no longer remained quiet: they took to arms.

The series of Samnite wars that ensued decided the fate of Italy, affecting directly in the process almost all the peoples of the peninsula as they attempted to preserve their own neutrality or prevent the supremacy of either main contender. Even the overseas adventurer, Pyrrhus of Epirus, became involved. By 268, however, the issue was settled. By then the Romans had made themselves masters of the whole peninsula,[261] fortunately for themselves since four years later they were at war with a major external power.

To achieve their hegemony the Romans had employed their devices of 338: confiscations of territory, incorporation of communities, and imposition of alliances. Owing, however, to the

3 Peninsular Italy

poverty of the sources and in particular the loss of Livy's second decade describing the period from 293 to 218 details are for the most part irretrievable. Only for the colony foundations is the surviving record of the Romans' activities anything like complete.

There is no way of proving the common assertion that normally each people as it was conquered was obliged to cede one-third of its territory to Rome. But there can be no doubt that her confiscations were very large and showed a tendency to get larger. In the third century Rome seized the entire territory of the Sabini and of the Senones, most of Picenum (apart from Asculum) and huge tracts of Etruria, Bruttium, and the Sallentine peninsula. The Aequi, Hernici, Paeligni perhaps, Praetuttii, Samnites, Vestini and Volsci are also all recorded as surrendering unspecified amounts of their territories.[262]

Rome did not retain all of the sequestrated territory for herself. Much of it was given over to newly founded Latin Colonies. Nevertheless a good deal of it remained permanently hers, with the result that by 268 Roman Italy had grown impressively. The annexation of the Sabine country as a result of the conquests of M'. Curius Dentatus (291/290), for instance, almost doubled the size of the Ager Romanus at one stroke; together with other seizures it gave Rome a solid belt of territory, that she could call her own, right across the central part of the peninsula from sea to sea.

The growth of Roman Italy is illustrated by the availability of Roman public land in various parts of Italy later and also by the creation of new Roman Tribes: the Oufentina on Volscian soil in Latium Adjectum and the Falerna in northern Campania in 318; the Aniensis on Aequian land in the valley of the river Anio and the Teretina amongst the Aurunci in the Latium-Campania border zone in 299; and after the First Punic War the Velina amongst the Praetuttii and Picentes, and the Quirina amid the Vestini and Sabini in 241.[263]

The territories of the new Tribes were not entirely denuded of their previous inhabitants and these were absorbed, slowly perhaps but surely. Besides these natives, however, the territories of the Tribes also accommodated large numbers of Roman *coloni*, each with his own allotment of land. The viritane distributions that settled these *coloni* are for the most part unrecorded, but the Sabine country is one region known to have received a good many of them.[264] Etruria, Umbria and Picenum seem to be others.

The number of small Roman settlements (*fora, conciliabula*) that such immigration generated was large, and caused the map of Italy to resemble a veritable patchwork, perhaps even more than is commonly thought. The diaspora of the Roman citizen body also lessened its cohesiveness and complicated its administration, since Rome's elected magistrates for the most part discharged their duties in Rome itself. There must have been local village officials to manage the elementary needs of the Roman rural settlements, but for the more demanding supervision of judicial procedures *praefecti iuri dicundo*, itinerant prefects resembling English circuit-judges, were used. They were appointed annually by the praetor in Rome, each of them being assigned to a specific assize-district (*praefectura*).[265]

These *praefecti* acquired exceptional importance in the third century owing chiefly to the kind of territory incorporated then. The huge additions to the Ager Romanus were made in central Italy and in the border areas of Samnium, regions where the tribal dispensation prevailed and the city-state was unknown. The natives lived in rudimentary hamlets and villages (*pagi, vici*) and these when annexed by Rome were unsuitable for immediate transformation into *municipia*. Rome, nevertheless, had a good reason for annexing them. To ensure against any repetition of the coalition of north and south that had so direly threatened her at Sentinum in 295, she needed a broad belt of Roman territory across central Italy stretching from the Tyrrhenian Sea to the Adriatic.

Details of the organization of the areas annexed by Rome are very scanty. But the identity of at least some of the peoples incorporated is revealed either by casual allusions in the extant literature or by the type of constitution they had after the Social War. The Italian communities incorporated after that conflict had *quattuorviri* (or in some cases *duoviri*) as their chief local magistrates, and this means that those whose magistrates were named differently from this had probably been constituted as Roman communities earlier.

Thus it is possible to infer that the following communities were incorporated before 90, all of them initially with partial citizenship, since none of them was Latin-speaking (it is, in fact, recorded of a number of them that their citizenship was *sine suffragio*): Volscian Privernum, Fundi and Formiae *c.*329 and Arpinum in 303, each of them apart from the first-named positively known to have had a trio of *aediles*; Hernican Anagnia, Capitulum and Frusino in 306, the first two with epigraphically attested *praetores*; Aequian Trebula Suffenas in 303; Sabine Trebula Mutuesca, Amiternum, Nursia, Reate, and probably Cures, allegedly in 290, of which at least the first three had *octoviri*; Vestinian Peltuinum and Aveia, of which at least the former had three *aediles*, probably *c.*290; Praetuttian Interamnia, it too with *octoviri* and probably *c.*290; Umbrian Fulginiae, administered by *uhtur* and *marones*, also possibly *c.*290; Pentrian Samnite Atina, Allifae and Venafrum, doubtfully assigned to *c.*270; Faliscan (?) Capena, which had a *praetor*, at an unknown date; and Etruscan Caere, where the chief local magistrate was a *dictator* (Etr. *purth*), probably *c.*270.[266]

The Volscian, Hernican, Faliscan and Etruscan communities on this list were in areas where the city-state had long existed, and it is probable that they were promptly made *municipia sine suffragio* with the same degree of autonomy as contemporary Capua. Whether the same should be postulated for Trebula Suffenas and Fulginiae is much more doubtful; and for the communities of the Sabini, Vestini, Praetuttii and Pentri (if these latter were, in fact, annexed *c.*270) it is safe to say that municipalization was at this time entirely out of the question. These peoples lived in small villages and the city-state was foreign to them. Their settlements in the third century were quite unsuitable for transformation into self-governing urban common-wealths; and epigraphic evidence proves that some Sabine communities were not constituted as *municipia* until the time of the Empire and may indicate that Vestinian Peltuinum never acquired that status at any time.[267]

It must, therefore, be assumed that these settlements after their incorporation, as well as before it, were organized as *pagi* of limited autonomy and that the Sabine *octoviri* and Vestinian *aediles* were native *pagus*-officials that had adopted Roman titles and discharged functions not unlike those of the local officials in the *fora* and *conciliabula* of the Roman *coloni*.

Throughout the whole region assize-districts (*praefecturae*) consisting of one or more settlements were established, each *praefectura* being named after the settlement in it that actually housed the prefect. Thus there is record of the *praefectura* of Amiternum, of Aveia, of Reate etc., and ultimately this led to the word *praefectura* being used as the title for a species of community, one that lacked the extensive autonomy of a *municipium* or a *colonia*, but was the residence of a *praefectus iuri dicundo* and as such a place of greater consequence than an ordinary *forum* or *pagus*, let alone a *conciliabulum* or *vicus*.[268] It should be borne in mind, however, that the word *praefectura* properly meant the prefect's assize-district, not the settle-ment in which he resided.[269] Apparently it was not until after the Social War that the word came to be used officially as the desig-nation for a particular kind of community.[270]

The *praefecti iuri dicundo* greatly helped to expedite integration. Their duties, as their title implied, were primarily judicial, being especially concerned with the working of Roman law among the full citizens, *coloni* for the most part, subject to it. The partial citizens had their own legal systems, as at Arpinum where testamentary procedures, for instance, differed from those at Rome.[271]

But in a region like the Roman corridor across central Italy, where settlements of *cives optimo iure* were mixed up with those of partial citizens, the prefects necessarily came to be much involved with the latter. Moreover, as the settlements generally lacked full autonomy, the prefects no doubt sometimes found themselves performing administrative functions as well as judicial. It has been suggested that it was they who helped the authorities at Rome to keep track of the *cives sine suffragio*.[272]

In the Sabine country the duties of the prefects must have assumed a new dimension when the partial citizens were elevated to the full citizenship. This happened quite early, as early as 268 according to Velleius. Probably not all the Sabini were made *cives optimo iure* that soon, however, since the Roman Tribe in which later most of them were registered, the Quirina, did not even exist until 241. The likelihood is that only Sabini living in *praefecturae* west of the river Himella in or near the settlements of Cures and Trebula Mutuesca were upgraded in 268: they were registered in Sergia, one of the tribes that did exist at that date. The Sabini further east probably did not become enfranchised until 241, or perhaps even later.[273]

In any case, whatever the date, the granting of full citizenship to the Sabini was an epoch-making event. It was the first time that Rome had made *cives optimo iure* of a whole community that was not Latin-speaking. The reason for her action was probably the desire to have the corridor across Italy as solidly Roman as possible; and full citizens rather than partial ones seemed more likely to make it so. The Romans needed more *cives optimo iure* at this time anyway in order to redress the balance of full to partial citizens that the spate of incorporations *c.*290 had upset. Secondly, they chose to upgrade the Sabini rather than other Italians because they could perhaps be assimilated more easily owing to the affinity that existed between

Romans and Sabini. The story of the Sabini helping Romulus to get Rome started can be dismissed as fiction, but, like the tales about Numa Pompilius, Atta Clausus and Appius Herdonius, it indicates that Sabini had been in Latium and close neighbours of Rome from her earliest days. Romans even believed, whether correctly or not is immaterial, that their own name for themselves, Quirites, derived from Cures, the Sabine community that had given them their early king Numa Pompilius, the very king who had taught them how to retain divine favour. This belief enjoyed wide currency in the third century, and before the end of that century it had hardened into the firm tradition that Fabius Pictor, Rome's first historian, knew. It may have been the growing latinization of the Sabini that helped to foster the legend. By 300 many western Sabini had abandoned their native tongue for Latin, and before the century was out the eastern Latini were adopting it too. Latin was even spreading among their Vestinian neighbours in the valley of the upper Aternus,[274] although as the Romans did not have any tales or tradition of mutual relations with these they did not have similar feelings of kinship with them. If the choice of Sabini for elevation to the full Roman citizenship was due in even the smallest degree to their latinization (and Strabo hints that it was), it was a significant portent foreshadowing Roman practice in later times.[275]

In 268, however, it was a kind of culmination, for it seems that the Romans now decided to call a halt to the policy of incorporating whole communities in Italy. 'Old' citizens seemed in some danger of being swamped by 'new', and it is clear that Rome in 268 hesitated long before creating any more new Tribes,[276] probably to give time for many more 'old' Romans to settle in central Italy and thus make the authentically Roman presence there stronger. Finally two more rustic Tribes were brought into being, in 241. But these were the last. The risk of 'new' Romans preponderating in future new Tribes was now altogether too real. Accordingly the number of Roman Tribes was frozen at thirty-five and became canonical.[277]

Among the Roman citizens registered in the rustic Tribes were the settlers of the Citizen Colonies. Down to the end of the Second Punic War, and even slightly beyond, these settlements were *coloniae maritimae*, even though the three founded between 300 and 268 seem to have been intended to police communications by land as much as to repel raiders by sea: Minturnae and Sinuessa (295) controlled the coastal route around the end of the Mons Massicus and Sena Gallica (*c*.289) the southbound route to the Colfiorito pass across the central Appennines.

As already noted, the Citizen Colonies were extensions of Rome established on the coasts of Italy. But they were not held in high esteem. Although autonomous, each was a very small settlement consisting of only three hundred settlers who had been given minuscule plots of land. It was supervised by a pair of chief officials (in imitation, no doubt, of Rome's two consuls), who seem to have had the unpretentious title of *duoviri*, possibly because the range of their judicial authority was quite restricted. The low regard felt for these Citizen Colonies made it difficult to find recruits for them, and from their earliest beginnings Rome was obliged to accept non-Romans as settlers in them.[278] On the whole, it is not surprising that she founded so few colonies of this type.

Rome showed no similar reluctance to found Latin Colonies, establishing at least eighteen of them in the seventy-year period from 338 to 268. Every four years or so, on the average, she planted a new Latin Colony, and this was a prodigious effort, for the 2,500 to 6,000 settlers required for each foundation were for the most part recruited from her own citizen body, even though Latini and perhaps other Italians were accepted as settlers.[279] Collectively the Latin Colonies constituted the Nomen Latinum, for the settlers in them had to give up their Roman citizenship and accept Latin status instead.

Latin Colonies were always strategically sited – to control a traffic artery, to guard a river crossing, to supervise a fertile plain, to shield the territory of a Roman rustic Tribe from attack.[280] The actual townsite of a *colonia* normally housed only a part of its population, but it also served as a place of refuge for all and consequently was strongly fortified with massive walls.[281] The territory of a *colonia*, being intended to sustain the whole community, was usually ample.

Listed in chronological order the Latin Colonies clearly indicate the course of Roman expansion. Cales (334) countered Samnite-controlled Teanum Sidicinum and protected a new Roman rustic Tribe, Falerna (318). Fregellae (328), Luceria (314), Saticula, Suessa Aurunca, Pontiae (313), Interamna Lirenas (312), Sora, Alba Fucens (303), Narnia (299), Carseoli (298), Venusia (291), Beneventum (268) and Aesernia (263) encircled and even dismembered the Samnite League, penetrated the mid-Italic region, and safeguarded the territories of the new Tribes Oufentina (381), Teretina (299) and Aniensis (299). Hadria and possibly Castrum Novum (*c*.289), Cosa,

Paestum (273) and Ariminum (268) helped to strengthen the Roman grip on Picenum, Etruria, Lucania and the Ager Gallicus respectively,[282] protected the coasts of Italy, and ensured some security for the Tribes Quirina and Velina when they came to be created later (241). Clearly it was the Latin Colonies, not the Citizen variety, that Cicero had in mind when he talked about *coloniae* being 'bulwarks of empire' (*propugnacula imperii*).[283]

But great as was their strategic and military importance, it was their impact on the linguistic and cultural pattern of the peninsula that most matters for the present study. Initially the colonies were communities varying in size from 8,000 to 20,000 persons, since they included not only the settlers but their families as well. All spoke Latin, even the non-Romans among them using that language either as mother-tongue or as lingua franca. The despatch of groups of such size to so many different points would have disseminated their language under any circumstances, but the situation in third-century Italy was especially favourable to its diffusion. It is true that the colonists were not pushing a frontier forward against primitive nomads in the manner of pioneers in nineteenth-century North America or Australia. But a colony was regularly assigned a territory larger than was needed for the allotments of its settlers, and many of its earlier inhabitants continued to live on it. The political and social barriers between them and the colonists gradually gave way and in a comparatively short time, probably within two or three generations, the natives had been absorbed and become indistinguishable in speech and most other respects from the descendants of the colonists.[284] Something of the sort must also have happened in Citizen Colonies; but, as they were so much smaller and fewer than the Latin variety, their effect on Republican Italy was less marked.

The Latin Colonies were Roman in more than speech. Ethnically they were largely Roman and, even though they no longer possessed the Roman citizenship, they retained their Roman political habits. Each colony, like Rome, had a pair of annually elected chief executives, and these bore the very Roman title of *praetor*. Their physical arrangements were equally Roman. The townsite of a *colonia Latina* had its *forum*, *comitium* and temple of the Capitoline triad; and in some the town was even divided into wards named after the wards of Rome. The buildings themselves were Roman in style and decoration. The influence of the surrounding natives occasionally emerges: it can be seen, for instance, in inscriptions from Luceria and Venusia, in coin-weights and types from Ariminum, and in coin legends of Aesernia. But in general life in a Latin Colony from the material point of view was very Roman.

The Latin Colonies, it has been said, really provided the instrument for the romanization of Italy, and certainly they could have taken little time in latinizing thoroughly the Latium-Campania border region, where there were many of them. Even in other regions they must have radiated Roman influence well beyond the immediate confines of their own territories. On the other hand, it must be remembered that in the third century there were still extensive areas of peninsular Italy without Latin Colonies, and after 268 not many more such colonies were founded there.

The Nomen Latinum was by far the most useful and trustworthy group of allies, inevitably so and not merely for ethnic reasons. The Latini needed Rome just as much as she needed them. Situated sometimes at great distances from Rome and from one another, usually in the midst of populations that were resentful of Rome's conquest and of the colonists' presence, the colonies had to maintain their Roman connection in order to survive. For Rome they were a most effective instrument of power.

Rome's other allies in Italy were much less homogeneous than the Latini, and they seem to have differed from the Nomen Latinum in another particular also. Each non-Latin ally had its own treaty to define its relations with Rome. There is no sign of a similar practice in the case of the Latin Colonies.[285] Perhaps their rights and obligations were thought to be indicated, even though not protected, by the Foedus Cassianum that Rome had signed (in 493 ?) with the old Latin League and that, although abrogated in 338, was still carefully preserved at Rome down at least to the time of Augustus. On the whole, however, it is more likely that the status of the Nomen Latinum was made explicit by a unilateral pronouncement of the Roman Senate.

Be that as it may, the non-Latin allies as distinct from the Latin displayed a multiplicity of treaties, as well as of languages, sentiments, cultures and constitutions. Ancient authors often allude to these allies and, even though no complete and definitive list of them survives, their number must have been very large. Positive evidence exists for the allied status of Hernican Aletrium, Ferentinum and Verulae; Sidicine Teanum; Campanian Abella, Nola and Nuceria; Italiote Heraclea, Neapolis, Rhegium, Tarentum and Velia; Apulian

Arpi, Canusium and Teanum; Faliscan Falerii; Etruscan Volsinii; Umbrian Camerinum, Iguvium and Ocriculum; Picentine Asculum; mid-Italic Marrucini, Marsi, Paeligni, and Vestini; Sabellian Bruttii, Frentani, Hirpini, Lucani and Samnites; and Messapian Iapyges. But there were undoubtedly many more who have escaped individual notice, such as the states of Etruria mentioned, but not identified, by Aristotle.[286] In fact, one can confidently assert that by 268 there was no community south of the Pisa–Ariminum line, apart from Rome herself, that was truly independent.[287] All were linked to her in some way or other.

Technically the allies were independent, living their own lives in their own way. They showed infinite variety. Some were organized tribally, others were commonwealths of the urban mini-type. States with a rigidly stratified social organization (such as those of Etruria) lived in close proximity to those described as democratic (such as those of Sabellian Italy). A few had 'equal' treaties with Rome, while the overwhelming majority did not. All alike, however, were in the same general condition of not being able to pursue an individual foreign policy or go to war with one another: instead they were required to follow Rome's lead and provide her with armed support whenever she called for it.

Local administration in all of them was almost bound to be in the hands of the well-to-do, the families of property and prestige, who alone could afford to hold office; and Rome undoubtedly preferred that this should be so, since it ensured smooth functioning of her arrangements. Their permanently privileged position gave the local élite a vested interest in the system, and the key to Rome's success in controlling Italy was her manipulation of these Italian magnates (*primores Italiae*; *principes populorum Italicorum*). Should they not prove either submissive or co-operative enough, stern measures might be needed, and the Romans were prepared to be tough.[288] Instances of Roman severity are recorded in the third century. But in general the allied states were neither restive nor turbulent: their leaders accepted Roman paramountcy.

How the many treaties differed from one another in detail is not known. Presumably they were all without time-limit, but they could not have been identical in wording since particular duties were evidently specified for certain of the allies. States on the coast, for instance, might be required to furnish naval aid, if necessary, rather than military. Then again what Livy calls an 'equal' treaty must have been couched in different terms from one that was not, even though it seems unlikely that any were undiplomatically labelled 'unequal': the inferior character of a treaty had to be inferred from the tenor of its clauses. Cicero implies that one sign of an 'equal' treaty was that it did not include the so-called *maiestas* clause, the clause that obliged the non-Roman signatory 'to uphold the greatness of the Roman People without reservation'. But Cicero himself provides evidence that an 'unequal' treaty was not bound to include the clause.[289] It was certainly written into the treaties that Rome signed later with Aetolia and Gades, and possibly into those with Mitylene and Cnidos. But these states were all outside Italy, and there is actually no evidence, much less any proof, of the *maiestas* clause ever being included in an Italian treaty, despite the fact that states with 'equal' treaties were very rare in Italy, numbering perhaps no more than three, Camerinum, Heraclea and Neapolis.[290] Those that did have such treaties were evidently proud of their exceptional status, although clearly it did not make them the equals of Rome. In fact, just like other Italian states, they have to be reckoned among the dependents of Rome.

By 268 then peninsular Italy, like Julius Caesar's Gaul two centuries later, was divided into three parts; and Rome evidently intended the tripartite arrangement with its Roman, Latin and Italian areas to be permanent. The peninsula looked like a natural geographical unit with a good defensible boundary in the north Appennine watershed that runs almost due east from the gulf of Genoa to the upper Adriatic, and Rome's victory in the war against Pyrrhus (280–272) had greatly increased her stature throughout the country and strengthened her grip on it. Hence in 268 it seemed to the Romans that the entire country south of the Pisa-Ariminum line could be made their exclusive sphere of interest, and they, therefore, sought to consolidate it firmly.

They felt that they could now afford to end their policy of incorporating whole communities. The elevation of Sabini to full citizenship in this very year (268) had increased the number of Romans to the point where they would no longer need to be augmented periodically by the admission of foreign groups into their body politic. From now on their own natural increase, together with servile manumissions and the enfranchisement of individual foreigners, would be sufficient to maintain their citizen numbers – and their hegemony. Furthermore, no matter whereabouts in the peninsula their full citizens resided, the censors would be able to enrol them in the Roman rustic Tribes and thus keep track of them: all that they needed to do was to fragment the territories of the Tribes instead of keeping them solid and unbroken. This policy evidently was adopted in 268, for the upgraded Sabine partial citizens of that year were registered in Sergia even though this entailed having one part of that Tribe's *territorium* separate from the tribal core.[291]

The decision to incorporate no more entire communities may well have been prompted by the fact that any community annexed by the Romans henceforth would inevitably speak a language other than Latin and would, therefore, have to get the partial citizenship; and the Romans distrusted *cives sine suffragio* as perfidious, with some reason, no doubt, seeing that Satricum, Capua, Calatia and Atella had all tried to rebel at critical periods of the Second Samnite War (326–304).

It would probably be more useful to have Italian communities as allies than as partially enfranchised *municipia*. Rome was, after all, relying on the local aristocrats to make her system in Italy work, and they preferred even a sham independence to incomplete Roman citizenship. The contrasting behaviour of rebellious Roman Capua and stalwart allied Nola later in the Second Punic War indicates that the dignity of an allied notable was better satisfied by his being the first magistrate of an ostensibly sovereign state than a second class citizen of Rome.[292]

The decision taken in 268 to stop incorporating Italian communities means that Caere, so far from being the first *municipium* without the vote (as Gellius mistakenly says), was probably the last. A hundred-year truce signed with Caere in 353 broke down *c.*273 and Rome promptly attacked and captured the place, and confiscated half its territory. Caere itself was incorporated and granted *civitas sine suffragio*, probably at this time.[293]

It was perhaps also at this time that citizens without the vote, instead of being allowed to serve in military units of their own, were required to serve in Rome's legions (see Appendix III). This made it necessary for Rome to keep a roster of them which must have been compiled from information supplied by the voteless communities, perhaps through the *praefecti iuri dicundo*. The roster is known to have included also the names of native Romans degraded by the censors for misconduct. It was probably the coincidence of this new military dispensation with the annexation of Caere as a *municipium sine suffragio* that caused the registers of partial citizens to be known as Caerite Tables (*tabulae Caerites*).

To offset any disadvantage that might result from the cessation of integral incorporations, Rome seems to have tightened her bonds with the Latin Colonies. At any rate *coloniae Latinae* founded from 268 on appear to have stood in a special relationship with her. There were twelve such colonies, starting with Ariminum in this very year and ending with Aquileia in 181, and it is difficult not to see in them the twelve colonies singled out by Cicero for their exceptional status. It looks as if their links with Rome were closer and more intimate than those of earlier Latin Colonies, one symptom of this being the titles that the two colonies founded in 268 gave to their local magistrates: Ariminum and Beneventum, if only for a time, had consuls as their chief executives instead of the praetors usually found in Latin Colonies. The townsites of these two colonies also seem to have been divided into wards bearing the same names as wards in Rome.

Evidently Rome was going to rely on her Latin Colonies, not on communities of partial citizens. Any Italian elements that seemed worth cultivating more closely could now be recruited into the colonies and converted into Latini rather than into *cives sine suffragio*.

It was in 268 likewise that Rome took a step that was bound to ensure her ultimate control of the economic life of the peninsula. Down to 300 her economic role, although important, had not been dominant. In fact, she had not even found it necessary to issue coins of her own until after the Third Samnite War (298–291). Her earliest currency took the form of heavy ingots and clumsy coins weighing one Roman pound each that were produced by pouring molten bronze into moulds. But even now she was not the only central Italian state that minted. A number of others also issued bronze pieces of similar crudity. By 268, however, Rome had made herself the military and political mistress of the whole peninsula, and at the same time she had become economically more sophisticated. Therefore she now began to strike coins, instead of merely casting them, and no longer only in bronze: some of her coins were now of silver. These issues were clearly intended for circulation throughout Italy. One consequence was that a number of Italian states now ceased minting, probably not because of any positive order from Rome to do so, but out of a prudent desire to avoid the appearance, and the expense, of competing with her.[294]

Thus by 268 peninsular Italy had been arranged and organized so as to be effectively under Roman sway. But, contrary to what is commonly asserted, it had not been converted into a Roman confederacy. It did not even remotely resemble a federal union. There was no federal council, no machinery for bringing the Italian states together for joint consultation or even for dealing communally with Rome.[295] Nor was there in the third century much unity of sentiment: Pyrrhus, being an invader from overseas, had not deterred Italians – Samnites, Lucani, Messapii, Italiotes – from joining him in large numbers. Shared military experience under Roman direction may have engendered some camaraderie and feelings of ethnic kinship. Common trading interests and other material considerations may have led to some regional groupings within the system. The Romans may even have encouraged a military league or two to promote military efficiency. But, in general, the Italian states supplied military aid individually, not jointly; and it took many a campaign and the stern trials of the Punic Wars before pan-Italian patriotism began to stir.

It would be truer to say that the Roman system in Italy was divisive, not federative. So far from forming a confederacy, non-Roman Italy was a congeries of Rome's subject allies. Not one of them was genuinely independent, and all of them were controlled by Rome and linked to her by their bilateral treaties.

The system judiciously entangled allied Italy with Roman Italy so as to make it hopeless for any single community, acting alone, to challenge Rome's hegemony. Joint action by all presumably would have been successful, but it was most unlikely to materialize. Gradation of privilege – full Roman citizenship for some, partial for others; intimacy with Rome for Latini, foreign status for other Italians – ensured an ongoing conflict of interests. Full citizens had little reason to agitate for the elevation of those without the vote. The favoured Nomen Latinum was hardly likely to make common cause with an anti-Roman Italian combination. The Italians were so heterogeneous in language, culture and sentiment that the better disposed would hardly join in a revolt of the recalcitrant. Moreover, as all were under obligation to help Rome at her bidding, a revolt by one would automatically find itself opposed by the combined forces of all. Masterly statecraft enabled Rome to devise and apply a policy which a later age, resorting to Rome's own language, tersely described as *divide et impera*.

There is, however, another side to the story. It has been well said
that control is part of the machinery of freedom.[296] Rome imposed
control, but she also provided protection. At times it must have been
very comforting for Italians to know that in times of trouble Rome's
power was there to support them. Some of them are even said to
have become part of the Roman system in the first place precisely
because it bade fair to be a haven. Rome's strength may not have
been loved, but it was certainly respected and even, to judge from
some Italiote coinage issues, admired.[297] Above all, Rome put an
end to fighting between Italian states with incalculable benefit to
all.[298]

CHAPTER IV

THE IMPACT OF THE
PUNIC WARS

Rome had scarcely completed her organization of the peninsula
when the whole structure was put to the severe and prolonged test of
the First Punic War (264–241). She at once took the precaution of
strengthening both coasts of Italy, the Adriatic with a Latin Colony
at Firmum in Picenum and the Tyrrhenian with Citizen Colonies at
Castrum Novum and Pyrgi in Etruria. Later in the conflict she
reinforced both coasts still further, the Adriatic with another Latin
Colony, at Brundisium in 244, and the Tyrrhenian with two more
Citizen Colonies, at Alsium in 247 and Fregenae in 245. For security
within Italy Rome established yet another watch-dog Latin Colony
over her old enemies the Samnites, at Aesernia in 263, and also found
it necessary to destroy Etruscan Volsinii at the war's outbreak
(265/264) and Faliscan Falerii at its end (241), forcing the survivors of
both places to migrate and re-establish themselves on far less
defensible sites. In addition, Rome had to suppress a mutiny of 4,000
socii navales and 3,000 runaway slaves.

The course of the war and its outcome vindicated the soundness of
the system that Rome had fashioned in Italy. For the most part the
Latini and the Italians did what was required of them. Had they acted
otherwise, it is difficult to see how Rome could possibly have coped
with so exhausting an ordeal.

The behaviour of her allies was probably dictated more by
prudence than by patriotism. Celtic and Epirote assaults before 265
had possibly aroused some pan-Italian sentiment in them, but it was
little more than embryonic. Even Rome was not particularly keen to
promote Italian solidarity for fear that it might take an anti-Roman
turn. Such a fear was not unreasonable in view of the fact that the
fruits of victories regularly went to Rome. She emerged, for
instance, from the First Punic War as an imperialist power with
overseas provinces, whereas the Latin and Italian states were obliged

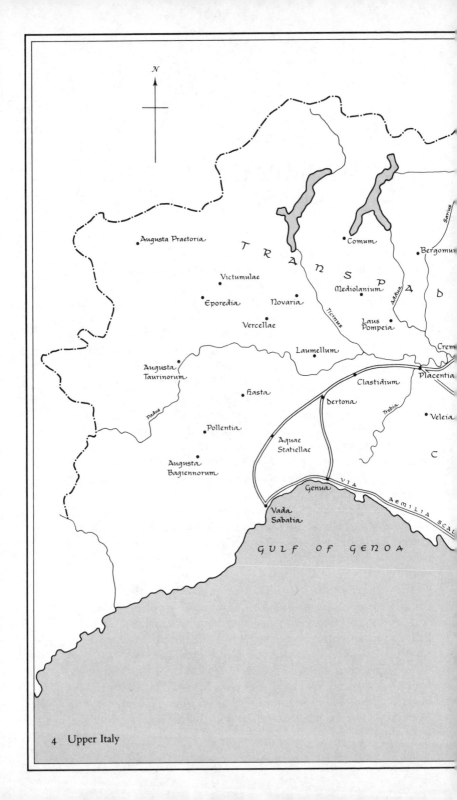

N

Augusta Praetoria

T R A N S P A D

Comum

Bergomum

Victumulae

Mediolanium

Eporedia

Novaria

Vercellae

Ticinus

Addua

Laus Pompeia

Laumellum

Crem...

Augusta Taurinorum

Padus

Hasta

Clastidium

Placentia

Dertona

Trebia

Veleia

Pollentia

Aquae Statiellae

C

Augusta Bagiennorum

V I A

Genua

A E M I L I A   SCAU...

Vada Sabatia

G U L F   O F   G E N O A

4 Upper Italy

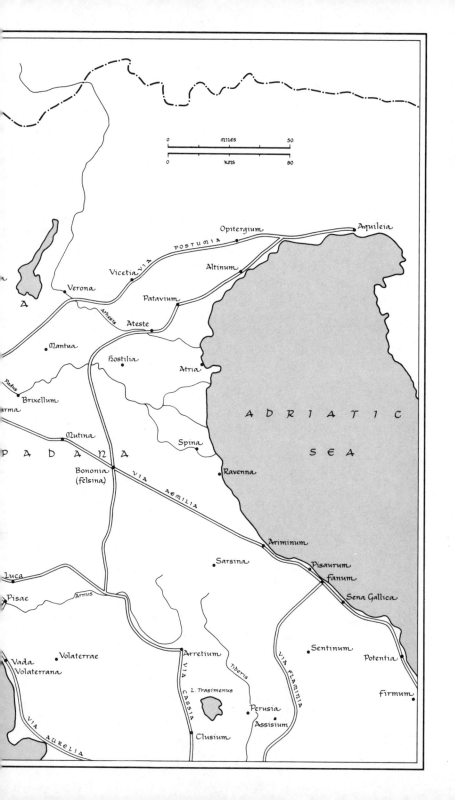

ADRIATIC

SEA

PADANA

VIA AEMILIA

VIA POSTUMIA

VIA FLAMINIA

VIA CASSIA

VIA AURELIA

Aquileia

Opitergium

Altinum

Vicetia

Verona

Patavium

Ateste

Mantua

Hostilia

Atria

Brixellum

arma

Mutina

Bononia
(Felsina)

Spina

Ravenna

Ariminum

Sarsina

Pisaurum

Fanum

Luca

Sena Gallica

Pisae

Sentinum

Potentia

Vada
Volaterrana

Volaterrae

Arretium

Firmum

L. Trasimenus

Perusia

Assisium

Clusium

Athesis

Padus

Arnus

Tiberis

MILES   50

KMS   80

to remain with their *status quo ante* and without additions to their territories. They must have been disappointed at this, to use no stronger term, and it probably required the dangerous invasions of the Gauls in 225 and of Hannibal in 218 to frighten them into taking a more resigned view of Rome's hegemony.

Whatever the attitude of the Italians, the horizon of the Romans had undoubtedly widened. By the year 241 they no longer regarded the watershed of the northern Appennines as the natural boundary for Italy. In 266 they had made dependent allies of the Umbrian (?) Sarsinates who lived on the northern slopes of that mountain barrier and who had once, so it was said, dominated both Mantua and Perusia. Rome may also have signed a treaty with Ravenna (another Umbrian community?) situated just to the south of the delta of the Po. Such activities showed that the Romans were already thinking of the Alps, rather than the Appennines, as the true bulwarks of Italy, a change of view imposed perhaps by the menace of the Cisalpine Gauls. As a consequence, once the First Punic War was over, the interval (240–219) down to the Second Punic War (218–201) was largely taken up with a systematic effort to subjugate Cisalpina.[299]

A direct initial thrust through the central passes of the north Appennine watershed seemed to the Romans both difficult and perilous, since they did not control the approaches to them. They therefore went around the extremities. At the western end hard skirmishing in the years after 241 won them control of the bay of Spezia and the port of Genoa in or near the territories of the Ligurian Apuani and Ingauni respectively. But it was at the eastern extremity that the really heavy fighting took place, against the Gallic Boii. Here Latin Ariminum guarded the gap around the mountains and allied Sarsina guarded the Mandrioli pass across them. The Romans also had a good base and starting point there in the so-called Ager Gallicus which they had seized *c*.280 and settled with viritane *coloni* *c*.232. Latin Spoletium (241), controlling the Valle di Spina and the Colfiorito pass over the central Appennines, ensured their communications with the region. The disunity of the Cisalpine populations was also in their favour, and they succeeded in winning over and making allies of the Cenomani and Veneti.[300]

The Boii, aided by the terrain, which, in the latter half of the third century, was still extremely difficult because of its dense forests and extensive marshes, proved dangerous foes. In 225, enlisting the support of the Insubres and of transalpine mercenaries (*gaesati*), and

possibly of some Taurini, they poured across the central passes of the
north Appennine watershed, thereby avoiding Ariminum. They
then advanced down the western coast of the peninsula almost to
within striking distance of Rome.

This massive Gallic invasion is responsible for one of the most
important documents of the Roman Republic. A list of the forces
that Rome in her alarm planned to deploy should it become
necessary is preserved by Polybius. It derives from Fabius Pictor,
who actually served in 225, and reveals that in that year Rome could
mobilize over half a million men of military age, of whom rather
more than half were Latini or other allies.[301]

The crisis of 225 was possibly the first occasion that Rome sought
to draw up a list of all the forces at her disposal. But whether that be
the case or not, the compilation of the roster could not have been a
simple or straightforward matter, for normally Rome did not
supervise, much less conduct, any census in non-Roman Italy.
Perhaps on this occasion each people was ordered to let the Roman
consuls know the maximum number of its military effectives; but, if
so, it is not easy to see how Rome could or would have been able to
verify what was reported to her. The roster looks like an emergency
makeshift and it may have been resented as a device for squeezing
extra troops out of the Italian communities. Possibly it was a factor
in the Capuan revolt nine years later and in the resistance of twelve
Latin Colonies to Rome's insistent demand for men in 209.

In the event, the victory at Telamon ended the Gallic threat in 225.
The Romans then took the bold decision to carry the war into the
heart of Cisalpina by advancing from Ariminum. It was now that
Flaminius enhanced his fame by crossing the Po to attack the
Insubres in their homeland (223); and at about the same time M.
Claudius Marcellus began his illustrious military career with victory
over a motley host of Gauls at Clastidium (222). This opened the
door to more distant Piemonte and the mountain strongholds of the
Ligures and won for Marcellus himself the *spolia opima* because of his
hand-to-hand defeat of Virdumarus, chieftain of the Anamares.
These successes made the Romans masters of Cisalpina; and, the
better to discharge the role, they began construction in 220 of a great
military highway, the Via Flaminia, from Rome to Ariminum via
the Scheggia pass and Fanum on the Adriatic coast.[302] Another
highway running north from Rome along the Tyrrhenian coast may
have been built even earlier than this, the Via Aurelia, named

perhaps after C. Aurelius Cotta, consul in 252 and 248 and censor in 241: but as it led into the difficult mountain country of Liguria, it was not as suitable as the Flaminia for troop movements to Cisalpina.

The Romans also followed their usual practice and expropriated a large tract of Cisalpine territory. On it they founded two large Latin Colonies in 218, Cremona and Placentia, on the northern and southern bank of the Po respectively. These colonies were well sited to prevent any renewed co-operation of Boii with Insubres and to keep attackers north of the river. The new colonies also provided some control of the approaches to the central passes across the north Appennine watershed. Rome, in effect, had extended her hegemony of Italy as far north as the river Po.

It was at this juncture, however, that Hannibal arrived to undo most of what Rome had achieved in upper Italy. She managed to retain Cremona and Placentia but very little else, and Hannibal was able to invade the peninsula proper.

Hannibal in the Second Punic War counted heavily on non-Roman Italy. Like that other great enemy of Rome, his contemporary Philip V of Macedon, he was reasonably well informed about Romano-Italian relations and hoped to make them serve his cause. He planned to shatter Rome's system in Italy, not so much by capturing Italian cities (for he had no illusions about his inability to storm well-walled strongholds), but by persuading them to throw in their lot with him. Once he had isolated Rome and rendered her helpless, he would be able to impose his own Carthaginian peace. Hannibal was, in fact, hoping that by his victories over Rome he would undermine her morale and by his favours to Italians he would entice them to his side.

In Cisalpine Gaul this strategy was more than a little successful. From the moment of his arrival Insubres, Boii and Ligures supported him enthusiastically. In 216 the Boii annihilated L. Postumius Albinus and a Roman army in the Litanian forest, and throughout the war, and even after it, Carthage continued to find Gauls and Ligures willing and eager to fight against Rome.[303]

In peninsular Italy, however, it was another story. South of the Pisa-Ariminum line not a single community could at first be induced to join Hannibal despite his spectacular triumphs at the river Trebia (218) and Lake Trasimene (217) and despite his victory parade through Campania after inflicting the latter disaster. It was not until he overwhelmed the Roman army at Cannae (216) that large-scale defection from Rome began.

Capua may not have been the first, but was certainly the most important peninsular community to go over to Hannibal, and it was at once joined by Atella, Calatia and the Sabatini, all in Campania. In Apulia Aecae, Arpi, and Herdonia and in the Sallentine peninsula Uzentum threw in their lot with him. Among the Samnite tribes, the Hirpini (led by the important settlement of Compsa) and the Caudini both defected; about the Carricini no record survives. Most of the Bruttii and very many Lucani followed suit.

Other Italians, if they did not actually revolt, began to waver, especially the Etruscans, on whose soil he had won his great victory at Trasimene. Rome thought it prudent to take hostages from Arretium and other Etruscan states as guarantees for their good behaviour, and throughout the war she regularly stationed one and sometimes two legions in Etruria. Perhaps it is significant that there is very little record of Etruscan states apart from Perusia supplying combat troops for Rome's armies; and even the materiel they supplied may have been sent more out of prudence than goodwill. It is also to be noted that individual Etruscans are known to have fought for Hannibal. Umbria also needed watching by Rome. Obviously in peninsular Italy lukewarm irresolution, if not positive rebellion, was sufficiently widespread to cause considerable concern.[304]

Nevertheless, the universal revolt that Hannibal was hoping for did not materialize. In fact, no tribe or community went over to him in its entirety except in Campania and the far south. Latium, central Italy, Picenum, most of the ports, and the Nomen Latinum everywhere made no move to support him; and in the upshot neither did Umbria or even Etruria. Concluding that he could expect no help from the northern and central regions of the peninsula, Hannibal never visited them again after Cannae except for his brief diversionary feint at Rome in 211 in a futile attempt to relieve Roman pressure on Capua. He could not persuade, and he lacked the power to dragoon them.

To compound his disappointment even Campania and the south were far from whole-hearted in their support of him. In Campania Cumae, Nola, Nuceria and Acerrae remained firmly loyal to Rome no matter what it cost them, and for Nuceria and Acerrae the cost was high. On the borders of Campania Teanum Sidicinum stood firm for Rome and Caiatia parted company with its fellow Caudini by refusing to join Hannibal. Further south, some of the Lucani stayed with Rome. So did many Bruttii: Petelia and Consentia actually held out against him with desparate courage for as long as they could. Amongst the Samnites the most powerful tribe, the Pentri, remained loyal to Rome despite the hardships that this entailed. The Frentani, including Larinum, also stood by Rome; and apparently so did Teanum Apulum and Canusium among the Apuli. The Messapii, exposed like the Bruttii to his full might and fury, did prudently give him aid, and some of them actually volunteered their services to him. But even the Messapii for the most part acted only under duress. This was also true of the turbulent Italiotes who, generally speaking, joined him only with reluctance, justifiably fearing that, if they did not, he would let loose the dreaded Bruttii upon them.[305]

It was in the Oscan-speaking districts that Hannibal found his greatest support; but even there it was far from fervent and usually due to his looming presence. Communities joined him lest he destroy either them or their harvests. Hannibal must have been sorely disappointed with the Italian response to his overtures, all the more so since the communities that did go over to him did so grudgingly, whereas those loyal to Rome displayed almost incredible stout-heartedness. Capua supported Hannibal with at best lukewarm conviction; Petelia resisted him with unyielding resolution. Wherever his troops went they found a sullen and chilly reception and sometimes scorched earth; Rome's troops could count on aid and comfort everywhere. Clearly morale was on the side of Rome.

It is no exaggeration to say that Rome was saved because of the help she received from her Latin and Italian allies; and it is worth recording, even if the surviving literature which embodies the Roman tradition is little concerned to publicize it.[306]

Appian is probably exaggerating when he says that Italy fielded twice as many men as Rome herself.[307] But Italy did almost certainly supply more than half the troops opposing Hannibal, and some of them were of excellent quality. The Nomen Latinum and the mid-Italic region provided exceptionally good soldiers. It was a contingent of Pentrian Samnites who inflicted the first defeat (admittedly a minor one) upon Hannibal in the field; and the sources refer repeatedly to the feats of Latini, the Paelignian cohort, and the soldiers of other tribes. Even the Etruscans fielded some combat troops, although their quality was not always reliable.

Rome got more than fighting men from Italy. The strongholds of the peninsula were placed at her disposal and she put them to good use. In Cisalpina the Latin Colonies Placentia, Cremona and Ariminum, in the centre Etruscan Arretium, and in the south Campanian Suessula and Latin Beneventum, Luceria and Venusia were powerful bastions.[308] Other places provided shelter and comfort for Roman troops: Apulian Canusium, for instance, gave asylum to the remnants from Cannae. Nor were Bruttian Petelia and Campanian Acerrae alone in their defiance of Hannibal: Latin Spoletium, Italiote Tarentum (its citadel at least), Campanian Nola, Apulian Salapia and other places were similarly resolute.

Italian loyalty can hardly be attributed to affection for Rome or even at this stage to 'national Italian patriotism'.[309] Time and habit had not yet fully reconciled the Italians to their dependent status, much less imbued them with a Roman outlook. Nor had the seeds of pan-Italian patriotism sown by Brennus and Pyrrhus burgeoned as yet into mature and robust growth. The year 209 made that clear. By then Hannibal's worst seemed definitely over. Sicily, Capua and other centres had been recovered; the situation in Spain was well in hand; Hannibal was confined to the deep south; and Hasdrubal had not yet arrived in the north from Spain. For the second year in a row the outlook was sufficiently reassuring for Rome to make do with fewer legions, twenty-one in 210 and 209 as against twenty-five in 211. With such a combination of favourable circumstances Italian particularism promptly revived, even amongst Rome's closest allies: in 209 twelve of the Latin Colonies refused her further military aid on the ground that they were exhausted.[310] It was perhaps fortunate for Rome that Hasdrubal reached Italy shortly afterwards, for the alarm that he aroused before his defeat and death in 207 prevented the movement started by the recusant twelve from spreading further.

The attitude of Rome's allies was based on self-interest, not pan-Italian patriotism. For all Hannibal's blandishments and temporary favours Italians were far from convinced that he either could or would promote their fortunes. A stranger from overseas, of alien ways and unintelligible speech, was hardly the one to correct those aspects of the Roman system that rankled most. He might guarantee, but was more likely to curtail their autonomy, and he was perfectly capable of inflicting his fearsome Gallic troops upon Italian communities. Moreover, even if Hannibal were seriously intent on ameliorating the Italians' lot, his dispensations were not likely to be lasting. Sooner or later he would be gone: but the Romans would still be there, able and anxious to reimpose their authority and to chastise those who had played them false.

This estimate of probabilities was dramatically confirmed in 211 when Rome recovered Capua and at once demonstrated that her power to punish exceeded Hannibal's to protect. Rome confiscated the entire Capuan territory (except apparently Casilinum), dismantled the Capuan state, executed the rebel ringleaders, and deprived all but two Capuans of various rights: some lost their property, others their freedom; the city itself was not razed, but it was reduced to the status of a mere *pagus*, tolerated because of its physical usefulness.[311]

After what happened to Capua Hannibal was able to retain communities only by force; and his force had become a wasting asset. Increasingly he found himself unable to prevent the Romans from recapturing communities that he had won over or brutally coerced. Even places of great symbolic prestige, such as Tarentum (209) and Locri (208), were retaken; and Hannibal, who did not shrink from terrorism when it suited his purpose (as at Nuceria in 216), now felt himself obliged to destroy captured or surrendered towns that he could not defend. This policy of despair robbed him of whatever scanty remnants of credit Italians might still be disposed to accord him. Their self-proclaimed champion had become the nightmarish monster of his own dream, a scourge bringing rapine, death and destruction to the Italian countryside.[312]

Material considerations reinforced the calculating commonsense of the Italians. During the half century before Hannibal's arrival the Romans had maintained law and order within the peninsula and had repulsed Punic, Illyrian and Gallic raiders attempting to assault it. This *pax Romana* was, of course, intended primarily to serve Roman interests. But Italians profited from it. By 218 widely dispersed settlements no longer needed to feel exposed and enhanced prosperity was general, for Italians as well as Romans. There must have been many, especially among the *principes populorum Italicorum*, who were relatively contented with the state of affairs and grateful to Rome for their well-being. Even her secular Samnite enemies shared in the general betterment, to judge from the embellishment of the sanctuary at Pietrabbondante.[313] Roman hegemony guaranteed orderliness for the annual transhumance of Samnite flocks, a factor that may well have contributed to the decision of the Pentri to stand by Rome when the other Samnites (Caudini and Hirpini), less dependent on well-policed drovers' trails, opted for Hannibal.

The Italians were also stiffened by the resolute nature of Rome's resistance to Hannibal. She might make heavy demands on them, but she imposed even greater burdens on herself. When extra-ordinary efforts were called for, Rome exerted herself to the utmost, fielding additional legions and shouldering grievous economic duties. The sturdiness of her example was a stimulant, and many an Italian joined the surviving consul from Cannae in refusing to despair of the Republic. Even Rome's enemies found her tenacity impressive.

But Hannibal's failure to smash the Roman system in Italy did not mean that he was without effect upon it. In fact, he altered it profoundly by helping to weld it more tightly together. His hammer blows did not destroy, but actually strengthened Rome's hegemony and removed it even further from challenge. Before he came, Rome and her allies had been tested in the First Punic War and in the Gallic invasion of 225. They now had to face a much sterner trial and they met it triumphantly.

To meet the succession of emergencies at the start of the war Rome acted with resolve and vigour. She moved swiftly for the common good and took far-reaching decisions without much, if indeed any, consultation with her Latin and Italian allies. There was, in fact, no time for that, and the allies acquiesced.

The dependent status of the allies would hardly have permitted them to protest against this Roman assumption of authority in any case. But in all likelihood they were not disposed to challenge it. Most of them must have recognized that this was no time for consti-tutional quibbling. The enormity of the menace imposed passive acceptance of Rome's orders. The inevitable consequence, of course, was growing encroachment by Rome upon allied rights.

This was perhaps neither foreseen nor intended, but it was none the less real, and it was not confined to military and political matters. Rome's direction of the war effort affected all aspects of Italian life. In the economic sphere ultimate decisions concerning the mobil-ization of resources and the payment therefor were bound to rest with the Romans. But even in cultural and social affairs, where Roman pressure could conceivably have been less, the consciousness of the Italians that their own conduct must not be too aberrant from the Roman tended to promote conformity. Thus, far from splitting Romans and Italians apart, Hannibal helped to bring them together, and he left behind him more 'national Italian patriotism' than he found.

The increased Roman influence on the economy of Italy is easy to detect. Even in prehistoric times the land had been thickly dotted with human settlements whose geographical proximity to one another promoted mercantile exchanges. Rome's expansion over the peninsula intensified this intermingling of the economies of the Italian settlements. Hannibal's invasion distorted the pattern of this age-old interdependence. The devastation of some districts, the enemy occupation of others, the diversion of men and resources to serve the needs of war, the interruption of imports, and the break in agriculture brought chaos to the established routines of everyday life and disrupted normal channels of trade. The ultimate beneficiary was Rome, for it fell upon her as the directing state to play the leading role in preventing an economic collapse. She did so very largely by harnessing as far as possible the activities of her hard-pressed allies to her own, and thus ensured that the economic effort matched the military.

The general belief that economic considerations played a rather small part in shaping the policies of the Roman Republic is no warrant for believing that Rome's leaders were utterly oblivious to them, least of all when faced with a crisis of Hannibalic proportions. Unprecedented in its magnitude and immediacy, it called for incomparably higher expenditures of money, as well as men, than the First Punic War, and Roman ingenuity and stamina were taxed to the limit by the difficulty of finding the needed resources, with Hannibal spreading havoc in Italy and his allies interrupting supplies from abroad.

Strenuous efforts must also have been demanded of the Italians, who had to raise, outfit, pay and maintain the troops they fielded, while at the same time making provision for home defence.[314] The sources occasionally mention the economic contribution they made, but more usually ignore it. They concern themselves with the efforts made by Rome.

These in truth were determined enough. Rome did not, of course, mobilize resources with the totalitarian single-mindedness of modern states when they go to war. In third-century Italy the

economy, and men's understanding of it, were too simple and
rudimentary for that. Rome had not yet learned to finance war by
mobilizing the credit of the state and leaving actual payment for later
generations to worry about, although it is to be noted that for some
operations in the Second Punic War she did resort to borrowing. In
general, Rome, and no doubt the other states of Italy too, had to pay
for the war as it was being fought. Somehow hard cash, actual coins,
had to be found to maintain government, to provide essential
supplies and services, and to safeguard state security. Among the
devices to which Rome resorted was the doubling of the *tributum* in
215 and the exaction of special contributions from the well-to-do a
year later.

The coins themselves supply evidence of the enormous financial
drain.[315] When the war began Rome was still using the same kind of
currency as sixty years earlier. The unit of reckoning, as in other
central Italian states, was a clumsy and ponderous coin, the so-called
libral *as*, weighing one Roman pound (= twelve Roman ounces). In
the south, however, and especially in Magna Graecia, these crudely
cast pieces were not very acceptable, since struck coins of precious
metal had long been common there. For these districts, therefore,
Rome had silver didrachms put into circulation early in the third
century: they were stamped ROMANO and weighed about six
Roman scruples. But they were probably neither minted in Rome
nor regarded as forming part of her native currency system. The
long First Punic War had surprisingly little deleterious effect on
Rome's coinage, and once it was over the Roman treasury was
strengthened by the reparations payments from Carthage and
tribute from Illyria. Thus, when the Second Punic War broke out,
the official Roman currency unit was still the bronze libral *as*; and
Rome was also still issuing silver didrachms (now inscribed ROMA
and called *quadrigati*) for use in Italiote regions.

The system could not, however, long withstand the encounter
with Hannibal. His war gobbled up huge amounts of metal, for all
sorts of purposes besides minting. Bronze, for instance, was needed
for weapons as well as coins and was at once in short supply. Silver,
too, soon became scarce: Carthage in the west and Macedon in the
east prevented supplies of that metal from reaching Italy. The
Romans had no option but to tinker with the currency. During the
first seven years of the conflict they halved the size and weight of the
as no less than three times. This brought the weight of the coin down

from twelve ounces (324 grammes) in 218 to two ounces (54 grammes) in 211.[316] Its ostensible value, of course, remained unchanged. For silver the stringency was worse and debasement of the metal in the *quadrigatus* was but a transitory palliative: by 212 minting of the coins had ceased altogether. After Trasimene in 217 Rome sought to boost morale by dipping into her precious stock of gold: she issued a few staters, her earliest coins in that metal. For propaganda they depicted the solemn determination of Roman and non-Roman Italy to remain firmly united against Hannibal's onslaught. Another expedient quickly adopted by Rome was to use the coins of other states, even those of Carthage, overstriking them with mint and value marks of her own.

The great crisis came in 213. By then not only was Capua ranged against Rome, but notable Italiote centres as well – Thurii, Heraclea, Metapontum, and Tarentum (apart from its citadel). In addition, Philip V of Macedon and the leaders of Syracuse had entered the war against her, and the failure of Syphax's revolt in Africa was freeing Punic troops for use against the Scipios in Spain. All this meant that in 212 Rome would need to field even bigger armies, amounting in all to twenty-five legions, and besides them would have to maintain powerful naval forces in the Adriatic. These called for unprecedented financial outlays. But the sacrifice was worth making. Syracuse was captured, Capua recovered, and Macedon tamed. War booty and the improved strategic balance brought ampler supplies of metal, and from 211 on Rome was able to put enormous numbers of coins into circulation. They included vast quantities of the new sextantal *as*, but also coins of silver and gold. Hence it looks as if Rome used the occasion for a drastic overhaul of her currency system.

The *as* remained the unit of reckoning, but the silver and gold issues were carefully brought into close relationship with it. The silver unit became Rome's most celebrated coin, the *denarius*: its name and its X marking proclaimed it officially equivalent to ten *asses*. The gold pieces were in three denominations, weighing one, two, and three scruples, with marks to show that they were worth twenty, forty, and sixty *asses* respectively. Rome also resumed the practice of putting distinctive silver coins into circulation in southern Italy. For this purpose she used the so-called *victoriatus*: it was slightly lighter than the *denarius* and bore no mark of value; being only half the weight of the defunct *quadrigatus* that it replaced, it was obviously intended as the equivalent of one drachma.

The new system proved durable. In the years after 211 shortages of silver did occasionally oblige Rome to trim a little the weight of both the *denarius* and the *victoriatus*. But she did not need to make any more radical changes in her currency during the war, least of all after success in Spain made large stocks of metal available. Actually the reorganization of her coinage system *c.*211 turned out to be a momentous step. For the *denarius* quickly established its superiority over all other coins in Italy: it was used, or imitated, everywhere.[317] It did not by itself, of course, romanize the country, but by accustoming Italians to Roman standards and methods of reckoning it helped to make them receptive to other Roman ideas and practices. Their economic activities and those of the Romans became inextricably mixed up and their social life was transformed in the process.

The changes brought by war were not confined to the material sphere. The spiritual life of Italy was affected too, and the new directions it followed were largely Roman in inspiration and guidance.

The Romans themselves were loth to believe that their early disasters at Hannibal's hands were due to their own ineptitude or unpreparedness. They attributed them to divine wrath. Somehow they had lost the favour of heaven and it was essential for them to regain the *pax deorum*. The allies inevitably shared this concern, for their religious attitudes were not fundamentally different. Indeed many of their cults and rituals were similar to, if not identical with, those of the Romans. Therefore the Italians too were anxious to re-establish a right relationship with the supernatural powers.

The prevailing anxiety and unease sought relief in widespread resort to mysticism, astrology, and all sorts of other irrational and superstitious practices. The Roman state itself set the example by assiduously cultivating and even importing religious rites that it hoped would be propitiatory.[318] Traditional cults, revived where necessary, were scrupulously observed and new and sometimes outlandish ones were hopefully introduced. Omens and prodigies were vigilantly noted and carefully expiated. Supplications were proclaimed, erring Vestals punished, temples dedicated. The rite of the sacred spring, Italic in inspiration but made Roman for the occasion, was resuscitated. The *lectisternium* ritual was introduced from the Greek world, the worship of Magna Mater from the

Asiatic. The god Apollo and his Sybils' utterances were invested with exceptional significance. There was even resort to human sacrifice, care being taken, however, to select victims who were not Roman, Latin or Italic.[319]

It is clear from Livy that Roman and non-Roman Italy alike were prey to superstitious preoccupations, and in such a spiritual climate the measures adopted by the stronger were bound to serve as models for its dependants.

Rome's language could hardly fail to gain from her assumption of political, military, economic and spiritual leadership throughout the crisis. Unquestionably there had been a gradual spread of Latin before the year 218, even though lack of evidence makes it impossible to trace in all its details. In southern Etruria the *conciliabula* on the soil of Veii are not the only settlements to have yielded Latin documents. Funerary inscriptions in Latin of the early third century, or even earlier, have also been found on the soil of Caere. Surviving inscriptions similarly testify to some latinization in the districts inhabited by Sabini and Marsi, the result, no doubt, of the establishment of Rome's corridor across central Italy. The effect now of the Hannibalic War was to bring it into districts where it would otherwise have penetrated much more slowly. It is to be noted that Livy alludes to the language situation in Italy much more frequently in his account of the Second Punic War than in his account of any other period. He records how Hannibal got into trouble at Casilinum through linguistic difficulties and himself tried to exploit language differences to spring a surprise at Salapia. The Romans for their part were on their guard against being betrayed by language: after capturing Hasdrubal's messengers they provided them with an Oscan-speaking escort when sending them through Sabellian districts for further interrogation.[320]

Hitherto the common people in non-Latin districts had probably had few occasions in their daily lives to use Latin, or even to hear it spoken much. But even in ordinary times, and still more during the Hannibalic crisis, no Italian community could afford to be without persons who knew the language, especially in influential positions. It was essential to maintain close relations with the paramount power if local interests were not to suffer. This was especially true in time of war. Quite ordinary Italians were bound then to be brought into contact with Latin, even though they were serving in their own cohorts or *turmae*. The officers of those units needed some knowledge of Latin in order to communicate with their Roman superiors; and it would be surprising if the rank and file failed to pick up some smattering from the Roman legionaries.

The thirty Latin colonies had also had time to help spread the language.[321] By 200 Brundisium was diffusing Latin in the Messapian region to judge from the dedication, in Latin, of a temple to a Roman-type divine triad at Manduria; and within a few years Quintus Ennius of Rudiae would be producing Rome's first epic poem. Ariminum seems to have performed a similar function in the north. At any rate, nearby Umbrian (?) Sarsina could make its own gift to Latin letters in the person of Ennius' contemporary, the comic playwright Plautus. Latin literature was fairly launched.

CHAPTER V

THE HEGEMONY OF
THE ROMAN REPUBLIC

The capitulation of Carthage brought power and prestige to Rome, but it did not bring peace. Hannibal's adventure had loosened Roman control of upper Italy and, spurred on by his brother Mago and other Punic officers, Gauls and Ligures remained in arms there even after the Carthaginian surrender.

Hannibal had demonstrated to the Romans that the Alps, far more than the Appennines, were the true natural rampart for Italy, and they could see for themselves how upper Italy might serve as a base for overland operations beyond Italy, whether westwards towards friendly Massilia and their new possessions in Spain or eastwards towards hostile Macedon and the Hellenistic monarchies. Rome, therefore, moved at once to reimpose her authority on the far north, even at the cost of continuing warfare.

The Gauls resisted fiercely, their innate pugnacity now exacerbated by the desperate consciousness that it was a battle for survival. Even Rome's allies among the Celts, the Cenomani, joined the struggle against her for a short period between 200 and 190. That decade opened with the sack of Placentia, the Latin Colony that had remained impregnable throughout Hannibal's war. It closed with the submission of the Boii, the last of the Gauls to surrender.

The Romans were thus left free to deal with the Ligures further west, much more stubborn enemies than the Gauls. Some Ligures are said to have remained in arms even down to Augustus' day, although most of their tribes had been conquered by the year 150. Not that the Romans had by then brought the Alps under their control:[322] for the next hundred years and more they could not even use the mountain passes except on payment of transit tolls to the mountaineer tribes.

Simultaneously with their reassertion of control over Cisalpina, the Romans were restoring their authority in peninsular Italy. They had already shown at Capua in 210 what was in store for Italian supporters of Hannibal; and, as soon as Carthage made peace, they proceeded to the grim work of punishment. Some Italians were executed, others sold into slavery, and yet others deprived of their property. Rome also resumed her earlier practice of seizing land from guilty communities, but she did not revive her policy of wholesale incorporations: so far as is known, no community was annexed with partial, much less with full Roman citizenship. Nor does Rome appear to have distributed any of the territory she confiscated to her allies, although she did use some for Latin Colonies. Evidently the escape of the allies from Punic domination was to constitute its own reward.

The territory seized was mostly in the south, Sabelli (with the notable exception of the Pentrian Samnites) being the principal sufferers. Not that the Italiotes and Messapii escaped scot free. The archaeological evidence suggests that even where the native inhabitants were not ruthlessly expelled impoverishment and depopulation were likely to be common.

Some of the confiscated land was quickly transformed into Latin-speaking country by being distributed to demobilized Roman soldiers, either *viritim* or in *coloniae*, a few of which were of the Latin variety. But a certain amount of it was retained as Roman state domain so that it could be leased out and contribute thus to Roman public revenues. In Campania the land leased was predominantly agricultural, but elsewhere much of it was devoted to pastoralism. The lessees (*possessores*) were Romans for the most part, but did include some Italians and even perhaps some of the original owners. The enterprises of the lessees required more than a little capital, but of this there was no shortage in second-century Italy. For, besides consolidating her position in both upper and peninsular Italy, Rome was soon drawn into conflicts of the Hellenistic world and within fifty-three years had made herself mistress of the entire Mediter-ranean basin. The profits and opportunities from her overseas empire in the form of booty, bullion, slaves, reparations, tribute and commercial exploitation brought a steady flow of wealth into Italy. The accumulation of investment-seeking capital there was enormous and it led to a marked growth of the commercial class.

The effect of all this on the life and economy of Italy was dramatic.[323] Social changes were inevitable in second-century Italy in any event, owing to the diffusion of Hellenistic influences throughout the Mediterranean world. But in Italy their speed and scale were breathtaking. Subsistence agriculture on small holdings tended to get replaced by cash crop farming of huge estates. In the south there was a massive increase of transhumant pastoralism, a development with sinister implications since the flocks were mostly tended for absentee owners by armed slaves who were little better than brigands and made living conditions so unbearable that the freeborn natives drifted elsewhere. In many regions peasant farmers were a vanishing breed.[324]

Generalizations, however, are misleading. Conditions varied greatly from one part of Italy to another. Sturdy peasants and yeomen did not disappear everywhere by any means, and many areas of the Italian countryside remained populous and agriculturally productive. There is abundant archaeological evidence for the prosperous condition of Latium and Campania (even including Capua) in the second century.[325] Even in the south Hannibal's devastation and Rome's vengeance had not brought complete ruin and depopulation, though the freeborn population did dwindle sharply in Apulia, Lucania and Bruttium. Nor had deforestation as yet brought its desolation nor malaria its ravages.

The mistress of Italy was in an advantageous position to exploit the changed conditions. Rome had emerged from the Hannibalic ordeal relatively stronger than the Italian states, and the morale and self-confidence of her governing class now exceeded all bounds. She proceeded to extend her power and influence; and, as her stature grew, her Italian allies became ever more palpably her dependants.

Profiting from her war-time tradition of leadership, Rome continued automatically to play the larger role that the conflict had thrust upon her, and the Italians, although no longer constrained by the proximity of peril to accept her fiats without protest, had nevertheless to conform to them. She was in a position to ignore complaints and impose her will as she saw fit.

Where she was most likely to issue orders was in connection with military activities and the peninsula being now pacified (except for some Ligurian areas) this often meant service abroad. The allies must have resented this, for no matter how ready they might be to help defend Italy and even to recognize that operations at either end of the Mediterranean kept Hellenistic monarchs and other possible enemies at a safe distance, many of Rome's enterprises must have struck them as imperialist adventuring.

Nor were Rome's orders confined to the military sphere. As self-appointed guardian of law and order in Italy, she was always ready to stamp out 'conspiracies' wherever she claimed to find any. Thus, social unrest in Etruria and Bacchanalian cultists everywhere could be suppressed as dangerous to the communal well-being; and other cases of high-handed Roman interference in the internal affairs of non-Roman communities in the second century are not hard to find.[326] Her actions might be well intentioned, as for instance when she took energetic measures to minimize the effects of floods, fires, famines, earthquakes and other natural disasters of a wide-ranging kind. But such paternalism tended to sap the spirit of independence and self-reliance of the Italian communities.

Rome now bestrode Italy like a colossus. The Second Punic War, like any great conflict, had enhanced both the material power and the moral authority of the state that had directed the winning side, and Rome, whether consciously seeking to do so or not, could now hardly help impressing Italy with her character, her speech and her customs. Even Cisalpina, which now began to be brought firmly within the Roman system, was not immune.

In fact, the conquest of Cisalpina was by now far enough advanced for the Romans to organize it to suit their own interests. As usual they decided to 'divide and rule' and to vary their treatment of the conquered. Their arrangements in the two areas into which upper Italy is divided by the river Po differed sharply.

South of the Po, in today's Romagna, Emilia and Liguria, Rome confiscated large tracts of territory. For the Gauls the consequences were overwhelming. The Lingones simply vanished and never again played any part in the history of Italy. The Boii, although they did not completely disappear, also suffered heavily. A good half of their territory was seized and many of its inhabitants slain or expelled. But a certain remnant of the tribe, the young and the elderly according to Livy, seem to have been left as subject allies on a low-lying area in and around Brixellum (the Ager Boicus of Festus?).[327]

Much of Cispadana,[328] like Cisalpina in general, consisted of undrained marshes and uncleared forests, and before 200 it could not have been really densely settled: indeed, in some areas it may not have been properly settled at all. There would thus be plenty of land available for new settlers provided that it could be made habitable. First, however, it had to be made secure.

The Roman instrument for this purpose was, of course, the

colonia, and Rome at once reinforced the two Latin Colonies already on the Po, Placentia and Cremona. She also planned some new colonies. No doubt she would have preferred them, too, to be *coloniae Latinae*, but by now there was difficulty in finding settlers for colonies of this sort. The calls upon Roman manpower immediately after Hannibal's war were heavy. Men were needed to strengthen old colonies and to found new ones in peninsular Italy, and the armies in Macedon and elsewhere were also calling for men. Besides this, native Romans realized how valuable their citizenship had become, and they were reluctant to surrender it merely to obtain allotments in Latin Colonies, least of all in a region as distant, difficult and dangerous as Cisalpina. The offer of huge parcels of land (50 *iugera* a man and even more for *equites*) succeeded in attracting 3,000 volunteers for Latin Colonies in the Boian lands. Many of them, it may be suspected, were non-Romans; indeed to judge from the name of the colony that was founded, Bononia (thought to derive from the Celtic word meaning 'base' or 'foundation'), some of them may even have been Gauls. In any case, 3,000 settlers barely sufficed for this one colony, which was established in 189 on the key site of Etruscan Felsina controlling the Raticosa pass across the Appennines. Ultimately Bononia became a very fine city, but at its foundation it was the smallest Latin Colony recorded since Cales and Luceria in the fourth century; and even its comparatively modest number of settlers could not at this time be found for a projected second colony in Cispadana, and the plan for one had to be dropped.[329]

Additional Latin Colonies being thus out of the question, the Romans resorted to colonies of the citizen variety. Such colonies hitherto had been miserable affairs on the sea coast peopled by a handful of settlers endowed with the barest minimum of land; and such establishments were hardly indicated as bastions for the protection of Roman territory in the north. Accordingly the Romans devised Citizen Colonies of a radically different sort, comparable in all respects, except their citizenship, to Latin Colonies. They would not be confined to the littoral and they would be agrarian rather than maritime settlements. Their settlers would be numerous, all enjoying Roman citizenship, a feature bound to attract Italian volunteers and render it unnecessary to offer allotments on the Bononian scale. Even so, the parcels of land, although modest, were more than twice as large as those in the old *coloniae maritimae*.

The first pair of such new model Citizen Colonies were probably Potentia and Pisaurum in 184. They were established south of Ariminum in the Ager Gallicus, a part of Cisalpina in Roman eyes. The settlers each received six *iugera* of land, but how many of them there were is not recorded. The next year two more Citizen Colonies were founded, both north of the Appennine watershed, at Mutina and Parma in the region now known as Emilia. Each consisted of 2,000 settlers and the allotments were five and eight *iugera* respectively. These colonies were, no doubt, intended to control the northern approaches to the Abetone and Cisa passes.

The Romans also now brought the Ligures living west of the river Trebia on both sides of the Appennines under their sway. Some Ligurian tribes fell victim to the unprovoked assaults of Roman commanders hungry for 'triumphs'. Others were forced to leave their mountain strongholds and occupy less defensible sites, as far away as Samnium in the case of the Apuani.[330] The Romans may have seized less land from the Ligures than from the Cispadane Gauls, but even so it was extensive, stretching to the Monferrato region and the river Stura. Here, too, the Romans had difficulty in finding recruits for Latin Colonies and, as amongst the Boii, were able to found only one. This was at Luca in 180. Another colony three years later at Luna, where each of the 2,000 settlers seems to have received six and a half *iugera* of land, had to be of the citizen variety. Both of these Ligurian colonies were south of the Appennine watershed, but they were nevertheless serviceable bases for the deeper penetration of northwest Italy,[331] and it was perhaps to this end that communications with them across Etruria had been strengthened a few years earlier with Citizen Colonies at Saturnia and Graviscae, in 183 and 181 respectively.

All the *coloniae* were quickly linked to Rome by military highways whose construction called for grading and ditch-digging, as well as for paving, and helped to drain many of the marshes that had proved so formidable an obstacle to easy movement in the Po valley in Hannibal's day.

With provision thus made for defence, and land reclamation taken in hand,[332] closer settlement became possible, and thousands of new settlers were brought to Cisalpina and allotted land south of the Po. From the many towns that later bore the title of *forum* one can reasonably postulate a succession of viritane distributions.[333] But only one, that of 173, is actually recorded. It has left abundant traces of centuriation and they indicate that it was a very large operation, extending from the Celtic areas in the east to the Ligurian districts further west, perhaps as far as the neighbourhood of Dertona. There was so much land available that now, perhaps for the first time, non-Romans participated in a Roman viritane distribution. The non-Romans (who were Latini) received only three *iugera* apiece as compared with the ten given to Romans and, so far as is known, they did not get Roman citizenship as a result of the operation. But there is no record of their resenting the discrimination nor any account of how they survived on such meagre holdings. The Roman beneficiaries of 173 seem all to have been registered in the Tribe Pollia.[334]

Some sections of Cispadana still contained ostensibly independent, sovereign communities. Umbrian (?) Ravenna, for instance, is known to have had a treaty with Rome, and the same must also be true of Sarsina, it too probably an Umbrian community. As already noted, the Boii in and around Brixellum also seem to have been attached (or, to use the Latin expression, 'attributed') to nearby Roman or Latin communities that supervised their administration without formally annexing them.

The Romans called the peoples living north of the Po Transpadani, perhaps to indicate that they constituted a special category: they were certainly treated very differently from the natives south of the river.

The Veneti continued to be allies of Rome, after 200 as well as before it. Rome also reached an amicable understanding with Etruscan Mantua. The Cenomani were also old allies but not equally reliable, and were consequently accorded less respect. After their abortive move against Rome in 200 they were disarmed in 197 and forced into a very unequal alliance. The same fate befell the Insubres a year later.

Thus, from the beginning of the second century, all of the Transpadane peoples east of the river Ticinus were allies of Rome, autonomous in local matters, but clearly subject to the Roman hegemony. They supplied troops when Rome called for them, they submitted to Roman arbitration when they quarrelled, and sometimes they even had to tolerate Roman interference in their internal affairs. The dependent status of the Gauls was even made explicit in their treaties, since these stipulated that no Cenomani or Insubres were ever to become Roman citizens, an exclusion ostensibly reassuring the Celts against inroads on their manpower, but more probably due to Celtophobia.[335] The latter may also explain why a group of central European Celts that sought to settle peacefully in Venezia Giulia was ejected by the Romans in 186 and barred from any renewal of their incursion by a Latin Colony established at Aquileia in 181.[336]

Rome did not seize any land in northeastern Transpadana. There were no viritane distributions there and of the two Latin Colonies one (Cremona) dated from before the Second Punic War and the other (Aquileia) was not on territory taken from Italians: it lay in the no man's land between the Veneti and their (Celtic ?) enemies, the Carni.

In the region west of the Ticinus, on the other hand, the Romans did confiscate land. Here the Celtic and Ligurian tribes remained in arms much longer than the other Cisalpine peoples, either because they were less accessible or because the Roman conquest was more desultory.

Roman seizure of territory in what is today called Piemonte began as early as the first half of the second century. The areas seized are not specified, but they evidently included at least some of the district known today as the Lomellina, immediately north of the Po near modern Vercelli. It was probably here that Rome in 172 settled the 'many thousands' of Ligures victimized by the unscrupulous M. Popilius Laenas. Other Ligures also got land from the Romans. According to the Elder Pliny, who, however, supplies no details, distributions were made to the Ingauni on no fewer than thirty occasions.[337] Not that Lomellina became thoroughly Ligurian; the peg-top jars (vasi a trottola) found there in some quantity provide evidence of Celtic inhabitants.

No record whatever survives of the submission of the Taurini to Roman authority. The Salassi, immediately to their north, came under assault by Ap. Claudius Pulcher in 143, ostensibly to prevent them from diverting the water of the river Cervo (?), but more probably to get control of the nearby gold-mines of Victumulae, which the Romans were certainly exploiting a few years later.

Piemonte remained a war theatre throughout the second century, and by its end Rome had pushed her dominion forward in the far northwest to the foothills of the Alps.

Although largely pacified and organized, and although inhabited by many Roman citizens, Cisalpina remained distinct from the peninsula to the south. Officially it was Gallia, even though conceded to be geographically a part of Italy. As a war zone in which Roman armies were needed almost every year throughout the second century, Cisalpina is depicted as a sort of provincial area, and, in fact, early in the first century, it was officially pronounced a Roman province. But whatever its political vicissitudes, romanization made the same steady headway there as in the rest of Italy.

In all parts of Italy Rome's economic predominance was as conspicuous as her military and political. The common view of the Roman ruling class, as more or less indifferent to economic considerations when framing state policy, can be very misleading. No state when contemplating a course of action deliberately ignores the probable material outcome of its decision, and it is inconceivable that the Romans did so. But, even if Rome's rulers had been largely unmoved by such factors, they could not have escaped the consequences of their own supremacy. Their hegemony was bound to extend into trade and commerce owing to the economic advantage that political power always brings. In the second century it enabled Rome to suspend direct taxation of her own citizens. The burgesses of other states were probably not so lucky, although they too must have reaped some benefit from the wealth that reached Italy from Rome's overseas empire and percolated into its remotest corners.

With by far the largest single concentration of population, Rome by her very size set the pattern and determined the volume of all mercantile activity, and the many entrepreneurs and business men from non-Roman Italy behaved just like Romans at Delos and elsewhere, and were actually mistaken for such. Rome had become the world centre of capitalism.

The economic domination of Rome is clearly indicated by the common use of Roman coins in non-Roman Italy, ultra-Roman though their types were. Native issues did not disappear, but they lost ground steadily to Roman, especially those of silver. Rome's coins now circulated everywhere; and her new coins were now all on a Roman standard, since she soon stopped issuing any of a special type for use in hellenized districts. By c. 170 minting of the *victoriatus* had ceased and, even though *victoriati* continued to circulate in Cisalpina and elsewhere, they were henceforth reckoned as worth only two *sestertii*, clear proof that Italy was not only using Rome's coins, but had also adopted the Roman method of reckoning and pricing. By 141 the *sestertius* was everywhere the normal unit of account and prices were regularly quoted in it, though actual *sestertius* pieces do not seem to have been minted and therefore could not have been in circulation until forty years later.[338]

Well engineered and solidly paved traffic arteries carried the Roman military, political, economic and social presence even into the more recondite parts of Italy during the second century.[339] Thus, three roads crossed Etruria from south to north. The most easterly of them, the Via Cassia from Rome to Arretium, may date from 187. It is usually reckoned earlier than the middle road, the Via Clodia, which traversed central Etruria and may have been built *c.* 183 at the instance of the politically dominant Claudii Marcelli to service Saturnia, the newly founded Citizen Colony. The third road, the Via Aurelia along the Tyrrhenian coast, could belong to the third century, being named perhaps after the censor for 241; but it was extended in the second century by the Via Aemilia Scauri of 109, which started at Vada Volaterrana, followed the Ligurian coast to Vada Sabatia and then ran north via Aquae Statiellae to Dertona deep inside Cisalpina. By 109 Cisalpina had an extensive network of highways and they were linked to the road system of the peninsula. A paved extension of the Via Flaminia had been built north-westwards from Ariminum to Placentia in 187: it replaced an earlier, unpaved road and was named the Via Aemilia after the consul for the year. It serviced Bononia, Mutina, Forum Lepidi,[340] and Parma, and its impact was such that to this day the district is known as Emilia. At Bononia the Via Aemilia joined a second Via Flaminia, built by the other consul for 187, the son of the man responsible for the original Via Flaminia of 220: this second Via Flaminia went south across the Appennines to join the Via Cassia at Arretium; and soon it was extended northwards as well to Aquileia, with the result that this Latin Colony was linked to Rome by continuous highway.

Many other roads are recorded in the second century. One of them ran down the Adriatic coast: its name is not known, but it was obviously of great importance and may date from before the year 200. A second Via Aemilia, of the same date as its Cisalpine homonym, followed the route of the later Via Traiana across Samnium to reach the lower Adriatic. The consul of 148 built a road, named after him the Via Postumia, from allied Genua across the Giovi pass to Dertona. Dertona became a nodal point of great importance in the heart of Cisalpina.[341] It was linked to Placentia (by an extension of the original Via Aemilia in 148 or earlier), to Pollentia (by a Via Fulvia, perhaps in 125), and to Vada Sabatia on the Ligurian

coast (by the already mentioned Via Aemilia Scauri). Two Viae
Popiliae (of 133 ?), one from Capua to Rhegium and the other from
Ariminum to Aquileia, seem quickly to have been renamed Viae
Anniae, after the consul for 128, who probably not only completed
them but also built yet another Via Annia (in the vicinity of Falerii).
A road into the interior from Pisa may belong to 123: it was called the
Via Quinctia and named after the consul for that year. A Via Caecilia
(of 117 ?) that branched off the Via Salaria and reached the centre of
the Adriatic coast by way of Amiternum is also recorded.

The roads helped Rome not only to maintain law and order, but
also to carry her customs into all parts of Italy, including the Po
valley. She became, as Cicero notes,[342] the cultural leader as well as
the political mistress, and it is this that largely accounts for the speed
with which the Hellenistic civilization penetrated all Italy. Greek
influence, by no means negligible even in prehistoric times, had
become much more marked during the heyday of Magna Graecia,
and not least in Rome: in the opinion of fourth-century Greek
observers the city actually resembled an Hellenic *polis*. But, from the
late third century on, the operations of the Romans had brought
them into direct contact with the kingdoms of Alexander the Great's
successors east of the Adriatic and exposed them, and through them
the whole of Italy, to the full impact of the world they found in and
around the Aegean. Hellenistic sculpture, painting and architectural
details, Hellenistic writing and modes of thought came to be quickly
noted and eclectically imitated at Rome, and Rome's hegemony
ensured their rapid transmission into other parts of Italy.[343] The
country became a sort of western reflection of the Aegean world
with Roman overtones and grew culturally much more homogeneous. From 200 on art becomes a very uncertain guide for
differentiating one Italian people from another.

In Italy the Roman peace made for an active and continuous social
and economic development, observable above all in the gradual but
steady growth of rural settlements into centres of greater consequence and of more monumental aspect.

The inspiration clearly came from Rome. The many new temples,
for instance, owed much to her example.[344] Naturally this is best
illustrated in Roman or Latin Italy, in places like Civitalba or
Monterinaldo in Picenum where there were structures with
magnificent sculptured pediments that could vie with the new
basilicas rising around the Roman Forum, or like Cosa in Etruria

1 Thirteen aligned altars, dating from the 6th to the 4th century at Lavinium, the shrine city of the LATINI and of Rome, whose magistrates sacrificed there upon entering and leaving office. Castor and Pollux were among the deities worshipped.

2 The end altar, lower and older than the other twelve and the first to be disused. The entire sanctuary seems to have been abandoned in the 2nd century.

3 One of the town gates at Norba, Latium. The massive blocks of polygonal limestone and the rounded bastion illustrate the powerful defences that protected LATIN COLONIES.

4 Limestone relief of a
(transhumant?) shepherd of the
SABELLI. Primitive art from rustic
Italy. 3rd–1st century.

5 The HERNICI of Ferentinum
built their town wall with both
squared and polygonal blocks as
can be seen from this arched
gateway, the so-called Porta
Sanguinaria.

6 Small head in terracotta from the country of the AEQUI. The Italic peoples seem to have attached great importance to such votive representations of the human head. 3rd century? From Carsoli.

7 Terracotta votive head similar in date and provenance to the preceding, but more obviously 'classical' in appearance. It illustrates feminine head-dress among the AEQUI.

8 The polygonal wall protecting the citadel at Arpinum of the VOLSCI was pierced by this pointed gateway. The Gothic effect was achieved by corbelling.

9 The AURUNCI greatly
venerated the goddess Marica,
the mother of King Latinus
according to Virgil. This votive
statuette in terracotta from her
shrine near the mouth of the
river Liris dates from
prehistoric times.

10 Votive head in terracotta
recently found at Teanum of the
SIDICINI. The tall head-covering
and the curls are typical of the
region. 6th–4th century.

11 Tufa stele from the SIDICINI.
The name of the deceased is
written retrograde in Oscan: NI
KATTIIS NI (Numerius Catius, son
of Numerius). 2nd–1st century.

12 For several centuries the CAMPANIANS of Capua dedicated crude, stereo-typed, statues of tufa, representing a seated *kourotrophos* with one or many more swaddled infants on her lap. She may be the goddess of fertility or the matron donor. This specimen dates from *c.* 400.

13 This 3rd-century tomb-painting from Cumae shows a woman and her attendant, a scene familiar from Greek vase-painting. But the florid treatment is very CAMPANIAN.

14 CAMPANIAN metope in tufa found near the triangular forum in Pompeii with an unusual representation of Athena brandishing workmen's tools. The other figures may be Hephaestus nailing Ixion to the wheel. 3rd century?

15 Aligned SAMNITE tetrastyle temples at Schiavi d'Abruzzo in the country of the Pentri. They face southeast, like those at Pietrabbondante, and belong to the 2nd century. The smaller and more recent one without a *podium* was built by G. Papius (? the Samnite commander in the Social War).

16 Recomposed section of the entablature of the larger and earlier SAMNITE temple at Schiavi d'Abruzzo. Although the frieze is Doric, the temple columns were Ionic. 2nd century.

17 Typical three-disc SAMNITE corselet, probably of the 4th century. The common view that this type of cuirass developed out of the prehistoric one-disc heart protector is false.

18 Small wooden head from the sanctuary of Mefitis at the Vale of Amsanctus in the country of the Hirpini SAMNITES. *c.* 300?

19 Mefitis, as the provider of water and protectress of the fields and flocks, was also a great favourite of the LUCANI. Their chief sanctuary to her at Rossano di Vaglio, seen here from the air, was in use from *c.* 350 to *c.* 50.

20 Bronze figurine of Hercules and a snake (hydra?) from the country of the LUCANI. The Italic peoples were very fond of Hercules. 4th century.

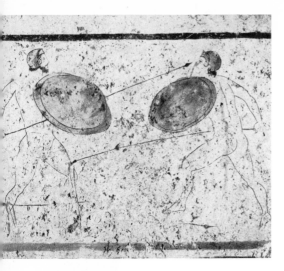

21 The tomb-paintings of the LUCANI show many scenes of gladiatorial combat, often with gruesome details. This one from Paestum dates from *c.* 300 or a little later.

22 Coins inscribed with the name BRUTTII in Greek suggest that this people may have been organized in a federal state. They copy Greek issues. This early 3rd-century tetradrachm shows OBV. the head of Amphitrite, and REV. Poseidon, naked, with his right foot on top of an Ionic column.

23 This fragmentary relief was found on the territory of the MESSAPII. Obviously Hellenistic in inspiration, it may be the work of Italiote craftsmen. Early 3rd century. From Lecce.

24 The potters of Apulia adhered for centuries to their own traditions. The 'trozella' ware of the MESSAPII is named after the discs on the handles. This vase from Rudiae belongs to the 5th or 4th century.

25 The vases of the DAUNII were likely to have eccentric shapes and distinctive decoration. The above specimen is from Canusium; *c.* 500?

26 No less eccentric were the *askoi* of the DAUNII, smothered with plastic decoration. From Canusium; *c.* 300.

27 The pottery of the PEUCETII was less flamboyant. It includes black Gnathian ware, like the *oenochoe* shown here decorated with Erotes among flowers and tendrils. 350–300.

28 In Apulia even vases of a conventional type had their own characteristic aspect. This large volute crater by the Darius Painter shows on side (a) the death of Hippolytus, and on side (b) the standard representation of a shrine, this one with a seated figure and offerings. From Rubi; *c.* 335.

29 Typical 4th-century Apulian *lebes*, decorated with a Dionysiac scene and symposium, and with a frieze of figures on the lid. From Rubi.

30 Bronze knucklebone which probably served as an Oscan pound weight (13 ozs/ 379 gms). The partly defaced inscription in the Oscan alphabet reveals that it belonged to the FRENTANI. First published in 1968.

31 Bronze statuette representing a woman of the MARRUCINI wearing local costume, who is making an offering to a divinity. From Rapino. Date unknown.

32 Ovid came from a prominent family of the PAELIGNI. This inscription, in Paelignian dialect but Latin script, commemorates his kinsman, Obellius Ovidius son of Lucius. From Pentima. 1st century.

33 Inscription of the cismontane VESTINI from Peltuinum, which had become a Roman *praefectura* administered by three local aediles, here named. The dialect is Vestinian, written in an early Latin alphabet; *c.* 200.

34 A favourite deity of the MARSI was Angitia, healer of snake-bites. Her shrine stood in a sacred grove near Luco dei Marsi, where its remains can still be seen.

35 Red figure *kylix* of the FALISCI. The two figures are probably Dionysus and Ariadne. The inscription reads, from right to left, FOIED VINO PIPAFO CRA CAREFO (= *hodie vinum bibam cras carebo*: in effect, drink and be merry for tomorrow we're dead). From Falerii Veteres. 4th century.

36 The so-called Porta di Giove at Falerii Novi. The town wall, as at Latin Cosa earlier in the century, was strengthened with towers; but for the FALISCAN town squared masonry was used, not polygonal. 3rd century.

37 Bronze currency bar of the
UMBRI: the inscription is
probably the name of its owner
(Fucius Sestinius). The bull in
relief confirms Pliny's assertion
that the *aes signatum* had herd
animals stamped on it. 3rd
century.

38 Symbolic of the cultural
independence of prehistoric
PICENUM, and of the readiness of
its inhabitants to defend it, is this
richly decorated bronze helmet:
when worn it had two crests.
From Pittino di San Severino.

39 The spiral discs hanging
from this pectoral were much
used for personal adornment in
pre-Roman PICENUM: they
remained in vogue for centuries.
From Canavaccio.

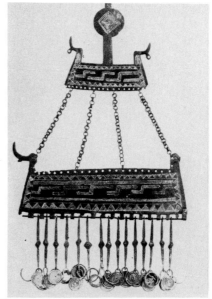

40 Rectangular stone houses of the LIGURES at the hill fort on Monte Bignone.

41 The *situlae* of the VENETI are typical of their production at Ateste and of their continuing use of orientalizing design as late as the Boldù-Dolfin specimen shown here, of the 4th century.

42 Votive bronze tablet of the VENETI, probably depicting their goddess Reitia. 4th or 3rd century. From Caldevigo, near Este.

43 The VENETI were much involved with the breeding and training of horses, as this votive tablet from Ateste illustrates. 4th or 3rd century.

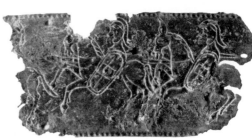

44 Stone *stelai* have been found among the VENETI only at Patavium. On this one two horse-soldiers are seen trampling a decapitated enemy. Late 4th century.

45 Bronze CELTIC helmet, with incised decoration and an iron crest. Probably 4th century.

46 A CELTIC silver phalera of the 3rd century. From Manerbio.

47 Warrior GAULS, nude except for their torques, belts, shields and the *chlamys* on the one on the left. They are in flight after sacking a sanctuary, symbolized by the *patera* and overturned vase at their feet. From the frieze of the 2nd-century temple at Civitalba.

48 Inscription of the LEPONTII, found in 1966 at Prestino in Lombardy. It is probably on an architrave and may belong to the 1st century. The retrograde writing, when transposed, reads: UVAMOKOZIS: PLIALEO·U: UVITIAUIOPOS: ARIUONEPOS: SITES: TETU and may mean 'Uxamogostis Plialessu dedicated the sanctuary to ? ?' (the third and fourth words being dative plurals).

49 Remains of a stone house of the RAETI at Montesei di Serso, near Trento.

50 Inscribed stags' horns from a shrine of the RAETI at Magrè, northwest of Vicenza. The writing is left to right on the middle one, right to left on the other two, and seems to consist exclusively of names apart from the last word on the second and third, *tinake* (Etruscan *zinace*?). 3rd century or later.

51 *Denarius* of the Social War insurgents, symbolizing the struggle between Roma (the wolf) and Italia (in Oscan *vitelio*; cf. Latin *vitulus*: the bull). In the exergue (in Oscan): G. Papius, the name of the Samnite commander.

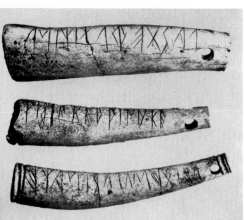

where the Capitolium and other monuments are so impressive. But non-Roman and non-Latin Italy was not very far behind. Amongst the Pentrian Samnites, for example, shrines sprang up in some profusion: significant remains of them have been found at a number of places and above all at Pietrabbondante, where the ancient sacred precinct was expanded into a spectacular complex of buildings intended to serve all Pentri (and perhaps all Samnites). The temples were not necessarily built to Roman measurements, but in style, lay-out and decoration they owed much to Rome. This did not mean that Rome had abandoned her practice of not interfering with native religions: she was not imposing her own cults. The large temple at Pietrabbondante was not dedicated to the Capitoline triad even if it did have three *cellae*.[345]

The Pentri may have been in a specially favoured position because of their loyalty to Rome against Hannibal. But even in the regions that had supported him native worship was not suppressed. The shrines to Mefitis at Lucanian Rossano di Vaglio and at Hirpinian Amsanctus continued to function and attract devotees. The archaeological evidence does indicate, however, a falling-off in the prosperity of ex-rebel districts. There was no spate of new temple building among the Bruttii and Lucani comparable with that among the Pentri, and their existing shrines gradually declined: that at Rossano di Vaglio seems to have been abandoned altogether in the first century.[346]

Another symptom of ubiquitous Roman influence was the political terminology. The titles *aedilis* and *quaestor* were adopted in many parts of Italy, and local councils were likely to be called *senatus*, even in Samnium. The constitutional nomenclature is patently Roman even in its distinguishing epithets.[347]

From the wholesale conversion of partial citizens into full ones, the spread of Roman law and Roman social attitudes can confidently be postulated.[348] It is generally agreed that most, if not all, the Italian communities incorporated originally without the vote had acquired full citizen rights by *c*. 100; and from the Sabine precedent of 268 one can argue that this upgrading presupposed some degree of romanization. Admittedly after the Sabini only one occasion is actually recorded when partial citizens were elevated, namely in 188 when Volscian Arpinum, Formiae and Fundi obtained full rights.[349] But this is reported by Livy in so casual and matter-of-fact a fashion as to suggest that promotion to the higher status was normal enough hardly to be worth mentioning. Partial citizenship may almost imply as much by its very nature, since it looks like an earnest for full citizenship to come. It certainly seems that no matter how reluctant the Romans sometimes were to extend their citizenship in the second century, they were not averse to upgrading it.

Roman political rivalries may account for this. Roman nobles in search of large followings of clients were prone to engineer the registration of *cives sine suffragio* as full citizens in the Roman Tribes. It could be done with relative ease, since in most areas the partial citizens were intermingled with full ones, and by now must often have been indistinguishable from them. It merely needed a compliant censor to get *cives sine suffragio* onto tribal rolls. They themselves were nothing loth, since after 200 the full Roman citizenship had become materially valuable. It is certain that Roman censors registered a great many partial citizens, whether by design or by accident. There is evidence of upgraded citizens in the Tribes Ufentina and Cornelia, and in 189, a year of bitter political strife, the censors T. Quinctius Flamininus and M. Claudius Marcellus were exceptionally easy-going: according to Plutarch, 'they admitted as citizens all who came forward to register, provided that they were of free-born parents'; and Livy indicates that *cives sine suffragio* were among the beneficiaries.[350]

The absorption of these contributed to the increasing Roman complexion of the population of second-century Italy. By the year 100 the free adult males in the peninsula may have numbered no more than in 225, but the proportion of Romans among them had risen sharply. The punitive measures taken against Hannibal's Italian supporters contributed to this no doubt, but are far from being the full explanation.

One factor helping to swell the Roman element was the universal mobility. A striking example of this was the forced migration of more than 40,000 Ligurian Apuani in 180 from the region north of Pisa to the district east of Beneventum. But this was merely one incident, even if spectacular enough to loom large in the surviving tradition. Large numbers of other Italians were also on the move, not on orders from Rome but spontaneously. Many of them poured into Latin districts,[351] and there was probably also some shift of enterprising, or desperate, migrants (including Romans) from peninsular to upper Italy when prospects there became fairer. Significantly there were also thousands of Latini and others moving into Roman communities. This immigration, clandestine though much of it may have been, seems usually to have been tolerated. Assimilation of Italians resident on Roman soil (whether in Rome itself, in her rustic Tribes and *municipia*, or in Citizen Colonies) was constant, the absorbed Italians including not only immigrants but also indigenous inhabitants of the areas concerned. By contrast, Rome herself was no longer losing citizens to Latin Colonies on the same scale as formerly, since few such colonies were founded after 200 and none at all after 180.

Military service also helped to change the make-up of the population in the second century. Even after Hannibal's defeat Rome was obliged to go on fielding large armies year after year owing to the growth of her empire and her new responsibilities as a world power. One effect of this is well known. It made permanent the alteration that the protracted wars with Carthage had set in motion, transforming it from a citizen militia composed of men of property, peasant proprietors for the most part, who served for short summer campaigns at no inordinate distance from their own homes, into a professional force for which the property qualification was first reduced and finally (in 107) abolished and whose proletarian soldiers served for years on end in far distant lands. Grave as were the political and social repercussions of this change (and no doubt they manifested themselves in the Italian states as well as in Roman Italy, for these had to meet the same, if not even greater military demands), its consequences for the population shift were more serious still. The incessant warfaring, even though it did not perhaps reduce the total number of Italy's inhabitants, undoubtedly did tip the demographic balance to the advantage of Rome. For, despite Polybius' repeated assertion that the armies were roughly fifty per cent Roman and fifty per cent Italian, the evidence indicates that in the second century Italian soldiers under arms outnumbered Roman, sometimes by as much as two to one. As these men in the prime of life were now serving less and less in Italy and correspondingly more overseas, for years on end – in the Aegean world, the Near East, Africa and above all in Spain, most dreaded of all war theatres – the consequences for the birth-rate in Italy were inevitable. The rate dropped, but it dropped further amongst the Italians than amongst the Romans, since proportionately more of them were out of the country. And it was not only their absence abroad that affected the birth-rate. The Italians also suffered disproportionately higher casualties in the fighting overseas.[352] It would also not be surprising if they served longer tours of duty abroad, since popularity-hunting Roman politicians were not agitating on their behalf as they were on behalf of Roman conscripts.[353] Some soldiers never returned to Italy at all, but on discharge simply stayed in the region where they had served and settled down there with native women. There is no positive proof that such expatriates were for the most part Italians, but there are indications that they may have been.[354]

Another factor distorting the make-up of Italy's population in the second century was the huge expansion of slavery. The 150,000 Epirotes enslaved in a single day after Aemilius Paullus' victory at Pydna in 168 gives some idea of its magnitude.[355] At that time all the adult Roman males together amounted to only just over twice that figure. Slaves brought to Italy ultimately were assimilated in the main into the Roman citizen body. Those of them liberated by Italian masters did not, it is true, automatically get Roman citizenship. But, as the masters were more usually Roman, most manumitted slaves did obtain it. Moreover, it may be suspected that even those freed by Italians often migrated, like their erstwhile masters, to Roman territory and there in the course of time managed to pass as Romans.

For various reasons, then, the Roman element in the population of Italy was growing at the expense of the Italian, and in at least one particular this state of affairs may seem surprising. During the second century the Romans on the one hand allowed individual Italians to flock into Roman territory and there be more or less unobtrusively absorbed into the Roman body politic, yet on the other hand they opposed official extension of the Roman citizenship to non-Roman communities and even passed alien acts repeatedly to expel immigrated Italians.[356]

The Roman ruling class can be held responsible for this inconsistent behaviour. When Italians acquired Roman citizenship, ordinary Romans were probably resentful insofar as it affected them materially (as, for example, when *novi cives* competed for cheap grain or for allotments of land), but probably content insofar as it relieved them of burdens (as, for example, when Italian newcomers were conscripted for service in Spain). In any case, the view of ordinary Romans hardly mattered: they did not decide policy.[357] What really counted was the attitude of the Roman upper classes, and it evidently differed from one period to another. Early in the century Roman nobles were eager to swell their following of adherents with immigrants and thereby increase their own influence in the Assemblies. Indeed, at first it was only in response to recriminatory protests from non-Roman communities, for whom mass emigration was making the *formula togatorum* an intolerable burden, that the Roman ruling class could be induced to have 'foreigners' periodically expelled from Roman soil.[358] After 139, however, when the introduction of the secret ballot made clients' votes less dependable and encouraged Italian magnates to aim at a greater share of political power, the Roman upper classes decided that it was time to stop enfranchising Italians.

Rome's language inevitably profited from her military, political, economic, social and demographic superiority. The crippling terms imposed on defeated Carthage and the subsequent activities overseas carried Rome's power and with it Rome's language far beyond the confines of Italy. Latin had long ceased to be a peasants' and soldiers' patois: it had acquired a literature of its own and could serve as the vehicle for diplomatic intercourse on a much wider, international scene. It began to assume the authority and usefulness of a world language.[359]

One of the rare allusions in ancient literature to a Roman language policy illustrates graphically how Latin emerged from its parochial status. According to Valerius Maximus, second-century Roman magistrates 'were very determined never to give answers to Greeks in any tongue but Latin; furthermore, whenever Greeks gabbled anything forth with all the volubility of which they are such masters, the Roman magistrates firmly insisted that an interpreter be used, and this not just in Rome, but in Greece and Asia as well.'[360]

In Italy, of course, the penetration of Latin was deeper and more widespread. Not only was it used for politics, but also for business and every kind of activity. The severe punishment of Capua, the disloyal communities and the twelve recusant Latin Colonies did more than re-establish Rome's authority and enlarge her already giant stature within the peninsula. It also promoted the fortunes of her tongue, which at once acquired something of her own prestige. Latin became an elegant language suitable for cultivated drawing rooms, and to learn it became for Italians the fashionable as well as the useful thing to do.

Before the First Punic War a well informed observer of the Italian scene, asked to name the principal languages of the peninsula, would have been bound to mention Greek, Oscan and Latin: he would even have gone further and prophesied the ultimate dominance of the last-named.[361] But, if pressed to guess precisely when Latin would attain its absolute primacy, he would certainly have been at a loss. Even after the First Punic War, it was hardly possible to conjecture confidently the speed with which Latin would outdistance Oscan internally and Greek abroad. To Ennius, the Messapian born in 239, it had seemed advantageous to be at home in all three languages.[362]

After the Second Punic War, however, there was no longer room for doubt and hesitation. By then it was obvious that the triumph of Latin would come in relatively short order. The polyglot Ennius appreciated at once that, even for cultural purposes, Latin, not Greek, was the tongue of the future: he used Latin for his poetry. And Ennius was not alone: the Greek-speaking Livius Andronicus also wrote in Latin.

Not surprisingly, therefore, the language shift in Italy gathered marked momentum in the second century. The first intimations of it were the increasing use of the Latin alphabet and widespread bilingualism of the sort reflected in Plautus' comedies, Lucilius' satires and other writings.

In the districts closest to Rome Latin had by now become the language of private conversation, even within the family. By 200 Hernican, Auruncan and perhaps Sabine were already extinct, and it was now the turn for Volscian: if not actually dead, it was clearly moribund.[363] In the south colonizations and viritane distributions had injected a significant Latin-speaking element into the Sabellian population: Cicero implies that Latin could be readily understood in southern cities.[364] The political obliteration of Capua had robbed Oscan of its one really substantial metropolis, and that language consequently tended to become a country-dwellers' patois, its doom unmistakably foreshadowed in the appearance of Oscan inscriptions with latinisms even in Samnium.[365] At the same time, the decline of the Italiotes had severely curtailed the use of Greek, and the Latin alphabet, even the Latin language, began to appear increasingly in documents from Magna Graecia.[366] Even Messapic was affected. Really marked romanization of the rather inaccessible Sallentine peninsula is not noticeable until the first century, but there is a specimen from there of Latin of the second century.[367] In central Italy Aequian and Marsic died out in the second century, and Latin had replaced Faliscan on inscriptions from Falerii Novi by the latter half of the century.[368] In Etruria Latin was spreading steadily northwards, especially in the districts closest to the Tyrrhenian coast. Second-century tombs at Tarquinii were as likely to contain Latin inscriptions as Etruscan.[369] Veii at the southern end of Etruria was solidly Roman, and *coloniae* and *praefecturae* provided pockets of latinity elsewhere. Use of the Latin alphabet became common in Etruria, and many Etruscans even discarded their names and substituted Roman *praenomina* and *gentilicia* for them. Further east and north in peninsular Italy the transition from Umbrian to Latin was also well under way, and, although religious conservatism insisted that the native idiom be used on the Iguvine Tables, even some of the latter are written in the Latin script. Picenum for its part had so many *praefecturae* that much of it must have been using Latin.[370]

The state of affairs in upper Italy was not very different. South of the Po this is not to be wondered at. There much Roman and Latin settlement had promoted speedy assimilation of the Cispadane natives and Latin spread rapidly, even if it was of a sort that later elicited critical comment from Cicero and Horace.[371] In Transpadana, where seizures of territory had not taken place, other factors must have been at work. Perhaps Latin-speaking immigrants from peninsular Italy had settled on the land that reclamation had made available there. But more important probably was the illiteracy of the Gauls and Ligures, whose languages, uncommitted to writing, could hardly hold their own against an evolved tongue that was. Above all, it must have been the superior culture, sophisticated technology and strong social organization of the Romans that paved the way for latinization of the far north. The change in the Gauls was already very marked by the middle of the century when Polybius visited the Po valley. He found them hardly different from the Veneti except for their speech: Celtic, so he seems to imply, had largely disappeared. The semi-nomadic freebooters of two centuries earlier had evolved into settled townspeople and farmers, who had long since adopted a money economy, and whose fertile lands produced an abundance of cereals and grapes and enough pigs to supply the entire Roman army with its pork. Coin hoards found in the region indicate that Roman coins, like the Roman language, were in common use there.[372] The Veneti were affected as well as the Gauls, although with them it was not a case of an inferior culture yielding to a higher. Latin made headway among them because of its practical usefulness. Many of the second-century inscriptions from

Ateste and other Venetic communities use the Latin alphabet and some of them are bilingual, and by the end of the century inscriptions in Latin are not uncommon.[373]

Thus the transition to Latin was in full, if uneven, swing throughout all Italy in the second century. Nevertheless, nothing like a universal language shift had as yet occurred. In fact, most of the non-Latin documents found in Italy belong precisely to the second and first centuries; and to complement this, the overwhelming majority of second-century documents in Latin come from Roman or Latin districts.

In areas distant from Rome it is unlikely that Latin was much used for private conversation even by Italians who were bilingual, no matter how prone they were to employ it for political and other public transactions. The native idioms were still showing some vigour despite the ubiquitous ascendancy of Latin. One region where this is securely demonstrable is Etruria, especially its more eastern and northern sections. There Etruscan is still found on the many second-century sepulchral monuments. Nor are the inscriptions merely formulaic and traditional, as a glance at those from the tomb of the Volumnii immediately confirms.[374] For all the widespread bilingualism Etruscan was still showing signs of vitality in many parts of Etruria as late as 100. Even Caere, reasonably close to Rome and a *municipium* of long standing, had not entirely discarded its Etruscan, interspersed with Latinisms though its native speech had become. Further north, Volaterrae and the districts around Clusium and Perusia seem to have been still solidly Etruscan. Perhaps it was their pristine glories and a lively awareness of their own idiosyncrasy that delayed assimilation of the Etruscans. This was certainly true of the Greeks of Ancona, who remained an isolated pocket of hellenism on the coast of Picenum. Far more conscious of Hellenic superiority than of Hellenic decline, they were determined not to surrender their Greek to a 'barbarous' tongue. The attitude of the Sabelli seems to have been different. They vaunted no particular linguistic superiority of their own and many of them (Apuli, Frentani and Lucani) adopted the Latin alphabet in the second century. They were not yet, however, ready to give up Oscan. It remained the daily speech, and in Samnium and Campania it continued to be written in the native alphabet. In the far north Venetic certainly was not dead, and in the far south increasing 'interference' from Latin did not prevent Messapic from continuing as the common language.[375]

In some regions of Italy the mountains seem to have been linguistic as well as physical barriers. Whereas Latin spread swiftly among the Aequi, Marsi and cismontane Vestini, it threaded its way through the Forca Caruso into the Paeligni, transmontane Vestini and Marrucini much more slowly. It is to be noted that the great majority of surviving inscriptions in Paelignian, the best documented of the mid-Italic dialects, date from the second and even the first century.

One is justified in concluding that throughout the second century the peoples and tribes of Italy remained conscious of their distinctness from the Romans, just as much at the end of the century perhaps as at its beginning. Their innate and continuing love for independence was the principal reason for their attitude, but it was not the only one. The Romans themselves were more than a little responsible. They made it clear, especially towards the end of the century that Italian communities were to remain, in law, non-Roman. As has been pointed out, the system that the Romans had devised for Italy was not a confederacy. On the contrary, it was only too likely to isolate the dependent allies from each other. They were all tied to Rome, but they were not linked to one another; and their mutual contacts were frequently limited and occasionally cool. To counteract this, it is true, there was the constant, regular, united action of Romans, Latini and Italians on many a battlefield. After 268 the peninsular states fought by Rome's side, even if not in Rome's legions, in every war, and this must have accustomed them to think in terms of Italy as a single unit for military purposes. But the extent to which authentic integration was thereby fostered in other matters is debatable. Any pan-Italian sentiment generated in the wars was probably tempered by the twin reflections that the sacrifices demanded of Italians were neither equal nor always equitable and that, in any case, the wars in which they had to serve were Rome's, not theirs; Italian states were not permitted to make war on their own account, either collectively or singly.

For the Romans the system of bilateral treaties represented a policy of common prudence that contributed to their own security by keeping possible foes disunited. The Romans are even said to have been opposed to having Latin as the language of all Italy lest it make for easier intercourse amongst the Italians and facilitate the organization of anti-Roman movements. But their attitude was probably more ambivalent than such a simplistic view suggests. They may have felt some anxiety as to where universal adoption of Latin might lead, but surely they must also have been pleased at the role that Latin now played. Certainly the common belief that the non-Latin states of Italy were forbidden to use Latin unless expressly authorised by Rome to do so is almost certainly incorrect (see Appendix V). Nevertheless, even though there probably was no Roman veto on the use of Latin, the dependent states were not encouraged to develop close mutual relations.

Furthermore, if the Roman system kept the Italian communities separate from one another, it tended in the second century to set them apart from Rome as well.[376] By then the legal distinction between Romans and Italians was officially paraded and Rome was no longer incorporating whole communities; and even though individual Italians contrived to obtain her citizenship, they often did so (after 177, at least) by furtive means.

As the century wore on, the legal difference between Romans and Italians seemed to become more emphasized. With the increase in the value of their citizenship, the Romans deliberately kept themselves apart and aloof so as to retain its advantages for themselves. Roman citizens, for instance, enjoyed the right of appeal, got bigger allotments of land, received larger shares of war booty, escaped direct taxation (after 168), had their military burdens eased, and in Rome itself were partly fed at state expense. The allies cannot be shown to have had any of these benefits. Moreover their communities were exposed to the capricious whims of Roman officials, and did not at the same time profit much from the wars that they had helped Rome to win. Only Rome gained provinces overseas, and she retained for herself the tribute they disgorged: Italians might trade in them, but only Romans could plunder them. The wars did not even provide the allied states with loot for the embellishment of their towns, unless a Roman commander – a Scipio, a Mummius, or a Fulvius Flaccus – tossed them an item or two as a lordly and condescending act of grace.[377]

Not surprisingly the disadvantages under which the allies found themselves led to some upsurge of native sentiment. But, on the other hand, it also made them eager for the Roman citizenship, even though that meant abandoning their own speech and customs; and by the end of the century they were demanding the citizenship with increasing insistence. Some of them were not without qualms about the consequences, should their demand be granted. The Etruscans, for instance, and possibly the Umbri, too, were more than a little worried about what would happen to their stratified societies when exposed to the Roman *ius civile*. Nevertheless, all the allies wanted the perquisites to which citizenship would entitle them. The Romans, for their part, determined to retain their privileged status, persisted in ignoring the allied demand. It took the Social War of 91–87 to redress the balance.

CHAPTER VI

THE CONSEQUENCES OF THE SOCIAL WAR

The event that more than any other helped to make Italy Roman was the Social War (91–87), so-called, even by contemporaries, since it was a conflict between Rome and her *socii*.[378]

It was brought about by the demand of the allies for Roman citizenship. This the Romans were unwilling to concede, largely because they realized that the citizenship by itself was not what the allied leaders were really seeking. In their own states these leaders were large land-owners and constituted the governing élite, the *domi nobiles*, and they naturally wanted assurance that, on becoming Romans, they would enjoy a similar status in Roman society. The risk that they would not do so was very real especially for those of them that came from tribal states. The tribal magnates could hardly have been unaware that the Italians, who, in the past, had somehow managed to gain admission into the Senate, had come almost exclusively from urbanized communities; and for them the idea of becoming merely part of the anonymous Roman mass was anathema, no matter how ready their humbler fellows were to welcome the *civitas sine suffragio*, for such in effect it was bound to be. The *primores Italiae* wanted their share of privilege, a meaningful role in public affairs, a voice in deciding, executing and profiting from state policy. Unlike their peasant followers, they could easily afford to go to Rome and there they hoped to become members of the Senate. As Justin says, they were after partnership in power (*consortium imperii*), not mere Roman citizenship.[379]

If they had not openly avowed such aspirations long before, the reason had probably been the uselessness of their doing so. Hitherto the Roman system of open voting had effectively ruled out any hope of their achieving office at Rome. But now the secret ballot, tentatively introduced in 139 and securely confirmed in 119, held out the prospect of change.[380] From now on enfranchised Italians of means would stand some chance of winning an election, provided, of course, that their entire home communities also obtained the citizenship and backed them. The time was ripe for even tribal notables to make their bid for a share of power.

But naturally the Roman governing class was also aware of the implications of the secret ballot. They were determined not to share their privileges or allow their highest council to be polluted with rural and above all tribal elements. Therefore they refused to revive the policy of integral incorporation that had been in abeyance since 268. The reply of the Italian leaders to this rebuff was to repudiate the entire Roman connection, some of them even going so far as to encourage a revival of native speech and culture.[381]

Hostilities broke out in Picenum late in 91 when the allied people of Asculum were stirred to furious rebellion against Rome's hegemony and slaughtered every Roman they could get their hands on, including an investigative praetor recently despatched to their area with proconsular power. Other mid-Italic and Sabellian *socii* had concocted plans beforehand with the Asculani and now promptly followed their lead. But Italians elsewhere and the Nomen Latinum everywhere, except in partly oscanized Venusia, either supported Rome or stayed neutral: there was some movement in favour of the rebels among the Umbri and Etruscans late in 90, but it ceased at once when the Romans offered them the citizenship.

The insurgent leaders had a plan for a new, non-Roman system in Italy in which decision-making would rest with them; and they lost no time in implementing it. In their states widespread latinization had by no means stifled the spirit of independence, or even entirely eliminated the native Italian vernaculars. Accordingly the leaders organized these states (most of which were tribal) into a kind of confederacy, calling it Italia, a name well calculated to appeal to all who resented the exclusive behaviour lately practised by the Romans. It had a council, on which each participating state was represented, and a federal capital (also called Italia) located at the Paelignian settlement of Corfinium, approximately at the geographical centre of Italy and certainly in the very heart of rebel country. To publicize the insurgent alternative to Roman hegemony the confederates also issued their own silver coins, not a few of which have survived: they imitate Roman issues in weight and types and were obviously designed to rival and if possible replace them.

The fighting at first went very badly for the Romans, and late in 90 they announced their willingness to extend their citizenship to peninsular communities. This concession, combined with help from non-rebel Italy and from the Roman provinces overseas, enabled Rome to survive the crisis and gradually get the upper hand. By the end of 88 only Rome's inveterate Sabellian enemies, the tough Oscan-speakers from Samnium and Lucania, were still in arms; and by 87 even these were obliged to make peace, without an ignominious unconditional surrender, however, since Mithridates, the king of Pontus, chose that particular moment to divert Rome's energies, and attention, elsewhere by invading her province of Asia.

It is commonly held that Rome won the Social War by yielding to the allied demand and bestowing the citizenship upon all of Italy. This is an exaggeration. In 90/89 Roman citizenship was not given to all Italy. The inhabitants of Cisalpina, apart from those in the four Latin Colonies there, did not get it;[382] and even in the peninsula Italians did not obtain the kind of citizenship that they really wanted. The immediate sequel made it very clear that the Romans had no intention of accepting the Italians, either their commoners or their élites, as equals in the body politic.

One area, and indeed the only one in Roman public life, where newly enfranchised Italians might hope to make their influence felt was in the public Assemblies. But to prevent their doing so, the Romans proceeded to gerrymander their registration in the Roman Tribes. Rome began to enrol the ex-insurgents in a handful of specially created new Tribes that were to vote last and would, therefore, usually not vote at all, since decisions were normally reached before all the Tribes had had their turn at the ballot baskets. At least two new Tribes of this second-class kind seem to have been brought into temporary being.[383]

Division within Rome's own body politic, however, soon put an end to this chicanery. The political rivalries at Rome, which had been steadily growing in intensity during the second century and which had erupted into bloody violence during the Gracchan interlude (133–121), now at once assumed a much greater dimension. With the expansion of Rome to include all Italy, civic faction-fighting inevitably exploded into full-scale civil war. This tragedy, however, proved to be the Italians' opportunity, for none of the contending parties could afford to ignore them. Already in 88, when armed strife broke out to decide who was to have the command against Mithridates, one of those eager for the appointment angled for Italian support.

He got the command and the Italians got improved status since in the very next year the Senate conceded the principle that they should be distributed throughout the traditional thirty-five Tribes; the scheme for a number of new ones seems to have been quietly dropped. Actual registration of the Italians, however, proceeded slowly for the time being since the dominating group in the Senate was in no hurry to bestir itself. But in 84 L. Cornelius Sulla, the ultimate winner in the fight for the command against Mithridates, was about to return to Italy and was threatening grim vengeance on those who had sought to deny him that honour. At the same time he was careful to promise that he would respect the new status of the Italians. Not to be outdone, his opponents now began to speed up the registration of the new citizens, obviously in order to procure their support. This action did not foil Sulla nor did it avert bloodshed, but it did mean that the Roman status of the Italians was now irrevocably recognized.

In the ensuing Civil War (83–80), self-interest dictated the Italians' choice of sides, but it is not possible to identify with certainty who supported Sulla and those who opposed him. He himself reckoned the Samnites his bitterest foes, with the Etruscans not far behind. But, even amongst these peoples and especially among the Etruscans, some men of influence elected to join him.[384]

Sulla's victory over his enemies (who included a strong Samnite force under Pontius Telesinus) near Rome's Colline Gate on 1 November, 82, left him master of the Roman state and arbiter of the destiny of his friends and, ominously, of his enemies. Towards the latter he was merciless. His vengeance was not confined to the execution of his more prominent adversaries. Hundreds, if not thousands, of ordinary people were murdered without compunction and thousands more were ruined by the ruthless seizure of their property.

Sulla's partisans reaped the benefit. He allowed his captains to buy confiscated land for a song and thus become landed millionaires, and he established his demobilized soldiers in various parts of Italy on allotments of land that he had seized and classified as *ager publicus*. There seems to have been some viritane distribution (at Volaterrae for instance), but in general Sulla preferred to settle his veterans in compact *coloniae*, where they could protect themselves from the outraged locals and establish strong-points for the maintenance of the arrangements from which they had profited.[385]

Sulla's colonies were especially to be found in Etruria and Campania. There is positive evidence of foundations at Arretium, Faesulae and Pompeii, and strong presumptive evidence for Clusium and Nola, both of which later housed 'old' (Sullan?) colonists alongside of 'new' (Triumviral?). Other regions where Sullan colonies were established were: certainly Greater Latium (Praeneste, Privernum), and probably Samnium (Telesia?), Lucania (Abellinum? Grumentum?) and Picenum (Interamnia Praetut-tirorum? Hadria?). At Pompeii Sulla's *coloni* and the locals were not kept physically separate, and a tense situation developed. At Arretium, on the other hand, *coloni* and natives appear to have been organized as separate juxtaposed communities, each with its own administrative apparatus.[386] The difference of treatment of the two communities may have been due to the divergence of their respective attitudes: in Etruria some local aristocrats had supported him, in Campania relatively few had done so, therefore he had no compunction about repressing existing élites there.

In all, Sulla is said to have settled 120,000 veterans, the overwhelming majority of them in *coloniae*.[387] Many of them turned out to be indifferent farmers, and some of them, at Praeneste and elsewhere, actually sold their allotments for cash almost as soon as they got them. But they were efficient disseminators of Latin. In some regions it may have been Sulla's veterans who gave the *coup de grâce* to the native vernaculars. In Etruria, at least, the decline of Etruscan, inevitable though it was, must have been greatly accelerated by them. He, probably more than any other single person, was responsible for the diffusion of Latin throughout the peninsula. His influence on Cisalpine Gaul seems much less marked. But there Latin had already made great headway without his help.

Sulla's integration of Italy, however, was not promoted by vindictiveness alone. He had a constructive as well as a brutal side to his nature. His reorganization of the Roman Senate made that august body less parochial and more representative of Italy. He doubled its size, increasing its membership from three to six hundred, an action requiring the creation of far more than three hundred new senators, since he also had to replace the two hundred or so that had lost their lives through war, murder and natural causes since 91.[388] Sulla presumably sought his new senators among the elements that he could trust. They seem to have been *equites Romani* and leading personalities, some of them from Rome, others from the newly enfranchised communities, including a few Etruscans and perhaps even a Samnite magnate or two.[389] His reform of the Senate could have had but little direct effect on the spread of Latin, since all of his new appointees were assuredly already quite at home in that language. But it did draw Italy into a more intimate association with Rome, and to that extent promoted romanization.

It has been pertinently pointed out that Sulla could not abolish his own example. If Sulla could achieve his ambition, other aspiring nobles could hope to do the same, and in the first century there was no shortage of men willing to try. The political rivalries of these contenders for power plunged the Roman state, which now meant all of peninsular Italy, into half a century of strife, bloodshed and chaos, with rebellious slaves and raiding pirates adding their share of violence. Between 80 and 30 as many as half a million people or more were uprooted and scattered. Brigandage and kidnapping were common, and the burden of debt staggering. Order was not restored until 30, when one of the would-be dynasts succeeded in making himself *princeps* of the Roman world, acquiring the designation Augustus three years later. By then Cisalpine Gaul too had been incorporated and all Italy converted into a Roman land.

Surviving accounts of the half century from 80 to 30 have much to say about the dissensions and disturbances, but little about the incorporation of the Italians that was simultaneously taking place. Yet incorporated they were.

It would have been a protracted process under any circumstances, but it was rendered even slower by the turbulence of the times and the unrestrained behaviour of the quarrelling rivals who bedevilled the demographic situation and existing social structure with their confiscations and colonies and rarely allowed censors to stay in office at Rome and register citizens. The metamorphosis was not really completed until the reign of Augustus.[390]

The law that extended the Roman citizenship was the Lex Julia of 90. Two other citizenship laws (of 89?) are also cited by name, the Lex Calpurnia and the Lex Plautia Papiria, but they were supplementary, dealing with details which the Lex Julia had either ignored or left vague. It was the Lex Julia that was the basis for the whole operation. It revived the policy that had been abandoned *c.* 268, and incorporated, not individual Italians, but entire communities, and specifically communities in peninsular Italy. Cisalpine Gaul, which had always been treated as if it were not of Italy even though in it, continued to receive special and separate treatment despite the spread of romanization there.[391] Its four Latin Colonies were converted into Roman *municipia*, although whether as a result of the Lex Julia or of the Lex Pompeia of 89 is uncertain. It was certainly the latter law that regulated other communities in Cisalpina, by bestowing the title of *Colonia Latina* upon certain of the non-Roman communities there (even though no *coloni* were sent to them or other formal rites of colonization carried out)[392] and by 'attributing' native settlements to Roman or Latin communities. The names of the titular Latin Colonies are not recorded, but they evidently lay north of the Po, the region south of the river being already in large part Roman; and they are good evidence of romanization since assuredly they would not have been given the title of colony had their character, sentiments and prospective behaviour not been strongly pro-Roman. As for Cisalpina as a whole, it seems to have been organized formally into a province at about this time.[393]

As far as peninsular Italy was concerned, the Lex Julia laid down the noteworthy proviso that only those allied communities that formally agreed to conform in all respects to Roman law could get the citizenship.[394] Apparently, once a community accepted and implemented this condition, it was known as a *municipium fundanum*,[395] and its constitution was then drawn up, apparently in close consultation with it. Ultimately, by means of a law passed in the Tribal Assembly, the Roman People authorized its admission into their body politic and from then on it was a regular *municipium*. Records of such enabling acts, named after their sponsors, survive. Thus, a Lex Cornelia, whose author may have been the celebrated Cinna, arranged for the entry of Bruttian Petelia. A Lex Petronia seems to have brought in several communities simultaneously: Latin Interamna Lirenas, Campanian Pompeii, and probably Messapian Gnathia.[396] Once the municipal status of a community had been officially regularized, its magistrates conducted a census in order that a list of its burgesses might be sent to Rome. The net effect of the Lex Julia was to make peninsular Italy a conglomeration of *municipia et coloniae*, to use the expression of Cicero, even though in his day there were still communities there that were neither.[397]

The process of incorporating all of peninsular Italy was, however, far more complicated than the above account implies. For one thing, the tribal states presented a problem, it being difficult to see how they could meet the stipulation that they formally accommodate their legal systems to that of Rome: it was hardly practical for a tribal state to get all its *vici* and *pagi* to express their conformity simultaneously. There was no option but to break up the tribal states. Accordingly, they were subdivided into urban mini-states, which could make the required declaration and which the Romans in any case preferred. Even so some areas were not sufficiently developed to make urban commonwealths possible, and in them Rome was obliged to go on using her old system of *praefecturae*.

Inevitably the number of new *municipia* to be constituted was very large, since Rome had to organize them not only in non-Roman Italy, but also in those parts of Roman Italy that before the Social War had been without either *municipia* or Citizen Colonies, it being unthinkable that *novi cives* should get 'home rule' while 'old' Romans were left without it.[398] Italy became much more urbanized in consequence. Before the Social War there may have been about 125 fully autonomous urban units in Italy. After than conflict there were at least twice that many. An exact count is not possible, since more *municipia* were constituted than are actually recorded.[399] Unfortunately no ancient writer supplies any dates or other information about the mechanics of municipalization, and details have to be divined from hints in Cicero or from inscriptions.

The new *municipia* differed from the pre-war variety in style as well as in number. Whereas the old *municipia* were still allowed their distinctive earlier constitutions, the new were restricted to two, both of them novel. The Tabulae Heracleenses, the Lex Mamilia Roscia, the Lex Tarenti and many inscriptions of the first century and later prove that the new *municipia* were administered either by a board of four magistrates known as *quattuorviri* or by a pair called *duoviri* (a title hitherto confined apparently to Citizen Colonies). Presumably diversity was avoided in order to limit eccentricities and remove anomalies or, at the very least, to simplify and expedite the whole operation. Probably there was less standardization than the nomenclature indicates: magisterial functions were not everywhere identical and there was great variety in the titles of the lesser local magistrates.[400]

The quattuorviral *municipia* were much more numerous and for the most part earlier than the duoviral, and they may have distributed magisterial duties differently and defined areas of competence with greater precision. But no ancient writer explains in precisely what respects the two types of *municipia* differed from one another.

The *praefecturae* of ante-bellum Italy, like its tribal states, were greatly affected by the transformation of the country into a vast mosaic of urban commonwealths. Ultimately most, and perhaps all of them became fully autonomous city-states with their own jurisdictional authorities. But the exact date when the *praefecti iuri dicundo* stopped being sent out from Rome is unknown. Some *praefecturae* certainly remained in being throughout the first century, and both the Lex Mamilia Roscia and the Tabulae Heracleenses indicate that even new *praefecturae* could be constituted then, particularly, no doubt, as a result of the break-up of tribal states. *Praefecturae* are still recorded in the reign of Augustus and even much later; Forum Clodii was still called *praefectura* in AD 174 and Peltuinum as late as AD 262.[401]

Historical conservatism may account for some of these late *praefecturae*. Certain communities probably went on being called *praefecturae*, when, in fact, they had ceased to be such, simply because that was how they were traditionally known. The *fora* provide an instructive parallel. Many of them retained the title Forum long after they had become *municipia*, some of them indeed down to the present day.

Hence it may well be the case that, just as some developed communities of Latium (Bovillae and Castrimoenium, for instance)[402] were sufficiently urbanized to be established as *municipia* almost immediately after 90, so too were the better evolved *praefecturae*: Urbs Salvia in Picenum may be an instance. A further consideration is that after 89 the epigraphically attested presence of a *praefectus* in a community does not necessarily mean that it was then a *praefectura* of the old type. For one thing, he might not be a *praefectus iuri dicundo*; for *praefecti* could all be appointed for other tasks. But, even if he were, he might no longer be an appointee from Rome: the *praefecti* at Aufidena, Casinum and elsewhere, although they seem to have had judicial functions, may well have been locally appointed natives instead of nominees of the urban praetor. Certainly the *praefectus* at Lucanian Bantia could not have been the praetor's delegate, since his judgements were open to appeal.[403]

Nevertheless, there were undoubtedly authentic *praefecturae* long after 90. Perhaps no particular urgency was felt in 90 about converting existing *praefecturae* into fully autonomous *municipia* since they were already Roman communities anyhow. The *praefecturae* in Samnium and Picenum, for instance, do not seem to have been municipalized until about the middle of the century, to judge from what Cicero has to say about Atina in 54 and Caesar about Cingulum in 49;[404] and the Sabine *praefecturae*, whose burgesses had been the first non-Latini to be made full Roman citizens, apparently had to wait even longer: Reate, Trebula Mutuesca, Nursia and Amiternum were all still *praefecturae* in Augustus' day.[405] Admittedly they then had native officials of their own with the Roman title of *octoviri*; but, as these are not described as *iuri dicundo*, it must be assumed that the jurisdictional functions were discharged by *praefecti*. It is not known when these Sabine *praefecturae* became *municipia*. But, whenever it was, they went on calling their local magistrates *octoviri*, although by then they did possess judicial powers and were presumably *octoviri* only in name.[406]

After 90, therefore, it was the communities, which were already fully autonomous (such as Latin Colonies and Italian city-states) or well on the road to being so (such as certain Roman *praefecturae* and Italian tribal *pagi*), that could be, and were, promptly made into *municipia*. Larinum, for instance, had instituted its quattuorviral system before Sulla returned from the east in 83 and so too, it seems, had Pompeii and Interamna Nahars.[407]

But the less developed Roman *fora* and *conciliabula* and the non-evolved *pagi* and *vici* were not sufficiently autonomous by 90 to vote the immediate acceptance of Roman law as stipulated by the Lex Julia. They needed first to be formally organized, and this took time. Scattered settlements and clusters of homesteads had perhaps to be combined, and certainly every newly created urban organism had to be provided with appropriate municipal buildings and with a *territorium* of its own. Delimitation of the latter was likely to involve contentious and possibly time-consuming adjustments to existing boundaries.[408]

The difficulty of organizing new urban communities into highly structured city-states is illustrated by the case of Lucanian Bantia. Its status before the Social War is not known. But an Oscan inscription, which although extant only in fragments is the most considerable document in that language, throws much light on conditions in Bantia after its incorporation. The document was important enough to be carved on the back of a bronze plaque which has an obsolete Roman law, in Latin, of c.100 on the other side. Thus it was obviously intended for public display and was probably compiled some time after 80, apparently by the Bantians themselves, to serve as a temporary and tentative municipal charter until they were ready for one drafted in Latin. The surviving sections of the document seem to be a compendium of the regulations relating to civil and penal jurisdiction, which was bound to be of concern to a community in process of change from Sabellian to Roman legal practices. But the constitutional arrangements of Bantia are also incidentally revealed. The instruments of civic government (local assembly, senate and magistrates) owe something to the institutions of Sulla's Rome and of nearby Venusia. Ultimately, perhaps before the end of the first century, a Latin constitution replaced the one drawn up in Oscan; whereupon Bantia became a regular duoviral *municipium*.[409]

The standardized terminology used by Roman *municipia* after the year 90 betokened no diminution of their autonomy. They suffered grievously, of course, in the strife and violence of the first century and were powerless against the intervention of overbearing warlords in their affairs. But, in the periods of more settled conditions, they went about their own business in their own way, seemingly without harassment from the central power. Cicero, at any rate, describes how the local magistrates administered civic finances, were in charge of public works, and managed communal property and the rents accruing therefrom.[410] Even for jurisdiction the urban commonwealths were not closely supervised, much less rigidly controlled from Rome. It is true that all *municipia* were bound gradually to assimilate their local law to that of Rome, with the result that they came to resemble Citizen Colonies in being subject to the ultimate authority of the Roman praetor. But it is apparent that local magistrates were allowed considerable discretion. A recently published inscription of the first century confirms Cicero's statement of 63 that Puteoli enjoyed liberty and its own jurisdiction: the magistrates of that *colonia* could put men on trial and even condemn them to death, seemingly without appeal.[411] Perhaps it was not possible to devise blanket regulations defining where local competence ended and the urban praetor's began.[412] But, for whatever reason, municipal magistrates were evidently not subject to his constant interference.

Lacking a trained bureaucracy, Rome had little option but to pursue a hands-off policy relative to the *municipia* and *coloniae*. This is strikingly illustrated by events at Pisa late in the first century. That *colonia* found itself completely without magistrates in the year 4, since political rivalries in the town had been too intense to allow the election of any. This surely was the time when Rome might have been expected to intervene and restore order. But, in fact, she did nothing of the sort, and Pisa was left to solve its problem as best it could.[413] Manifestly the *municipia* and *coloniae* that made up first-century Italy were to all intents and purposes semi-independent states.

The state of affairs in Cisalpine Gaul after its enfranchisement in 49 was not very different. It is true that it did not at once become a part of Italy. For a few years it remained a province, even though a very anomalous one, seeing that virtually its entire free population consisted of Roman citizens. In 49 Julius Caesar preferred to have Cisalpina remain a province, since so long as it had that official status he could legally station troops in it, and they were useful for overawing the peninsula immediately to the south. Its formal incorporation into Italy, therefore, did not come until 42, when the newly created Triumvirs wished to ensure that whichever of them remained in Italy should not have a provincial army at his beck and call in Cisalpina.

Parts of Piemonte, as it happened, were still unsubjugated in 42 and the boundary between Italy and Transalpine Gaul was not delimited until years later. But the settled parts of Cisalpina were largely romanized.[414]

Thus, as Virgil says,[415] the will of Jupiter had been fulfilled: all Italy had been made one. Nevertheless a dozen tempestuous years were to intervene before the country found anything resembling tranquillity. The Triumvirs promptly revived the evil methods of Sulla's dictatorship, reverting to his practice of proscription and copying his policy of seizing land on which to settle *coloniae* of ex-soldiers. Between 43 and 33 they established twenty or more of them.[416]

Cisalpina had immediate cause to deplore its incorporation, when veterans from Philippi (42) were presented with farm lands snatched from Cremona and Mantua; and the rest of Italy shared its distress. Even before Philippi eighteen towns had been selected to make provision for the demobilized, some of them in Cisalpina but most of them elsewhere.[417] The poets Virgil, Horace, Propertius and Tibullus and thousands of less celebrated persons had to surrender their property. Many 'new' Romans must have been ruined but it was probably not the case that recently enfranchised districts were special targets for confiscation. Appian and Dio insist that all parts of Italy suffered and even some Roman senators lost their land. So far from adopting a policy of palpable anti-Italianism, the contenders for power were more prone to voice pan-Italian sentiments; and undoubtedly the 'new' Romans, who were shrewd or lucky enough to back the successful dynasts, shared in their plunder.[418] In fact, the disorders, instead of polarizing Roman Italy into 'old' and 'new', may well have had the opposite effect and expedited its fusion, as the increasingly scrambled population wallowed in a misery that made bedfellows of them all. All were exposed to the same hazards and hardships; all were ready to follow a charismatic leader and when they served it was in the Roman legions. Their daily difficulties and perils engendered community of feeling. Italians and 'old' Romans alike lost their deep sense of separate identities.[419]

The despatch of *coloni* to so many parts of Italy had by now made the Roman body politic less cohesive, while the solidarity of the various Italian peoples had also been undermined owing to the acceptance of Roman ways by their leaders and the demise of their tribal states. Thus among both Romans and Italians particularism had lost much of its edge. Romans found it a welcome change to absorb Italians instead of Levantine freedmen, and the Italians for their part were content to be assimilated. They might regret the passing of the old order and the disappearance or transformation of their ancestral states, but they had reason not to repine. They had acquired the Roman citizenship and become members of the imperial nation. The sooner they now became Romans in fact, as well as in law, the better.

Accordingly romanization made rapid headway in the first century, now with the active co-operation of the Italians, instead of the more or less passive acquiescence that they had displayed in the second. This was true even of Sabellian Italy where, as Strabo remarks,[420] native vernaculars, regional styles of dress and the like simply disappeared. By the year 30, if not indeed a decade earlier, Italians and Romans had become virtually indistinguishable and the epithets 'old' and 'new' were no longer relevant.

The universality of Latin, which the growth of urbanism no doubt accelerated, is the clearest evidence of this. Even Greek had given way: it was, as Tacitus reveals, still the language of Neapolis under the Empire, but elsewhere its position had become very precarious indeed.[421] The other tongues were in much worse case than Greek. Inscriptions in Messapic became ever rarer in the first century and ceased altogether by its end.[422] Oscan, it is true, lingered on for a while after the first century in Pompeii and in areas that had been tribal before the Social War, but it had almost certainly disappeared from Picenum and was clearly doomed in other areas. The mid-Italic dialects had followed Sabine, Auruncan, Aequian, Volscian and Faliscan into oblivion, Paelignian perhaps being the last to go. In Umbria some communities had still been clinging to the native tongue in 90, but promptly adopted Latin after becoming Roman: at Asisium *marones* are recorded in Umbrian shortly before 90; but their sons a few years later used Latin for public pronouncements.[423] In Etruria, Etruscan ceased to be used for epitaphs in the first century; the last trace of it, for instance, in the sepulchre of the Salvii Othones at Ferentium belonging to 67. Speakers of Etruscan had not entirely died out by 30, but from then on it was left increasingly to antiquarians to keep the language alive.[424] In Upper Italy Venetic had died out by the end of the first century.[425] In fact, all Cisalpina seems to have been latinized by then, even if the Latin spoken there was likely to sound uncouth to purists from the south.

The Italian upper classes were more romanized than the lower, despite continuing cause for complaint in the discrimination to which they had long been subject.[426] In theory, they were eligible for all the Roman magistracies, and in this respect, down to 49, seemed outwardly to be better off than some old Roman families that had been persecuted by Sulla and by his fiat legally debarred from office. But, whatever the theory, during the first half of the first century, Italians, especially those from former tribal areas, stood little or no chance of winning the consulship: that office was effectively monopolized by the *nobiles*, the Roman families with a consul somewhere in their background. Such exclusion was of small concern to the Italian lower orders who could no more aspire to the highest magistracy than the Roman commons could. But the Italian gentry, qualified for the office as they were by their wealth and (so Cicero implies) by their liberal studies, must have resented it.

To the Italian magnates the consulship was for long tantalizing and elusive. But, so far from promoting anti-Roman feeling amongst them, this stimulated them to cultivate Roman ways even more assiduously. No sentiment of class solidarity caused them to cohere into a pressure group for the redress of their grievance: a notable from Umbrian Iguvium was not likely to make political cause with a local aristocrat from Lucanian Silvium. Italian bigwigs demonstrated their readiness for membership in the Roman élite by faithfully imitating its behaviour: they ruthlessly pursued their individual ambitions, seeking not to undermine the privileges of the Roman *nobiles*, but to obtain them for themselves.

The disturbed conditions of the first century soon gave them their chance. The contending dynasts of that tristful period found the talents of the Italians far too useful to let go to waste, and, as Velleius points out, the obscurity of their non-Roman origins no longer prevented Italians from coming to the fore. After the year 50 many of them attained the Roman consulship.[427]

CHAPTER VII
TOTA ITALIA

The last of the Republican contenders for power was Octavian. To him 'all Italy' (*tota Italia*), including now, of course, Cisalpine Gaul, 'spontaneously' swore an oath of allegiance in 32. At any rate, that is what he himself asserted many years later when, as the *princeps* Augustus, he compiled a kind of *apologia pro vita sua*.[428]

That an oath of allegiance, the so-called *coniuratio Italiae*, was sworn to Octavian in 32 is generally admitted; and it was largely this that enabled him to crush his rival Mark Antony one year later at Actium. But it would be naive to believe that the oath was either universal or spontaneous. Bononia is known not to have taken it; in fact, that city was exempted by Octavian himself because of its notorious Antonian connection. And Bononia was not unique. Ariminum shared its sentiments, and so perhaps did Placentia and Nursia. Moreover, after his victory at Actium, Octavian reproached a number of communities for their failure to respond and actually punished them for it.[429]

The spontaneity also left a great deal to be desired: one third of the Senate, for instance, instead of rushing to take the oath, promptly opted for Antony. Clearly, whatever its ostensible degree of romanization in 32, 'all Italy' was far from united, although it ought no longer to be described as 'a geographical term, and nothing more'.[430]

It was not until his victory at Actium that Octavian was able to make Rome and Italy truly one. This was certainly his aim. Not content to impose the potent, but possibly temporary, will of the victor, he was intent on bringing about a lasting reconciliation, a thorough fusion, of Romans and Italians.

The climate was favourable. Everywhere there was a yearning for peace. Weary of anarchy and violence, the average inhabitant of Italy longed for the re-establishment of law and order and a return to settled and stable conditions. To obtain integration was obviously desirable, moreover it seemed inevitable. The country had been moving steadily towards unity for generations, and the process now appeared within measurable distance of its destined end. The idea was in the air and the victory at Actium provided the opportunity to galvanize it.

Octavian could himself claim to be a symbol of Italo-Roman union. Roman by birth, and even ultra-Roman by instinct, he was, nevertheless, a son of rural Italy. His *patria* was Velitrae, where his family was of long standing and some substance. In 61 the family suddenly attained prominence in Rome when Octavian's father became praetor. His mother Atia also had a rural background. She was from a prominent family of Aricia, although she too had a close link with Rome. Her mother was Julia, the sister of Julius Caesar.

Thus Octavian, a patrician by Caesar's fiat since 44 and a consular by his own insistence since 43, could not unfairly represent himself as Italian, as well as Roman. And the same could be said of his wife. Her antecedents, Claudii and Livii Drusi, were doubly aristocratic, suitably mixed of patrician and plebeian elements. But her background was also partly Italian: Livia was the daughter of a certain Alfidia from Marruvium in the country of the Marsi.[431]

In promoting the unification of Italy, Octavian may have acted more from calculation than conviction. For the man from Velitrae may not have had much genuine feeling of solidarity with other countryside Italians. But he most certainly did need their help. Without it his bid for power was bound to fail: in March 44 he could hope for no other following. At that time the notables of Rome were committed to others, to his great uncle's murderers, to Mark Antony, to Lepidus. None of them rushed to the side of Octavian. He, therefore, had little option but to turn to the magnates of rural Italy; and turn to them he did, and very quickly.[432]

Octavian's rivals, of course, were also aware of the usefulness of Italian notables, and the consequence was that the latter now found themselves in the same situation as after Sulla's return from the east some forty years earlier. The competititon for their support enabled them to play a decisive role in the affairs of the Roman state. They got into the Roman Senate in droves, and the consulship was theirs for the taking. In the ten years from 43 to 33, of the thirty-five men to reach that high office no fewer than twenty-five were newcomers (*novi homines*), for the most part from rural Italy.[433]

The excessive number of consulships was due to the failure of most consuls to serve their full terms in the disturbed conditions of the decade after Caesar's murder. They came and went without much regard for the constitutional provision that the office should be held only by men who had reached a certain age and passed through the minor magistracies. The consulship became the prize of the tough, the unscrupulous, and the lucky; and they promptly exploited its possibilities for profit and prestige. Nor was it only the followers of Octavian, men like Vipsanius Agrippa or Salvidienus Rufus, that obtained preferment. His fellow Triumvirs had their nominees too; and soon the Senate was swollen to a thousand members and more with these parvenus.

After 31, however, patronage in Italy, and indeed in the entire *oikoumene*, rested exclusively with Octavian. To preserve his own pre-eminence, always his first and foremost concern, he continued to rely heavily on Italians whom he promoted to the consulship. The office itself henceforth would be held by men of whom he approved, and he made it a vehicle for the integration of the Italian upper classes. Admittedly these newcomers were not allowed to make policy, influential though many of them became. But this was now also true of the *nobiles* of patrician or plebeian families that had formerly guided the destinies of the Republic. All power now rested with Octavian. The Italians could at least now count on their share of a high and historic office whose dignity had been restored; and they could, and did, play a full part in the consultative process and in administrative activities at the highest level. The *primores* of Italy had attained parity with the *nobiles* of Rome.

To a certain extent the Italians owed their chance to the wastage of the old Roman families in civil war. By the twenties republican *nobiles* of the right age were in short supply and suitable quaestors were hard to find (in 24 for instance). But it was also the fixed policy of Octavian, or Augustus as he ought now to be called, to have a large Italian element in the imperial administration. The verse, one might almost say the propaganda, of the great contemporary poets, themselves sons of rural Italy, puts this beyond doubt. Virgil's *Aeneid*, composed precisely in the years immediately after Actium, symbolizes Augustus' early struggles and his task of unifying Italy. Horace's pan-Italian tone is less obvious, but it can be felt unmistakably in the poems published in 23, especially in the six so-called Roman odes.[434] That the sentiment of contemporary prose is similar is shown by Livy, and also probably by the *ingenia decora* that, according to Tacitus,[435] wrote on Augustan themes in the days before a growing tide of delation scared authors into sycophancy or silence: these writers are reflected in the pages of the Elder Pliny where the eagerness to identify Italy with Rome is constant.

The Italian magnates were, of course, pleased at their enhanced importance. The republican *nobiles*, however, were naturally less than enthusiastic. Augustus won them over with his aggressively pro-Roman stance and his ultra-Roman programme. Even before Actium he had been championing Roman institutions and values against threats and influences from abroad, especially those from the east. After Actium he became a veritable second Romulus, actively promoting a Roman renascence. Everything Roman won his warm support and earnest encouragement.[436]

To restore stability and decorum to Roman public life, Augustus assumed censorial powers and soon purged the bloated Senate of the disreputable elements so obnoxious to the Roman upper class, taking care, however, not to expel the worthy *primores Italiae*. In 29/28 the membership of the Senate was reduced to about 800. Augustus was actually aiming at the historic figure of 300, but this was to prove elusive, even for him, although he did manage ten years later to get the number down to approximately 600.

Simultaneously he rehabilitated the consulship, the Roman magistracy *par excellence*, by making it once again an annual office. Only two of the fourteen years between 43 and 29 had seen both consuls last for the entire twelve months. But in the next twenty-two years (from 28 to 6) there were only four occasions when consular pairs did not serve their full twelve-month terms, and in those four death by natural causes played a hand. Moreover, from 28 on, the formality of election by the People regularly took place, rigged in advance though the consulships were. This refurbishing of the consulship was no genuine restoration of the Republic;[437] but it did provide reassuring comfort to the *nobiles*.

In 23 Augustus gratified them still further. He himself had been holding one of the consulships for eight years running. Now in the middle of 23 he vacated it, since there was a reasonable certainty that suitable aristocrats would get it. Between 31 and 23 he had lowered the age limit for the quaestorship from thirty to twenty-five, and this expedited the eligibility of the younger members of noble families whose elders had perished in the civil wars. It now became possible for men of thirty-two to reach the consulship.

Another Augustan innovation that compensated the old aristocracy for the loss of so much of its former influence to Italians was the elevation of a number of notable plebeians to the patriciate. Their pride must have resented patronage from a municipal upstart, but their vanity was soothed with the tribute to their distinction.

More effective perhaps than anything else in reconciling the republican *nobiles* was Augustus' demonstrated ability to do without them. He was offering them a role in the ostensibly restored Republic; but, if they preferred to sulk on their estates, he could still run the state without them. This seems to have been the deciding factor. From now on republican aristocrats returned to prominence. Indeed, the list of consuls from 28 to 6 looks extremely republican with its large preponderance of *nobiles*.

But what was done could not be undone. The clock was not put back entirely. By now the Italian element was too securely established to be extruded. Accordingly, even though few consuls between 18 and 6 were *novi homines*, a number of them were nevertheless of Italian extraction. The descendants of the parvenu consuls of the forties and thirties had reached the age of thirty-two, and it was a mingling of the new aristocrats with the old that was to characterize the *novum saeculum* proclaimed by Augustus in 17.

The Italian element continued to grow. Augustus' careful reorganization of Rome's provinces and his regularization of the various provincial commands into a standing army called for a constant stream of able and experienced officials, of whom a certain proportion had to be men of consular standing since Roman tradition demanded that formations of more than one legion could be commanded only by ex-consuls. For some years before 6 it had been obvious that election of only two consuls a year was not going to generate all the ex-consuls needed. Augustus, therefore, instituted the six months' consulship, which meant not only two extra consuls every year, but also made room for more Italians. By the beginning of the Christian era it had become normal for consuls to be obtained from anywhere in Italy, even from regions that before the Social War had been tribal.

An even more potent factor in the integration of the Italian upper classes was Augustus' transformation of the Equites Romani into a secondary aristocracy, recruited from everywhere, with proportionately many more Italians than were to be found in the senatorial aristocracy.[438] The Equestrian Order already under him, although not fully organized until the reign of Augustus' successor, was to be found in every corner of Italy. Patavium alone could boast of no fewer than 500 Equites in his lifetime. He put the talents of the Equites to excellent use in special areas of the imperial administration.

Meanwhile the lower orders, too, were becoming ever more thoroughly mixed. There were, it is true, still some Italians that were 'attributed' to *municipia* or *coloniae* without being full burgesses of them. But, as Augustus' reign wore on, they became steadily fewer, and their status, technically non-Roman, was ignored and even forgotten.[439]

Augustus himself kept a careful tally of Roman citizens. Already in his days as Octavian, he had conducted a census (29/28); and before he died he was to do so twice again, in 8 BC and AD 14. Head counting was not popular with the masses, but as the registration of the Capuans demonstrated in 189, it could in itself contribute to romanization. It gave the Italians a sense of belonging to the Roman community.

Colonization, another Roman practice that Augustus assiduously promoted, had a similar effect. The land for the twenty-eight *coloniae* he claims to have founded in Italy, so he virtuously insists, was not confiscated, but bought and paid for. He also claims that they became very populous communities, and they must have served as powerful latinizing agents.[440]

The growing consequence of the *coloniae* is one symptom of the full acceptance by Italians of the idea that they were now Romans. Under Augustus, and with his constant encouragement, it gradually became a matter of pride for communities to be recognized as extensions of Rome. No doubt the prosperity of Augustus' own foundations boosted the prestige of *coloniae* in general, and his scheme for enabling the decurions of *coloniae* (but not apparently those of *municipia*)[441] to vote for the consuls and other magistrates of Rome without going to Rome to do so must have improved the colonial image. The *colonia* thus began to outrank the *municipium* in dignity, and gradually the formula *municipia et coloniae* came to be reversed. Ultimately *municipia*, once symbols of Italian distinctiveness, found it advantageous to get their title changed: they grew eager to be known as *coloniae*.

In the material sphere, the Augustan period brought improvement to existing Italian towns and the construction of new ones, and the ambition to follow the monumental trend set in Rome is evident. Roads, bridges and public works were also built, and it was fitting that in Augustus' unified Italy like monuments should be erected at either end of the newly restored Via Flaminia.

In architecture an Italian tradition had been well established during the Republic and coherently integrated with Hellenic components, and it was maintained not greatly altered under Augustus. But his building programme in Rome was carried out with incomparable quality of workmanship and with new materials that gave his monuments and structures unprecedented splendour. Moreover, they were built to exalt, not an individual, but the glory of Rome and the Roman people. The Italians must have felt that the glory reflected upon them as well; and the improved and enhanced centres of their own towns gave them an added sense of civic pride and unity with Rome.[442]

One factor contributing powerfully to integration was the peace that the Princeps had brought to Italy. The strife and bloodletting of the Republic's dying years belonged to the past; and just as reassuring was the strengthening of the frontiers. The northern boundary of Italy had remained shifting, fragile and porous until well after the battle of Actium. But by the year 6 the Alpine tribes had at last been subdued, the passes opened to normal traffic, and the frontier of Italy pushed forward well into the mountain zone and firmly delimited. The coasts of Italy had also been made safe with the establishment of naval squadrons at Misenum on the Tyrrhenian and Ravenna on the Adriatic. All residents of Italy could now breathe easily; and from this feeling of confidence they derived a sense of community.

Augustus' policy for the Empire at large further reinforced the Italians' sense of identity with Rome. He set Italy apart from the world of the provinces beyond its borders. It was Italy that mattered: Italy was the source of political power, the pace-setter in spiritual and cultural change, the leader in economic enterprise, the recipient of favours, the true heart of the Empire. The Roman world was being shaped by Italians, no longer the tolerated associates, but the active partners of the men of Rome in directing the imperial domain. Small wonder that they came to feel themselves authentic members of the community that had incorporated them.

By now, of course, Latin was in common use throughout the length and breadth of Italy. In fact, everywhere, except in one or two Greek communities, it was the only language used for official communication. And Italians not only understood it; they also wrote in it. It became the normal medium for any writing of literary pretension. Strabo, it is true, mentions farces performed in Oscan in Augustan times,[443] and Greek authors, like Strabo himself, used their own tongue even in Italy. But Latin, sanctioned now by its great poets, became increasingly the language of literature.

The native *pagi* of Italy had been assimilated. No doubt they exerted some counter-influence on Rome, and they certainly nursed memories of their independent days when their separate identities had been so marked and distinctive. But parochial nostalgia was no impediment to a feeling of solidarity with Rome, and did not keep Italy in a welter of aggressively competing cultures. The violence of the last century was a grim reminder of where fierce rivalries could lead. The Italians were content to be Romans. The fusion which Augustus had sought to promote had taken place.

Augustus himself evidently regarded the year 2 as the date when the unification of Italy was complete. It was a memorable year and marked out as such by the emperor himself. It is easy to see why. He was due to begin his sixty-third year in the year 1 and, like all educated contemporaries, he knew that the sixty-third year was everyone's great climacteric, the year of danger, disaster and perhaps even death.[445] Prudence, therefore, dictated that he have all his affairs, public as well as private, well ordered and settled before ever the critical year began.

Accordingly on 1 January 2 BC Augustus assumed the consulship for the last time (his thirteenth) and took measures that would keep the state flourishing no matter what his great climacteric had in store for him.

First, he provided even more securely for the succession. In 5 he had officially adopted his fourteen-year-old grandson Gaius Caesar as the 'son' to succeed him. Now in 2, when Gaius' brother Lucius in his turn became fourteen, Augustus similarly adopted him, and thus made doubly sure. Lucius was introduced to public life and designated consul-to-be for AD 4.

Later in the year 2 the two heirs apparent participated in the spectacular and elaborate ceremonies with which Augustus officially dedicated his new forum, now after forty years of desultory construction rushed to completion together with its temple of Mars Ultor.

It was likewise in the year 2 that Augustus tidied up the grain dole, prudently placed the Praetorian Guard under two commanders, had a contest instituted in his honour in Greek-speaking Neapolis, and strengthened the foundation of the emperor-cult in Italy. It has even been suggested[446] that this was also the year when he ceremoniously repopened the gates of Janus after their third closure during his reign, and drafted the record of his achievements in both war and peace that was to appear in the year of his death as the *Res Gestae Divi Augusti*.

But for Augustus the great moment came early in the year 2, on 5 February. On that day, he proudly recalls, he was pronounced officially and with great éclat Father of the Fatherland (*pater patriae*).[447] He was not the first Roman to win the honour. That distinction seems to belong to Cicero whom the Senate had hailed as Pater Patriae in 63; but no formal vote or decree ever conferred the title officially upon the great orator. Somewhat later Julius Caesar had also been styled Pater Patriae, probably officially. But Caesar seems to have accorded the title slight importance and may have assumed it largely in order to outdo, and silence, the boastful Cicero.[448]

Augustus evidently viewed the title in a very different light from his great-uncle. He esteemed it highly, representing it as the crowning achievement of his career. His winning of it is the note on which he closes the *Res Gestae*, just as though it was to this glorious climax that his whole life had been directed. It brought no specified or definable addition to his already immense powers. But, in a rank-conscious society like the Roman, it could contribute to his prestige, and he had long had his eye on it. Immediately after Actium it had been offered, and had even been unofficially given him in works of literature, in inscriptions and on coins. But for a thirty-two-year-old to claim to be Father of the Fatherland seemed absurd, and Octavian did not then formally assume the title. He could wait until he reached a more appropriate age. By the year 2, when he needed to prepare against his rapidly approaching great climacteric, the time was clearly ripe; and it was then accordingly that the official pronouncement came.

Some idea of the importance which Augustus attached to the occasion can be gleaned from Suetonius' account of it.[449]. First, a delegation from the Roman commons came to him when he was sojourning at Antium to offer him the title. But, instead of accepting it there and then, he returned to Rome, and there had it thrust upon him by a vast, laurel-garlanded throng as he was entering the theatre. Next, the Senate voted unanimously to join the Roman People in greeting him as Pater Patriae, for its members knew that to do so was to pray for the lasting happiness and prosperity of the state. Augustus, moved to tears, was heard to say that all his prayers had been answered.

Clearly the *patria* of which he was now the officially declared parent was not Velitrae. Nor was it Rome in the narrow sense of the city on the Tiber. It was the expanded Rome of the post-Social War era: it was Italy. To emphasize this the senator to make the motion was very carefully selected. He was M. Valerius Messalla Corvinus, a *nobilis* who openly boasted of his exertions on behalf of the Republic at Philippi, but who also was one of those fully reconciled to Augustus' new order. The choice of such a spokesman could not have been fortuitous.[450]

As it happened, Augustus survived the critical year and lived on for another fourteen. But for him they were years of catastrophe, not felicity. The two grandsons he had marked out to succeed him died, and their brother had to be sent into exile. The latter fate also befell their sister: she was the daughter of Augustus' daughter Julia who had herself been banished in 2, the year of Augustus' anti-climacteric precautions. Disaster also struck in the Empire overseas, in central Europe and in Germany where three legions were wiped out. The ageing Princeps was forced to rely more and more on his stepson Tiberius, whom he found antipathetic but whose services he could not do without.

Fortunately the conspiracies and struggles over the succession in Augustus' last year did not lead to a revival of dissension between Romans and Italians, much less to separatism. The unification of Italy stood firm, reinforced if anything by the measures taken in the last ten years of Augustus' life.

In AD 4 his third revision of the Senate left that body an assembly of the élite and the wealthy from every corner of Italy.[451] In the same year he compiled a register of all the residents of Italy with a fortune of 200,000 sesterces or more. This was regimentation, but it was also an indication of national cohesion, and it facilitated his institution two years later of the five per cent inheritance tax (*vicesima heredi-*

tatum) that was to help finance the bonus for demobilized soldiers.[452]

It may have been to make collection of this impost on legacies easier that Augustus organized the whole of Italy into eleven carefully defined Regions. The date, purpose, and principle of this subdivision are not on record. It is, however, the framework that the Elder Pliny uses for his description of Italy. It may have taken place in AD 6 and had been intended to promote general administrative efficiency.[453]

Whatever their purpose, the eleven regions gave a definite political organization and administrative reality to all Italy. They also enabled an unusually thorough census of the population of the whole country to be carried out in the last year of Augustus' life.

Probably no accomplishment of Caesar Augustus was of greater importance and consequence than his promotion of singleness of patriotism and national unity in Italy. That he, in fact, succeeded in unifying the country is eloquently indicated by the words with which, shortly after his death, the emperor's exact contemporary, the well-informed Strabo, the historian turned geographer, brought his extended account of Italy to a close:[454]

'The excellence of her constitution and rulers has prevented not only Rome from plunging into excessive discord and ruin, but Italy as well. In fact, after Italy came under Roman sway, the country, owing to the difficulty of administering so extensive a dominion, went on being racked by strife until it was entrusted to one man as to a father. Until then neither the Romans nor their allies had the good fortune to find peace and prosperity of the sort that Caesar Augustus brought to them by his assumption of absolute power.'

The romanization of Italy had been a protracted process spanning the last three centuries of the Roman Republic. Evidence does not exist for tracing it in all its details, but the broad outlines are clear enough. Decisive and key dates, quite obviously, were: 338 (the end of the Latin War), 268 (the consolidation of peninsular Italy), 211 (the suppression of Sabellian Capua), 173 (the distribution of Cisalpine land), 91 (the outbreak of the Social War), 32 (the oath to Caesar Octavianus) and 2 (the proclamation of a Pater Patriae).

Three phases can be regularly distinguished. Phase one was the military conquest of an area and phase two its political organization, normally featured by settlements of Roman *coloni* on some part of it;[455] these provided the greatest scope for Roman martial abilities and political talents. But the third phase was longer, infinitely more difficult to document, and above all of greater consequence: it was the assimilation of the subjugated people.

There is little evidence of the Romans attempting to force the pace. They could hardly have been displeased when others adopted their language, copied their ways and came to share their outlook. But they did not as a matter of policy encourage the Italians to do so, and they certainly did not impose their own way of life. In any case, the absorption of the Italians did not depend solely on the Romans. The behaviour and the attitude of the Italians themselves were in large part also responsible. For the Romans could hardly have imposed their military and political domination on the whole country had the Italians resisted them with sustained and determined unanimity. But this they never did, not in the Latin War, not at Sentinum, not at Hannibal's behest, not even in the Social War. A collection of independent states could no more present a united front in Republican Italy than in modern Europe, and by shrewdly graduating the political conditions imposed upon individual members of defeated groupings, Rome ensured that opposition to herself would be marked neither by singleness of purpose nor constancy of endeavour; and consequently all Italians ultimately became Romans.

Roman soldierly skill and administrative astuteness, however, are not the whole story. There were other factors at work, pervasive and persistent, even if not always very evident; and the part they played in transforming a polyglot land into a Roman unity is significant.

Paradoxical though it may seem, the very multiplicity of languages in pre-Roman Italy may have helped to promote its unification. Its Alpine rampart and the surrounding seas make the country a natural and largely self-contained geographical unit. But, at the dawn of its history, some forty different languages and dialects were spoken within its comparatively narrow confines. As its many tribes gradually became less simple and primitive and their mutual intercourse more constant and complex, the need for a *lingua franca* amid the babel of tongues grew increasingly urgent. This had become very apparent by the third century when Rome established her control of the peninsula. From that moment on the pre-dominance of her language was assured.

Already in the third century Philip V of Macedon had noted how extension of citizenship and settlement of *coloni* on confiscated land enabled the Romans to make themselves by far the most populous and widely spread nation in the peninsula. They were ubiquitous; and it was this constant cohabitation within Rome's cultural orbit, far more than her military superiority, that accelerated the diffusion of her language. Latin, clearly, was the only tongue suitable for pan-Italian use. Roman stimulation of and improvement of urbanism in Italy expedited its spread. In country districts the Roman *coloniae, fora* and *conciliabula* were ready-made centres of linguistic radiation. Italian urban areas, for their part, were even more susceptible to the influence of Latin, since neologisms, phonetic changes, and syntactic innovations catch on more swiftly in agglomerated centres than in scattered hamlets. It may well be that the rapid diffusion of the language in Umbria was due to the many towns there. The first step, almost invariably, was for Italians to discard their own alphabets and adopt that of the Romans.

Latin had long ceased to be a limited local vernacular and the growth of its literature meant improved lexical and grammatical standards. This increased its advantage over the Italic vernaculars, which were little better than loose, shifting patois in continuous retreat before an international tongue of stability, substance and authority.

Latinization in itself was not necessarily synonymous with romanization. But it was a principal romanizing instrument. The power to express and communicate, to form ideas and organize thought, and to give direction was highly developed in Latin; and when Italians used this newly adopted idiom they acquired, inevitably and often unconsciously, the Roman mentality that it represented. The use of Latin affected all that they did.

Nevertheless, the apparent readiness of the Italians to switch to Latin may well seem surprising. Of course, for a large segment of Italy's population there was no choice. These were the slaves. They and their descendants, entirely cut off as they usually were from continuing contact with their language of origin, were obliged to adopt the tongue of their masters, either to ingratiate themselves or to escape ill-usage; and their masters were Roman more often than not. For that matter some slaves of non-Roman masters were already Latin-speaking.[456] The 150,000 Epirotes enslaved in a single day in 167 give some idea of how numerous the slaves were, and by the sheer weight of their numbers they must have made a decisive impact on the linguistic development of Italy.

Another large group in Italy, even if not exactly forced into speaking Latin, had very little option about doing so. They were those who had been for whatever reason uprooted. There was much mobility of population, compelled or otherwise, both before and after Hannibal's war; and it assumed even greater proportions in the first century when contenders for powers settled thousands of their followers in different parts of Italy and ruthlessly scattered the previous inhabitants. Migrants were thus a familiar feature of the Italian scene. Whatever their ultimate destination, the language the migrants ended up by using, if they did not already possess it, was Latin. It was the language that could serve them, no matter where they went in Italy, a kind of passport to everywhere, like English in nineteenth-century USA. The discarding of their native vernaculars may have caused them some regret; but rootless people, bereft of spiritual as well as territorial moorings, were hardly likely to repine for long. Indeed, for many of them in the first century, and especially for those from former tribal districts, it was difficult to remain sentimentally attached to their original communities, for these had disappeared with the urbanization of Italy.

In the last analysis it was the failure of the Italians to feel strongly attached to their native dialects that accounts for their disappearance. The strength of linguistic allegiance varied considerably. The Italiotes, for all their petty particularism, had a sharp sense of their national identity; they were proudly attached to their native Greek and were clearly the people of Italy most tenacious of their mother tongue.[457] At the other extreme were the unlettered and fragmented Ligures, who appear to have been the least retentive. But all, literate and illiterate alike, eventually adopted Latin.

One possible reason was the failure of ancient societies to attach undue importance to a mother tongue. It was much less of a focal point than it is today. Even the Romans may not have accorded it the absolute assimilative power that modern governments attribute to their official languages. In Republican days, at least, they seem to have reckoned the adoption of Roman law by non-Latin peoples just as important as the acquisition of Latin, if not more so.[458]

There was little to impede its spread. No Italian community had a system of public education to give instruction in its own vernacular or to promote the linguistic consciousness of its members. Before the Second Punic War no language in Italy, apart from Greek, possessed a literature worth mentioning; and intellectual groups to stimulate native sentiments were unlikely. Circles of this kind did not materialize. Pontius the Samnite is said to have matched philosophic wits with Plato and Archytas, but he was not the founder of a Sabellian school.[459] Under the circumstances Italy was open to the overwhelming influence of Rome, with her close-knit social organization and the ability to make her presence felt. Once Italy had come under her control, the upper classes in other Italian societies, the natural guardians, one would have thought, of native cultures and speech, soon strove for social acceptance as well as for political favour from their Roman counterparts and were more disposed to learn the Latin language than to maintain and promote their own. Their behaviour undermined the linguistic resistance of the non-Latin peoples.

If language was not the expression of nationality to the same degree that it is today, it was because of the general lack of a strong national consciousness.[460] The concept of the nation-state did not exist in Republican Italy. There were leagues and confederacies in the Oscan-speaking districts, but they did not develop very far; and as tribal Italy with the passage of time grew politically more sophisticated, its tribes did not burgeon into nation-states. The evolving Italian tribes, instead of uniting more cohesively, tended to fragment into political entities of limited confines and parochial outlook. The Romans thought in terms of the city state. For them the urban commonwealth was the tidiest administrative unit, the most suitable setting in which civilization could come to full bloom.

The absence of nation-states meant that there were few, if any, national myths and traditions to help generate fervent national sentiment. Not that the various Italian peoples were indifferent as to who they were or where they came from. Many of them, besides the Romans, kept memories of the past alive. In Latium Praeneste, Tibur, Tusculum and Velitrae possessed at least some historical records. Among the Umbri Interamna Nahars preserved the story of its origin in the seventh century. The Samnites are described as keeping accounts, on linen, of glorious episodes from their past. The Sabini and the Etruscans are said to have had native histories. Moreover Etruscan families thought it appropriate to proclaim publicly the achievements of Tarquinian leaders of earlier days, even if in romanized versions of the first century AD, some of which still survive. Latin Brundisium, Sabellian Pompeii and Etruscan Arretium may also have produced *elogia* of this kind. But such activities are more expressions of parochial pride than of national renown.[461]

The action of a pre-Roman community in preserving, and even parading, records of its own achievements should not be taken to mean that it cared much, if at all, about the exploits of a larger body with which it shared a common language. The Italiote colonies, although very conscious that they were Hellenes, had no compunction at all about utterly destroying one another. The Etruscans accepted that prophecies by Tages and Vegoia concerned all Rasenna; but their national awareness extended very little further than that. Nor did cult and ritual do much to promote nationalism. In Italy, where the various religions had much in common and where the gods of different communities shared similar attributes and fields of action, live and let live was the normal religious attitude; and some gods, like Jupiter and the universal favourite Mars, were worshipped everywhere. The Romans appropriated other peoples' gods for themselves in the hope of gaining additional divine favour. The Italians, for their part, never had much difficulty in accommodating themselves to Roman religious beliefs and practices, and syncretism of Roman and Italian cults was common. Most of them, before ever the Romans established their control, had been touched either directly or indirectly by the religious ideas of the Greeks and had become acquainted with their gods. The Greek influence had not indeed standardized all the religions in the country, but it had rendered them unsuitable as rallying points for opposition to Rome.[462]

For that matter, not all Italians were disposed to oppose her fiercely: they were far too conscious of the alternative. The cultural vacuum left by the decline of the Italiotes and the Etruscans seemed likely in the fourth century to be filled by the tough and vigorous Sabellian stocks of the central Appennines, whose crude and undeveloped ways, well suited though they were to their own manner of living, were repugnant to the less primitive Italians living nearer the coasts. Cultivated progress and material advance appealed to these latter, and seemed more likely to be achieved under a Latin than an Oscan dispensation. Rome's military strength and political sagacity in the upshot prevented any Samnite hegemony, and it was she who assumed the moral, juridical and administrative leadership of Italy.

Roman values thus came to be accepted, and in particular the

Roman notion that the city-state represented the essence of civilization finally came to be shared by all Italians. Admittedly even in
Italy the urban commonwealth was not an original Roman idea. But
the Roman community was the most successful specimen of a
city-state, and the Italians certainly admired the way that the
Romans had exploited its possibilities. Small wonder, then, if they
regarded the Roman *res publica* as a pace-setter in statecraft and in
matters practical and chose it as their model. In fact, after the year
300 it was from Rome that new ideas for civic and social progress
proliferated throughout Italy. Eloquent testimony of this is the
widespread adoption of Roman political terminology by Italian
communities and the use of Roman coins and methods of reckoning
everywhere in the peninsula. It was largely by drawing on Roman
inspiration and by copying Roman improvements of Greek and
Etruscan techniques that Italians transformed their hamlets and
villages into towns and cities. Many parts of Italy remained
primitive and lagging in material progress until Latin Colonies or
Roman settlements were planted in their neighbourhood and
pointed the way to change.

    Moreover, Roman influence was not exclusively of the pragmatic
sort: it was reflected also in cultural matters. The Italic Hellenism in
art and architecture, that had become by 300 a varying, but integral
part of most local cultures in Italy, made them receptive to the
growing influences radiating from Rome. By the end of the third
century her culture, with its adapted Etruscan and Hellenic
components, and indeed with Italic elements as well, had come to
prevail.[463]

    By *c.*100 the trend towards romanization everywhere in Italy was
undoubtedly evident and probably irreversible: by then the whole
country was manifestly destined to adopt Roman ways sooner or
later. The Social War ensured that it happened sooner. The demand
of the insurgents for Roman citizenship proclaimed their willingness
for assimilation; and by the end of the century, assimilated they
were. Regional differences persisted, of course,[464] as they still do in
Italy, or in any other state. But by the year 2 *tota Italia* was
unmistakably Roman.

    It has been suggested that something may have been lost in the
process and that Rome's absorption of the Italians to a certain extent
curbed the originality and diversity of their genius. It has been
pointed out that in the days when the fusion of Italians and Romans

had barely begun, the Messapii produced the literary talents of Ennius and the Umbrian Sarsinates those of Plautus, whereas later, when integration was complete, Italian letters could only display the sterile mediocrity of the Empire.[465] But literature, like art, is unpredictable and it cannot be forgotten that some of the best literary works appeared under the patronage of Augustus, and were written by Italians.

In fact, Italian energies and talents, so far from being stifled, expanded further. It was Roman Italy, not Rome alone, that latinized much of the early Empire, disseminating Rome's language, institutions and values. Rome continued to bring into prominence and active office new men of high ability and enterprise from outside; in the first instance they came from the western provinces and the ultimate origins of many of them can be traced to Italy.[466]

Even long after the Roman Empire had run its course it was still largely from the Roman-Italian impact that the Latin cities and states of western Europe emerged, and a revived drive for discovery and expansion imparted a new significance and a new dimension to western civilization. In no small part this was the ongoing consequence of the remarkable feat of the Romans in inducing all Italy, from the Alps to the Ionian Sea, to share their loyalty to their City.

APPENDIX I

HONORARY CITIZENSHIP

The view expressed in Chapter 2 is the usual one, that Rome's earliest *municipia* were a consequence of her success in war. It rests on plain and matter-of-fact statements in Livy, and argues that communities that opposed Rome in the Latin War were annexed by her after her victory, some of them being granted her full citizenship and others merely the partial variety.

There is, however, a school of thought that not all the annexed communities were incoporated as *municipia*, but that that designation was reserved for those of them that were *sine suffragio*, the title being apposite exclusively for them since it was only their burgesses that assumed civic burdens without a corresponding right to civic privileges, such as the right to vote, to hold office, and to become a senator. It has, therefore, been suggested that the fully enfranchised communities, whose burgesses did enjoy such privileges, had a different and unrecorded title, such as *oppida civium Romanorum* or something similar.[467]

This conjecture is not convincing. It is based on the etymological assumption that *municeps* can only mean 'one who takes burdens' (from *munera* and *capere*).[468] This would be frail support even if it could be demonstrated that *cives sine suffragio* had no civic privileges whatsoever. This, however, is not the case. *Cives sine suffragio* did enjoy some civic privileges, the right of appeal, for example, and the private rights of all Romans (the *iura provocationis*, *conubii* and *commercii*).

Admittedly one cannot positively prove that the communities annexed with full citizenship enjoyed in the fourth century the title of *municipium* that was undoubtedly theirs in the first. But this is equally true of the communities annexed *sine suffragio* in the fourth century, since the word *municipium* is not used in surviving records of the Latin War settlement. The word *municipes*, however, is to be found there; and, significantly, it is used of the burgesses of Lanuvium who, it is generally agreed, became *cives optimo iure*.[469] It is, therefore, a reasonable assumption that the title *municipium* was given to all the communities annexed *c*.338, whether they obtained the right of suffrage or not.

But, be that so or not, it is abundantly clear that both those with and those without the full Roman citizenship had been deprived of their sovereign independence and had received in its stead a new status, a status imposed by the victor. This they must have resented, no matter how useful to them their new Roman condition ultimately turned out to be. It was not until much later that the *civitas* became so prized that the Italian communities were eager to acquire it and to bask in its prestige and concomitant advantages. Even as late as 216 burgesses of Praeneste, a Latin-speaking community, refused to accept Roman citizenship when it was offered them.[470]

If non-Romans in the fourth century regarded the full Roman citizenship as undesirable, it can be imagined what they thought of the partial variety.[471] Chapters 2 and 3 show how unpopular it was. All the stranger is it, therefore, to find the *civitas sine suffragio* sometimes depicted as a compliment and an honour. Aulus Gellius, for instance, says that the Romans bestowed it upon the burgesses of Caere for having given asylum to Rome's sacred objects at the time of the Gallic War (*c*.386); and Livy reports that it was conferred upon the burgesses of Fundi and Formiae *c*.338 to thank them for granting Roman troops unobstructed passage across their territories during the Latin War. Moreover, both authors regard the partial citizenship given to Caere, Fundi and Formiae on these occasions as no different from the *civitas sine suffragio* of *municipia* in general. Gellius not only calls the Caerites *municipes*, but even regards them as the prototypes for all *cives sine suffragio*, pointing out that later the lists of the disfranchised were known as the Caerite Tables; and Livy, for his part, stresses that Fundi and Formiae received exactly the same status as Capua.[472]

It is difficult to see, however, how either Gellius or Livy can possibly be correct. How could *civitas sine suffragio* be simultaneously a reward for some communities and a degradation for others? To suggest that it was a eulogy that immediately turned sour and became a stigma is to strain credulity: the irreconcilability is too glaring and the contrast too striking. One is forced to conclude that Gellius and Livy are referring, albeit inadvertently, to two very different kinds of citizenship.

Gellius himself supplies the clue to the enigma. He reveals that the citizenship awarded to the Caerites not only prevented them from voting at Rome, but also exempted them from all the obligations of ordinary Roman citizens. This is something radically different from the kind of *civitas sine suffragio* imposed upon incorporated *municipia*, the most striking and detested feature of which was precisely its insistence on the performance of civic duties, and especially military service.

Gellius cannot, therefore, be describing the normal *civitas sine suffragio*; he is referring to an honorary citizenship, and he virtually says so. His actual words are: 'the Caerites were permitted indeed to assume the honour of Roman citizenship, but were exempted however from its responsibilities and burdens'.

The nature of such honorary citizenship is clear. Its aim was to express Roman esteem for a non-Roman community that had rendered service to Rome; and, as far as the non-Roman community as a whole was concerned, it did very little more. It was of practical use only to individual members of the community who happened to visit Rome: there, although not allowed to vote or hold office, they could expect to be welcome and would not be required to discharge any of the burdensome duties of a citizen. Honorary citizenship was thus essentially a privilege extended to individuals in contrast to *civitas sine suffragio*, which was a status imposed upon a community collectively.[473]

That the honorary citizenship was called that in the fourth century seems more than dubious. The expression *civitas honoraria*, never very common, cannot be shown to be earlier than the Empire.[474] But the fourth-century Romans were undoubtedly familiar with the concept: perhaps they described it as *hospitium publicum*.[475]

Manifestly Gellius in the case of Caere has confused the two types of citizenship. Livy does not make the same mistake when dealing with Caere. But he is guilty of it in the case of Fundi and Formiae, both of whom received the honorary citizenship *c.*338, and perhaps also in the case of the 1,600 *equites Campani* who, according to him, received 'Roman citizenship' in 340 for refraining from making common cause with the Latini at the critical time.[476]

Honorary citizenship and *civitas sine suffragio* were, of course, alike in that both excluded their recipients from the right to vote at Rome. But they were sufficiently dissimilar in other respects for it to be surprising that Livy and Gellius should have confused them.

Livy's error is due to the fact that Fundi, Formiae and the *equites Campani* did indeed soon become partial Roman citizens, in fact so soon after getting the honorary citizenship that it was very easy for him to confuse the latter with the *civitas sine suffragio*. Honorary citizenship was authorized for the equites Campani in 340; they were pronounced *cives sine suffragio*, along with the other burgesses of Capua, just two years later (or six, if Velleius' version is preferred).

Fundi and Formiae received their honorary citizenship in 338 and their partial citizenship apparently in 329.

The short lapse of time will not similarly account for Gellius' error about Caere, since its burgesses were pronounced honorary citizens *c*.386, and were not made *cives sine suffragio* until *c*.270 (or possibly *c*.353).[477] Gellius, however, failed to note the time lag, being bemused by the fact that the Romans later designated as 'Caerite' the registers that listed citizens deprived of the vote (such as the 2,000 struck off the tribal rolls in 214).[478] From this Gellius deduced, erroneously, that the Caerite Tables were so called because Caere was the first community to be incorporated *sine suffragio*, presumably *c*.386;[479] and thereby he mistook the honorary citizenship awarded to it then for its subsequent partial citizenship. Nevertheless, Gellius was not unaware of the incongruity of saying that Rome honoured Caere by giving it the *civitas sine suffragio*, and for that reason he inserted the expression *versa vice* to explain why the Caerite Tables actually implied the exact opposite.[480]

ROMANO-CAPUAN
RELATIONS

In Chapter 2 it is stated that Capua, whatever its vicissitudes between 343 and 338, was undoubtedly incorporated by Rome with *civitas sine suffragio* after the Latin War and thus became part of the Roman body politic. The testimony of Livy and Velleius to this effect is explicit. Yet many scholars have expressed scepticism, largely because the Campani (= the burgesses of Capua) are often described by Livy and once by Diodorus as 'allies' between 338 and 216.[481] The critics point out further that it was not until 210 that *praefecti Capuam Cumas* began to be despatched annually to northern Campania,[482] and they take this to mean that the subordination of Capua to Rome really dates only from the time of its recovery from Hannibal in 211, the story of its incorporation about a century and a quarter earlier being a fiction inspired by the wish to justify the severity with which Rome punished its defection. Criticism of this sort reached the extreme with the suggestion that Capua, so far from being a *municipium sine suffragio* between 338 and 216, was in fact the equal partner of Rome in a condominium that embraced much of Latium and of Campania.[483]

Now for Livy and Diodorus to describe Campanian partial citizens as allies may seem strange. But it is not unparalleled. Elsewhere Livy himself refers to the Caerites and the Sabini as *socii* at a time when both were *cives sine suffragio*, and Tacitus even calls the full Roman citizens of rural Italy 'allies' in order to distinguish them from their urban fellows.[484] Quite possibly Livy called the Capuani *socii* to indicate not that they were non-citizens, but that they were inferior citizens, since the word normally denoted dependence. Diodorus, for his part, was writing in a language that had no expression of its own for *cives sine suffragio* and, therefore, described the Capuani by a Greek epithet that seemed to define their status with tolerable accuracy: he calls them *symmachi*, which, like its Latin counterpart *socii*, often had an implication of inferiority.[485] For that matter, Rome's partial citizens did strongly resemble her allies, especially those of the Latin sort who, like them, possessed the Roman private *iura*. Indeed, the Romans seem ultimately to have come to the conclusion that, since they had the Nomen Latinum, they could dispense with *cives sine suffragio*. Admittedly partial citizens differed from allies in that they served in wartime in the legions of Rome instead of in units of their own. But this may not always have been the case. Before 268 they may well have served separately (see Appendix III).

That *praefecti Capuam Cumas* were not elected until 210 is beside the point so far as the status of the Capuani before that date is concerned. After Capua's revolt in 216 it was elementary common sense for Rome to keep the place under a strict and constant surveillance: hence the annual appointment of *praefecti* after its recapture. But between 338 and 216 the Roman supervision had not needed to be so close, and Capua had been allowed to manage its own internal affairs with a minimum of interference from Rome. Prior to 216 intervention was necessary only when the discrepant legal systems of Capua and Rome made it so for the equitable administration of justice; and on such occasions *praefecti iuri dicundo* could be, and according to Livy were, sent to Capua.[486]

Actually the grounds for believing in the annexation of Capua *c.*338 are very strong. First, there is the numismatic evidence. For the 125 years between 340 and 216 not a single coin issued by Capua in its own name has ever been found, whereas Capuan coins for the mere five years between 216 and 211 are comparatively common.[487] It is incredible that a large city like Capua, whose notorious *superbia* made it prompt to display its sovereign right to issue its own coins in 216, would have entirely refrained from striking any for more than a century earlier, had it then had the right to do so. The conclusion is ineluctable: Capua did not coin between 340 and 216 because it was not then a sovereign state.[488]

Secondly, if the annexation of Capua *c.*338 is fictitious, it is difficult to discover when the fiction was perpetrated. The story could hardly have arisen after 210, for that was a period in the full light of history and very well recorded. In any case, it is certain that the belief that the Capuani were Roman citizens was quite widespread well before 210: the words of the contemporary and non-Roman Ennius leave no doubt on that point. And, in case Ennius' word is not enough, there is the evidence of another non-Roman, the careful and painstaking Polybius. He not only records the Capuani as part of the Roman armed forces in 225, but also reports that in 270 an attempt had been made to save the Capuan personnel of the contumacious 'Campanian legion' from punishment for their misdeeds at Rhegium on the grounds that they were Roman citizens and could not be executed without being allowed to exercise their right of appeal to the People. Admittedly what Polybius believed is not positive proof. But he can scarcely be brushed aside since he was acquainted with persons whose fathers and grandfathers had lived through the period that he was describing, and this provided him with the next best thing to actual eyewitnesses.[489]

Thirdly, one has to account for the failure of Q. Fulvius Flaccus, the proconsul who recaptured Capua in 211, to win a 'triumph'. His achievement created a sensation and was of the very sort to deserve the honour. In this very period the conquerors of Syracuse in 212 and of Tarentum in 209 celebrated 'triumphs'.[490] Yet the distinction was withheld from Flaccus. The reason must have been that, as his victory was won over Roman citizens, it was not eligible for a 'triumph'.[491]

Finally, there is the matter of the 1,600 equites Campani. Livy's actual words about them are inexact, but the sequence of events he records for them seems accurate (see Appendix I). It may seem odd that the equites Campani, who were obviously viewed with approval by Rome, should have been made cives sine suffragio along with their humbler fellows after the Latin War, and some scholars have actually suggested that the Capuan aristocrats became cives optimo iure then, while ordinary Capuans received only the partial citizenship.[492] But had that been so, one would have expected to find notable Capuani in the consular Fasti as well as notable Tusculani. In fact, there are none,[493] and this suggests that the equites Campani, like other Capuani, did not have the right to vote or hold office. This is actually proved by what happened in 215. In that year three hundred equites Campani, who were serving away from Capua and had, therefore, not participated in its rebellion, were pronouncd burgesses of loyal Cumae to ensure their exemption from any punishment that Rome might eventually inflict on Capua.[494] Rome assigned these equites to Cumae partly because it spoke Oscan and was near Capua, but also almost certainly because its partial citizenship exactly corresponded to that of the equites themselves.

The equites Campani could not have been very happy about being pronounced cives sine suffragio c.338, but there were compensations. None of them lost any land as a result of Roman confiscation of Capuan territory; on the contrary, each of them by Rome's fiat became entitled to a handsome annual stipend from the burgesses of Capua; and by Rome's favour they were also guaranteed ongoing control of the municipium. Furthermore, any of them who visited

Rome was apparently still entitled to the privileges of honorary citizenship which had been awarded them in 340; and, to judge from the amount of intermarriage between Roman and Capuan aristocratic families, it seems that more than a few of them availed themselves of this *hospitium publicum*.[495]

THE FORMULA
TOGATORUM

The military obligations of the Italian 'allies' were set forth in a document called, somewhat surprisingly, *formula togatorum* ('Roster of Toga-Wearers').[496] Allusions to the *formula* can be found in Livy and elsewhere, but the most explicit mention of it is in an official document. Sections 21 and 50 of the Lex Agraria of 111 speak about 'members of the allies or of the Nomen Latinum from whom in the land of Italy (the consuls) are accustomed to call for troops in accordance with the *formula togatorum*'.

The purpose of the *formula* presumably was to ensure that the military services of the allies were roughly commensurate with those of Rome herself, and to that end it prescribed the contributions which the various allied communities were to make to the joint defence of Italy.

In theory, each ally could no doubt have been ordered to give its all. In practice, however, no occasion was likely to arise when so much would be demanded of it. There were so many allies that total and simultaneous mobilization of all would never be needed. It would be sufficient to get some help from each, and it was the *formula* that stated the extent of the help.

Livy indicates that it stipulated the number of men for which a community was liable,[497] and this has been interpreted to mean that it laid down, once and for all, the maximum number of troops that Rome could demand from each ally.[498] This, however, could not have been the case. War and limited liability are in the last analysis incompatible, and Romans and Italians alike must have realized that in an extreme emergency an ally might have to commit its total military resources. Another very material consideration was the unsuitability of fixed and immutable quotas. Conditions were liable to change and communities might grow or wither away. Any system that ignored such possibilities, and made no provision for updating, was bound to lose its practical usefulness and ultimately break down altogether. In fact, the varying proportion of allies to Romans in the armed services at different times, together with other evidence, makes it pretty certain that the *formula togatorum* was not frozen.[499]

It was not a document of a federal kind; it was a list kept at Rome. Probably it took the form of a scale showing the number of men that the allies would be expected to supply for every legion fielded by Rome. But what determined the exact figure for an individual ally is unknown. Livy merely says that the consul requisitioned infantry and cavalry in accordance with the number of men of military age.[500] These served in their own formations (cohorts of infantry, *turmae* of cavalry); but the higher command was invariably Roman. Otherwise there is curiously little that can be said about the military contribution of the allies.

Even the meaning of the statement of the Lex Agraria that the *formula* concerned allies *in terra Italia* is uncertain.[501] In theory, this should exclude allies in Cisalpina which down to 42 seems officially to have been reckoned Gallia rather than Italia. Yet it appears unlikely that the Latin Colonies in upper Italy were not subject to the provisions of the *formula*, whatever the obligations of Mantua, the Venetic settlements and the other allies there.

Even in peninsular Italy it is not known for sure whether the handful of 'equal' allies were bound by the *formula*. The Lex Agraria seems to imply that there were states in Italy that were not listed in the *formula*; and Livy, with that 'most equal' ally Camerinum in mind, may mean that the essential difference between 'equal' and 'unequal' allies was the freedom of the former to decide for themselves what amount of aid to send when Rome called for any, whereas the 'unequal' had to supply whatever the *formula* specified.[502] Very probably the point is academic since, even if the contribution of an 'equal' ally was in theory voluntary, one can be reasonably sure that it was never less than what that 'equal' ally would have been required to supply had it been under the *formula*. That was the only sure way for an 'equal' ally to preserve its favoured status.

How the *formula* affected the so-called naval allies we are also not informed. It is generally believed that there was a group of allied communities, Italiote for the most part, whose duty was to provide ships and sailors instead of soldiers. Livy certainly implies that there was such a special category of allies, and it would be natural that, for operations at sea, states like Rhegium and Neapolis should be called upon to provide *socii navales* rather than soldiers. It is also reasonable to conjecture that these seamen were regarded as equivalent to part or all of the quota prescribed by the *formula* for their respective states.[503]

No ancient text reveals when the *formula togatorum* first came to be devised, but the name itself may throw light on the matter. *Formula togatorum* is an odd expression to use of a roster of peoples, not all of whom wore the toga.[504] One may, therefore, conjecture that, when it was first used, Rome's allies did, in fact, wear that garment; and the Romans went on using the expression even after their original toga-clad allies were joined by others who did not affect it. The years immediately after the Latin War, when Rome's allies were effectively confined to Latium, obviously constituted the period when Rome's allies were peoples familiar with the toga. It is, therefore, possible that the beginnings of the *formula togatorum* are to be sought in the peace settlement of *c*.338.

If this guess is correct, one might hazard the further conjecture that in those days the *formula* encompassed the communities of partial citizens as well as allies. Festus, it is true, asserts that *cives sine suffragio* served, like *cives optimo iure*, in the legions.[505] But he does not say that this had always been the rule; and in the years immediately after 338 a different practice may well have prevailed, for at that time the Roman state had no way of keeping track of its partial citizens: as they were not enrolled in the Tribes, the Roman censors and consuls knew little or nothing about individual *cives sine suffragio*. Consequently there would have been practical difficulties about enrolling them in the legions.[506] It seems likely, then, that at first communities with the partial citizenship, like communities of allied status, were assigned quotas which their local magistrates were required to meet.[507] In fact, there is evidence of partial citizens serving in units other than Roman legions. Capuan cavalry served separately at Sentinum (295); during the Pyrrhic War (280–272) Capuani served, together with allied Sidicini, in a formation of their own, the Oscan-speaking 'Campanian legion'; and at the battle of Ausculum in 279 the Campani, Sabini and Volsci all seem to have been in their own contingents (cohorts?) even though intermingled with the legions.[508]

It is possible that it was only after 268 that *cives sine suffragio* began to serve in the legions. By then Roman officials could probably keep themselves informed about them through the itinerant *praefecti iuri dicundo* and the Caerite Tables. By 225 the Capuani were evidently serving in the legions along with Rome's full citizens. But even then, some *cives sine suffragio* may still have been allowed their own formations, the Sabini for instance.[509]

THE DESTRUCTION OF
FALERII VETERES[511]

The revolt of Falerii in 241 is of more than passing interest since, apart from the defections provoked by Hannibal in the Second Punic War, there is no other example after 265 of a community rebelling against the Roman system in the peninsula until the uprising of Latin Fregellae in 125. For that reason the episode excited much comment even in antiquity, and as a result a fairly full account of it survives from a period otherwise singularly bare of extant records.

According to the ancient sources, Falerii rebelled. Yet it is inconceivable that as late as 241, at a time when Rome had just emerged victorious and powerful from a hard struggle with Carthage, any community in the peninsula would have had the hardihood, alone and unaided, to challenge her. It is probable that the so-called 'rebellion' amounted, in fact, to no more than a failure on the part of Falerii to meet, promptly and in full, all of the demands for troops that Rome had made upon it during the recent hostilities. Falerii may even have behaved in the First Punic War like the twelve Latin Colonies in the Second and have actually refused to go on helping Rome against the enemy.

Whatever the offence, the Falisci were made to pay for it dearly. A Roman army moved against Falerii and in less than a week had taken it by storm. In the final assault 15,000 of its inhabitants are alleged to have perished. Rome then sold off all the surviving slaves and confiscated a good half of the territory of Falerii. Finally, the remaining Falisci were subjected to the same indignity as the Etruscans of Volsinii about a quarter of a century earlier, after the destruction of their city: they were forcibly removed elsewhere. The entire community was obliged to leave its strong and picturesque site on the river Treia for an open, less defensible location on level ground about four miles to the west. Some of the survivors may have flouted the order by migrating from Italy altogether: at any rate, years later a group of Faliscan expatriates were living on the island of Sardinia.[511]

No doubt the fate of Falerii is described with some exaggeration: the figure of 15,000 dead is particularly suspect. But that New Falerii was a drastically reduced community compared with the Old is demonstrated by the physical remains of it still so splendidly in evidence around the ruined convent of S. Maria di Falleri: the entire circuit of the city-walls is just over one and a half miles in length and could have accommodated only a limited population.[512]

The reasons for Rome's severity can be only guessed at. Falerii, of course, could boast of a persistent record of hostility to Rome in earlier years, and it is possible that, as with Antium almost exactly a hundred years before, the Romans were determined to end forever its capacity to make mischief. Probably, too, they wanted Falerii to serve as a stern warning to their other allies in Italy of the retribution awaiting any defiance of Rome; and the lesson seems to have been heeded. But there may have been yet another reason.

In the very year that they destroyed Falerii Veteres the Romans founded, at Spoletium in Umbria, a Latin Colony which controlled the approach on the Roman side to the Colfiorito pass across the central Appennines and thus helped Sena Gallica to guard the communications with the Ager Gallicus and Ariminum.[513] It is unlikely that the two events were unconnected. The Romans at the time could hardly have been oblivious to the possibility, and even the likelihood, of military activity soon developing in Cisalpine Gaul; in the event, Roman operations in the Po valley did turn out to be the most notable feature of the interval between the First and Second Punic Wars. In 241, therefore, the Romans may have been seeing to it that any eventual northbound forces of theirs should have unimpeded and easy access to the potential danger zone.

That Falerii Novi continued to be a Faliscan town is proved by inscriptions. They reveal that it went on speaking its native dialect for the next hundred years or so. This, of course, does not prove that it was an 'independent' community then, and there are scholars who think that it was more probably a *municipium sine suffragio*.[514] This, however, seems unlikely. It is true that prodigies were reported from Falerii (Novi) during the Second Punic War and that the community then had a senate and quaestors instead of *marones* and *aediles* of earlier days.[515] Furthermore, Polybius' description of the conflict with Rome in 241 as a 'civil war' might suggest that he envisaged the place as 'Roman'. Polybius' expression, however, cannot be pressed since, whatever the status of Falerii after 241, he could not have thought of it as 'Roman' at the time that his 'civil war' destroyed it. For that Falerii Veteres was not Roman is not only unequivocally stated by Livy, but it is also positively proved by the 'triumph' that its destroyer celebrated in the following year. Polybius, therefore, was using the adjective *emphylios* with the meaning 'inter-Italian' rather than 'civil'.[516] Nor can much importance be attached to reports of prodigies from Falerii. Admittedly Roman magistrates were not supposed to expiate portents reported from non-Roman soil. Livy, however, makes it clear that they occasionally did so, especially during the Second Punic War.[517] For that matter, the omens in question may well have been observed on the Faliscan territory that Rome had seized, which must have been still called Falerii. The senate, quaestors, praetors and censors of Falerii Novi could, of course, be 'Roman' institutions. But they could equally well be instances of the adoption by an Italian community of Roman political terminology. In the second century it was common for Italian settlements to give Roman titles to their local magistrates, and local councils were liable to be called 'senate', even in so non-Roman a region as Samnium.

There is then no hard evidence for thinking that the Romans incorporated Falerii Novi with the partial citizenship, and, if they had done so, it is most surprising that the relatively detailed, surviving accounts of the treatment meted out to the Falisci in 241 make no mention of the fact, and that the many inscriptions from the place contain not even a hint of Roman status before the Social War. The inscriptions do, however, reveal clearly enough that, after that conflict, Falerii was a *municipium*: it was in the Tribe Horatia and administered by *quattuorviri*, officials who suggest, even if they do not positively prove, that the *municipium* was later than 90.

On the whole then, it seems probable that Falerii Novi after 241, like Falerii Veteres before that date, was 'allied'. In other words, there is no reason to think that the Romans made it an exception to their post-268 policy of incorporating no more Italian communities integrally as *municipia*.

It is worth adding that, when the Romans put an end to Falerii Veteres, they nevertheless left its temples to Juno Curritis, Mercury and other deities standing; and these shrines remained frequented cult-centres to the time of Ovid and beyond.[518] Spectacular specimens of their terracotta decoration can still be seen in the Villa Giulia museum in Rome. The Romans, clearly, were adhering to their regular practice of not suppressing the religious life and beliefs of the peoples they subjugated in Italy.

APPENDIX V

LATIN IN NON-LATIN COMMUNITIES

In 180 the people of Cumae, then a *municipium sine suffragio*, asked the Roman Senate for permission to substitute Latin for Oscan as their official language.[519] This has been interpreted to mean that no non-Latin community, not even one with partial Roman citizenship, could adopt Latin without first being authorized by Rome to do so.[520] But it is *a priori* so incredible that there could ever have been such a ban on the use of Latin that the action of the Cumaei is more probably to be explained by the special circumstances of the time.

The year 189 had witnessed the regularization of the long anomalous situation of the Capuani. Ever since 211 these had been living in a kind of limbo without a state of their own, their status being that of *dediticii*. In 189, however, those Capuani who could afford to do so went to Rome and there contrived to get registered by those notoriously liberal censors T. Quinctius Flamininus and M. Claudius Marcellus. Nor was this all: shortly afterwards they successfully petitioned for the *ius conubii* to be restored to them. The Capuani were thus in effect converted into full Roman citizens in 189.[521]

Such a status for them was inevitably resented by those *municipia* of partial citizenship which, instead of behaving like Capua, had loyally supported Rome throughout Hannibal's war. Three such *municipia*, Volscian Arpinum, Formiae and Fundi, were so outraged by the discrimination in favour of the traitorous Capuani, that they at once sought promotion to the full citizenship for their entire communities. A plebeian tribune was induced to propose a bill in the Tribal Assembly elevating the three *municipia*, and after some obstructionism from other tribunes the bill was passed in 188.[522]

The Volsci, however, had not been the only *cives sine suffragio* to display loyalty in the Second Punic War. Campanians, too, had done their duty. In fact, the fidelity of the Cumaei seems to have become a byword;[523] and not unnaturally the Cumaei now expected to receive no less favourable treatment than the Volsci. It was, however, too late to be registered by the obliging censors of 189: Flamininus and Claudius Marcellus had already closed the *lustrum*.[524] Unfortunately, too, the next pair of censors, M. Porcius Cato and his patrician *alter ego* L. Valerius Flaccus in 184, were notoriously reactionary and strict; they would be not only unwilling to give individual *cives sine suffragio* a tribal affiliation, but even more reluctant and dilatory about registering a whole community in the event that any tribune introduced a bill upgrading one.

The Cumaei, accordingly, had to wait for their chance until 180, a year when political rivalries were at fever pitch owing to efforts by the Fulvii to enhance their political prominence.[525] The atmosphere was now suitable for the aspirations of the Cumaei. But apparently they did not succeed in enlisting tribunician support. Perhaps the plebeian tribunes, mindful of the opposition that their predecessors had run into in 188, were not anxious to clash with Cato. At any rate, no tribune sponsored a bill to promote the Cumaei. Thereupon the Cumaei petitioned the Senate for permission to make Latin their official language.[526] The stratagem is obvious. It was absurd of them to suggest that they or any other Roman community (not even one with only partial citizenship) needed special authorization to use Rome's own language.[527] Clearly the ulterior object of the Cumaei was to impress on the incoming censors of 179 that Cumaei were so thoroughly Roman that their registration individually as *cives optimo iure* was fully justified and unexceptionable.

How far the Cumaei were successful it is impossible to say. They were, of course, immediately assured that they could use Latin if they had a mind to; but there is no record of how many (if indeed any) of them were registered as full citizens in 179. It is, however, quite probable that a significant number of them did then become *cives optimo iure* and obtain registration, perhaps in the Tribe Falerna. For the censors of 179, M. Aemilius Lepidus and M. Fulvius Nobilior, had a controversial plan for reforming the Centuriate Assembly and needed all the voting support that they could muster.[528] That to this end they registered partial citizens as full is suggested by the sequel: after the censorship of 179, as after that of 189, some non-Roman states found it necessary to complain that they had recently lost excessive numbers of their burgesses to Rome.[529]

NEW *MUNICIPIA*
AFTER 90 BC

The reason why, after the passage of the Lex Julia in 90, Rome made most of her new *municipia* quattuorviral, but also constituted some as duoviral has been much debated. The common view,[530] that new *municipia* were regularly made quattuorviral until Julius Caesar for some mysterious reason decided to have them duoviral, is far from satisfactory. Duoviral *municipia* were brought into existence before his day, and quattuorviral *municipia* were certainly constituted after it.[531] In fact, one may well wonder whether Caesar's role in the municipal ordering of Italy has not been greatly exaggerated.

Recently historical continuity has been invoked. It is argued that communities that had had a pair of chief magistrates in their pre-Roman days were likely to remain duoviral when they became *municipia*,[532] while those that had had something other than two chief magistrates were usually made quattuorviral. Events in the Social War are invoked to support this theory.[533] Towards the end of the year 90, so it is argued, the Umbri, hitherto neutral in the war, threatened to join the insurgents, but were bought off with the grant of Roman citizenship together with a promise that their communities would be allowed to retain their favourite quattuorviral type of constitution: Rome not only kept the promise, but subsequently imposed the quattuorviral constitution on all *municipia* wherever established, apart from Samnium and Lucania, where the insurgents preferred duoviral constitutions and were able to hold out long enough to make sure that they got them.

For all its undoubted ingenuity this explanation seems inadequate. Not only does it fail to account for *municipia* that had not even existed as autonomous communities before the war; it also does not reveal why only some, and not all pre-war duoviral communities kept their constitutions.[534] Nor does it appear very probable that the new quattuorviral constitution was Umbrian in inspiration. It is hardly likely that the Latin Colonies, most intimate and faithful of all Rome's allies, were forced to replace their traditional pair of

praetores with new-fangled quattuorviri and for no better reason
than to comply with the preference of near-rebel Umbri. In fact, it is
far from certain that the Umbri did prefer *quattuorviri*. The quattuorviral constitution, so far from being universal in pre-Roman
Umbria, was perhaps only to be found in those communities most
affected by Roman collegial practices. But of these only one
specimen is known and even it is uncertain.[535] A second-century
inscription in Umbrian shows Asisium with a pair of *uhtur* and a pair
of *marones* (one of whom, interestingly enough, was a Propertius);
but these two pairs may not have constituted a genuinely collegial
foursome in the manner of the twin pairs, *duoviri iuri dicundo* and
duoviri aedilicia potestate, that in imperial times made up the quattuorviral boards of some *municipia*. In this connection a recently
found inscription from Mevania, also in Umbrian, implies that *uhtur*
were distinctly the superiors of *marones* and, therefore, may not have
formed unitary boards with them.[536]

Among the new *municipia* after the Social War there must, of
course, have been some whose constitutional arrangements differed
hardly at all from those of their ante-bellum days. But this convenient state of affairs was more fortuitous than tralaticious. That is
not to deny that there were ongoing usages. But the historical
continuity manifested itself more in the preservation of Roman
practices than in the proliferation of Italian preferences.

It is reasonable to relate what Rome did after 90 to what it had been
her habit to do before that date. This had been to distinguish
communities that were Roman by origin (*coloniae*) from communities that were Roman by incorporation (*municipia*). Presumably
she kept the two categories when the whole of Italy was converted
into *municipia* and *coloniae* after the Social War, especially as she was
then contemplating no change at all so far as communities of Roman
origin were concerned. Each of these was to have, as heretofore, a
pair of chief executives. For communities reckoned Roman by
incorporation, on the other hand, her earlier practice did need to be
changed. There would be so many of them that chaos and confusion
would reign if each was allowed, as in former days, to choose any
constitution it liked. It would obviously be less bewildering and
more practical to standardize them, outwardly at least. Rome,
accordingly, decided on boards of four for them.[537]

A possible complication was the difficulty of deciding whether or
not a community was Roman by origin. Now that the population of
Italy had become so scrambled and settlements could be *coloniae*
merely by title, this was by no means as easy as formerly. The same
criterion, however, could be applied in first-century Italy as had

been used earlier in the Greek world, when the *metropolis* of a colony composed of heterogeneous settlers depended on which state the founder of the colony came from. In other words, a community was reckoned Roman by origin if Rome was responsible for its nucleation and organization as an urban entity, no matter whether she developed it out of a Roman *praefectura*, *forum* or *conciliabulum* or from an Italian *pagus* or *vicus*. Obviously any community that had not been really self-governing before the Social War, but was made into one by Rome after that conflict, was indisputably Roman by origin, regardless of its ethnic make-up and regardless of whether it had had an infusion of *coloni* or not. After 90 Rome was, in effect, founding *municipia* as well as *coloniae*, and she was not under the necessity of despatching settlers to them.

Accordingly, communities that were Roman by origin in this sense were made duoviral, just like *coloniae* of old. Usually they were constituted quite some time after the Social War, since they could not spring, as it were, from the goddess Roma, like Athena from the head of Zeus: they needed first to be organized.[538]

Communities defined as Roman by incorporation, on the other hand, became quattuorviral. They were by far the more numerous, and in many cases they could be constituted almost immediately, since they required no fashioning by Rome. They were the communities that, before the Social War, were already city-states (Latin colonies, Italian urban commonwealths, well evolved *pagi*) or Roman *praefecturae* very close to such in their degree of development.

Why Rome prescribed *quattuorviri* as the chief officials for these communities is not recorded. Probably her motives were mixed. Rome may have favoured the appellation *quattuorvir* in order to avert any cheapening of the title *praetor*, the title that most local magistrates would assuredly have claimed if given the choice.[539] Another reason was the likelihood that, in a developed community, four magisterial colleagues would promote more expeditiously than two the change from native law to Roman, a consideration that could be ignored in the case of a community of Roman origin, since its legal system was Roman, in theory anyway, from the start. A third reason for choosing the quattuorviral system may have been its flexibility: it could be readily adapted to virtually any kind of earlier constitution. (Even Italiote communities could be made quattuorviral: e.g. Locri, Rhegium.) But the principal reason for making a community quattuorviral was probably to ensure its easy and instant recognition as an entity that, far from being Roman by origin, had once been an independent political organism and thus possessed an individuality of its own. The organization of such communities into an ostensibly uniform group, all quattuorviral in type, may have rankled, but it did at least proclaim them to be no upstart, new creations. It helped to satisfy their self-respect by differentiating them at a glance from mere extensions of Rome, as duoviral *municipia* could be represented and as *coloniae* undoubtedly were.[540]

The title *colonia*, it must be remembered, was far from enjoying in the first century the high prestige that it acquired later under the Empire. Down to 185 Citizen Colonies were, as noted in Chapter 3, poor and unattractive institutions, for which Rome could not find enough recruits from her own citizen body in the fourth century, to which Romans were reluctant to go in the third, and from which the colonists promptly absconded early in the second. Even later in the second century, when Citizen Colonies were places of greater consequence, they still ranked lower than *municipia*, and very few of them were founded between 185 and 90. After the Social War, of course, Citizen Colonies were founded in large numbers, but, to judge from Cicero's attitude towards them, they were not objects of civic pride. Too often they were centres of disorder (as at Faesulae and Pompeii) or discordant impositions on historic communities (as at Arretium and Clusium).[541] In fact, in the first century the title *colonia* was tantamount to a badge of shame, proclaiming that a community had been humiliated and penalized, and it may have been to avoid any appearance of being *coloniae* that Capena, Acerrae and perhaps other ante-bellum municipia adopted the new quattuorviral constitution.

It needed the authority and crafty propaganda of the emperor Augustus to enhance the image of the *colonia*, and it was not until the first century AD that the *colonia* began to outrank the *municipium*.[542] Even then Praeneste, as late as the reign of Tiberius, petitioned to have its title changed from *colonia* to *municipium*.[543]

Actually, some communities were always eager to parade the fact that they had once been sovereign and independent. Carsulae, which seems to have been originally a duoviral *municipium*, managed to get itself transformed into a quattuorviral one. Aquileia, Falerii and Parentium, when given the title *colonia*, retained *quattuorviri* instead of switching to the *duoviri* appropriate to their colonial rank.[544] Fidenae, to avoid having tell-tale *duoviri*, revived a title from its remote past for its chief magistrates and called them *dictatores* (*sic*: plural). For Capena even its quattuorviral constitution seemed inadequate advertisement: it emphasized its former independent status by styling itself a *municipium foederatum*.[545]

There are apparent exceptions to the rule that communities created *ex novo* by Rome after the Social War became duoviral *municipia*, while pre-existing autonomous towns then incorporated by Rome were made quattuorviral; but they can be explained without much difficulty. Fidenae, Veii, Verulae and Herculaneum had all been city-states long before the Social War and were all duoviral *municipia* after it, not quattuorviral as might have been expected. The reason is that all four had ceased to exist as self-governing entities before Rome incorporated them. Fidenae had faded virtually into extinction after the fourth century; Veii had been dismantled as an autonomous Etruscan community in 396; Hernican Verulae had dwindled into insignificance by the end of the second century; and Campanian Herculaneum had been destroyed in the Social War itself. Thus all four places had to be resuscitated and organized afresh before Rome constituted them as *municipia*.[546]

This explanation is confirmed by the case of Etruscan Perusia. Immediately after the Social War Perusia, being a city-state, was made a quattuorviral *municipium*; in 40, however, it was destroyed by Octavian and, when rebuilt later, was made duoviral.[547] A similar fate appears to have overtaken Arna, near neighbour of Perusia. Its status immediately after the Social War is unrecorded. But in 40 it appears to have been destroyed along with Perusia. Thus it, too, became duoviral on its restoration after that date.

Another new *municipium* that at first sight seems aberrant is Tarentum. It had been an independent city-state for centuries, yet recently published inscriptions suggest that it was incorporated by Rome as a duoviral, not a quattuorviral, *municipium*.[548] The explanation is that before 90 there had been two communities at Tarentum, the old Spartan colony and Gaius Gracchus' Roman colony known as Neptunia. After 90 the two were fused; and as the new joint community had to be organized afresh, it was technically Roman by origin and therefore made duoviral.

The Roman practice seems to have been the same in Cisalpine Gaul after its enfranchisement by Julius Caesar in 49. There had been an increase in urbanization in the region in the second century and this made many Cisalpine communities ripe for prompt conversion into quattuorviral *municipia* in 49. They included the settlements upon which Sextus Pompeius had bestowed the title of *colonia Latina* in 89. There were also, however, settlements in Cisalpina, such as Bellunum, Forum Cornelii, Hasta, Industria and Pollentia, that had evidently not developed very far as urban communities. When they became Roman in 49 they needed to be organized and structured before they could be constituted as *municipia*. In other words, they could be defined as Roman by origin and were accordingly made duoviral.

NOTES

Documentation has been kept to a minimum.
Sources are not given for well-known events, references being supplied
only for statements in the text that seem to call for them.
Periodicals are cited by the abbreviations used in *Année Philologique* and
standard works by the following initials:

CAH	*Cambridge Ancient History*
CIL	*Corpus Inscriptionum Latinarum*
FHG	*Fragmenta Historicorum Graecorum* ed. Mueller
IG	*Inscriptiones Graecae*
ILLRP	*Inscriptiones Latinae Liberae Rei Publicae* ed. Degrassi
ILS	*Inscriptiones Latinae Selectae* ed. Dessau
MRR	*Magistrates of the Roman Republic* by T. R. S. Broughton
P.	P. Poccetti, *Nuovi documenti italici* Pisa, 1979
PCIA	*Popoli e civiltà dell'Italia antica*, by M. Pallottino *et al.* Rome, 1974–78
PID	*Prae-Italic Dialects* ed. Whatmough *et al.*
RE	*Realencyclopädie der Altertumswissenschaft* by Pauly, Wissowa, Kroll
SIG	*Sylloge Inscriptionum Graecarum* ed. Dittenberger
V.	E. Vetter, *Handbuch der italischen Dialecte*, Heidelberg, 1953)

Other publications, many of them with excellent bibliographies, are
named only once; when a publication is cited again, the note where its title
can be found is given in square brackets after the author's name.
Particular indebtedness is owed to A. La Regina [28, 58, 104, 313, 345,
351, 386, 390] and to R. Bianchi Bandinelli-A. Giuliano [139].

1 Dates throughout are BC unless otherwise indicated.
2 The positivistic view of the Romans from the first century on, that it was all foreordained (see, for example, Pliny *N H* 3.39), is, of course unjustified.
3 At this early stage in her history Rome seems to have been poor compared with Gabii, Politorium, Praeneste and Satricum (Montello).
4 Ps. Scylax 8 (in the fourth century: P. Fabre in *EC* 33 (1965), 353–66), and Polybius 3.24.16 agree that Monte Circeo was the southern limit. Modern scholars use the expression Latium Vetus: the Elder Pliny (*N H* 3.56) prefers Latium Antiquum.
5 But most of them had characteristics in common: such as basically Indo-European vocabularies, similar grammatical structures, same type of aspiration, a tendency to accentuate a word's opening syllable (with corresponding syncope and anaptyxis): see V. Pisani in *PCIA* 6.41f.
6 Tacitus *Ann.* 11.24; cf. *ILS* 212.

7 cf. Strabo 6.3.8, p. 283.

8 cf. M. Pallottino in *PCIA* 7.373f.

9 According to Livy (5.38f), the Gallic sack of Rome occurred in 390: but there is general agreement that 386 is the correct date.

10 The limits of the Ager Romanus Antiquus are uncertain: on average they were about five miles from the Capitol.

11 Gabii became such an ally: see P. Bruun in *Arctos* 5 (1967), 51–66. For some communities the loss of territory meant slow death.

12 Members of wealthy families occasionally received allotments to ensure upper class control of any new rustic Roman Tribe that might be created for the *coloni*: cf. Dion.Hal. 1.85.3. In 388 the beneficiaries included non-Romans from Veii, Capena and Falerii who had helped Rome and been rewarded with the Roman citizenship (Livy 6.4.4.; 6.5.8.).

13 The territorial Tribes of the Romans are not to be confused with the ethnic tribes of the Italians. For purposes of administration Romans living in the city of Rome were registered in four urban Tribes and those living in rural areas in rustic Tribes, ultimately thirty-one in number. No new rustic Tribes were created between 495 and 387, presumably because during its first hundred years and more the Roman Republic had been unable to enlarge its territory.

14 A *forum* was probably a community that possessed the right to hold a market (*ius nundinarum*), and to that end it was usually, but not invariably, situated on a highway: H. Galsterer, *Herrschaft und Verwaltung im republikanischen Italien* (Munich, 1976), 27. It was of greater consequence than a *conciliabulum*, although the latter too had some officials of purely local competence (Lex Mamilia Roscia 53, 55).

15 There is evidence of Greek influence on Rome from her beginning. By the fourth century the city-state was normal in Latium, and the Romans apparently had Greek help in surrounding their own town site with its Servian Wall.

16 On the *populi Latini* see R. Werner, *Der Beginn der römischen Republik* (Munich-Vienna-Oldenburg, 1963), 416–43. The tradition that they numbered thirty is not very old: A. Alföldi, *Early Rome and the Latins* (Ann Arbor, N.D. [=1967?]), 10–25. They can be called city-states although they did not much resemble a Greek *polis*: (see M. W. Frederiksen in P. Zanker (ed.) *Hellenismus in Mittelitalien* (Göttingen, 1976), 342). They could be very quarrelsome (see Livy 6.33.6).

17 Lanuvium, Tusculum and above all Praeneste had their own types of Latin: Plautus, *Trinummus* 608f., *Truculentus* 687f; Festus pp. 156, 157, 410L; Quintilian 1.5.56. The other languages of Italy also had local variants: e.g. Etruscan (Livy 10.4.9).

18 Intermigration is not positively testified but can be confidently assumed: an Antistius (from Gabii) held a magistracy at Rome before 338 (*MRR ad an.* 379).

19 Dictators are recorded at Alba Longa, Aricia, Lanuvium, Nomentum and Tusculum, and according to Licinius Macer fr. 10P. the dictator at Rome was of Alban origin. Praetors are recorded before the Latin War at Circeii, Lavinium, Setia. cf. A. Bernardi, *Nomen Latinum* (Pavia, 1973), 53, 58.

20 Livy (8.6.8.) does, however, regard the Latin conflict as virtually a civil war.

21 Livy 6.29.6; 7.18.2; 7.19.1.

22 Ardea, Circeii, Nepete, Norba, Setia, Signia, Sutrium are all said to have been *coloniae* of this kind before 338; and to them may be added perhaps Antium, Bola, Cora, Fidenae, Labici, Satricum, Velitrae.

23 Ideally half the *coloni* would be Latini and half Romans: cf. Livy 8.8.14.

24 Their speakers are usually called Italici although this word in Latin is by no means reserved exclusively for speakers of Osco-Umbrian languages. The dialects that fall between Oscan and Umbrian can be called mid-Italic.

25 The diaspora of the Italici presumably began before the seventh century; it was still under way in historical times. Testruna near Amiternum was its alleged starting point. (Dion. Hal. 2.49).

26 For the sacred spring see E. T. Salmon, *Samnium and the Samnites* (Cambridge, 1967), 35f.

27 Note the excellent remarks of C. Letta, *I Marsi e il Fucino nell'Antichità* (Milan, 1972), 24f.

28 A fifth-century document (? in primitive Oscan), recently found at Penna Sant'Andrea in the south Picentine country of the Praetuttii, alludes to *Safineis* (A. La Regina in *Posebna Izdanja* 24 (1975), 272; A. Prosdocimi in *SE* 46 (1978), 396); and sixth-century *bucchero oinochoai*, recently found at Nocera and Vico Equense in southern Campania are inscribed with what may be primitive Oscan in a south Picentine type of alphabet (*P.* 145).

29 On the origin of the Hernici see Virgil, *Aen.* 7.684 (with the comments of Servius and the Veronese scholiast); Macrob. *Sat.* 5.18.13f.; Sil.Ital. 4.226; 8.393. Festus, p. 89L derives their name from the Marsic word for 'stone'. Sabini were usually reckoned Umbrian (Dion. Hal. 2.49, citing Zenodotus).

30 Strabo 5.3.4, p. 231; cf. Livy 2.41.1.

31 The well-preserved walls of Aletrium are the finest surviving example of polygonal construction. Those at Ferentinum are almost as spectacular.

32 The relevant texts are Livy 9.42.11; 9.43.24. Hernican Anagnia and Capitulum are known to have had praetors; but those at Aletrium under the Empire may have been religious officials analogous to the *praetores Etruriae*: if so, the Hernican league may have been sacral. See *ILLRP* 271 (with the remarks of A. Degrassi both there and in *Scritti Vari di Antichità* (Rome-Venice-Trieste, 1962–71), 1.88; *ILS* 2681; *CIL* 10, p. 566).

33 *V.*226 (from Collemaggiore in the Cicolano district), if genuine, is an Aequian document of perhaps the second century. It shows Umbrian-style nomenclature (with the filiation between *praenomen* and *gentilicium*) and the Umbrian dative singular in -e, which persisted in this area into imperial times, (C. Letta [27], 34). It mentions a *meddix*

and may allude to the Talium recorded by Diodorus (20.26.3; cf.Salmon [26], 244).

34 Falerii Novi was sometimes called Aequum Faliscum (C. Hülsen in *RE* 6. 1970), presumably because it lay on level ground. The view that the Aequi attached high value to 'equity' is fanciful, but it was responsible for the tale that they invented Fetial Law (*ILLRP* 447).

35 'Volsci' may be cognate with the Greek word for 'marsh'. For their possible origin near the Fucine Lake see E. Manni in *Athenaeum* 27 (1939), 233f. The fall of the Roman Monarchy may have opened the way for their irruption into Latium: they are first heard of *c.*500.

36 *V.*222 from Velitrae (third century or earlier) is the only certain specimen of Volscian; *V.*223 is more probably Marsic than Volscian (C. Letta [27], 33).

37 They had two settlements called Satricum. Montello occupies the site of the one meant here; Boville Ernica in the valley of the river Liris is the site of the other.

38 Aufidius Luscus, chief magistrate of Fundi, used the title of *praetor* (Horace, *Sat.* 1.5.34), but this was snobbish affectation.

39 See e.g. Livy 4.28, 29; Virgil, *Geor.* 2.168.

40 For the identity of Ausones, Aurunci and Osci see Aristotle 7.1329b, Festus, p. 16L and Strabo (5.3.6, p. 233; 5.4.3, p. 242), who cites fourth-century authorities. Rhotacism accounts for the *r* in Aurunci. Polybius (34.11.7) differentiates Aurunci from Osci, probably because for him Opici (Osci) meant speakers of Oscan: i.e. Sabelli. Livy (8.15, 16) regards Aurunci and Ausoni as distinct, possibly because he thought that the close relationship of Vescia, Minturnae and Ausona made them ethnically different from Cales.

41 Allegedly they were related to the Siculi (Dion. Hal. 1.22) which might imply a Latinian language for them. But sixth-century inscriptions recently found at Nocera and Vico Equense (see n. 28) may mean that their language was an early form of Oscan.

42 The three settlements had a common shrine (? to Marica) called Trifanum: Livy 8.11.11.
43 *ILS* 4264; Livy 23.37.2; Strabo 5.3.6, p. 233; Horace, *Odes* 3.17.7; Virgil, *Aen.* 7.47.
44 Votive terracottas and tomb furnishings indicate that they reached the vicinity of Teanum in the seventh century. Once there they exploited the mineral deposits of the area.
45 Livy 8.22.1 (reading *Sidicinorum*); cf. Strabo 5.4.3, p. 242.
46 Strabo 5.3.9, p. 237; 5.4.10, p. 249.
47 Oscan-speakers evidently used the ethnic *Capuanus* (see *V.* 86, 88, 91); Latin-speakers avoided it (Varro *L.L.* 10.16.), preferring to use *Campanus* despite its ambiguity (for them, too, it could mean 'Campanian': Livy 23.17.10; 23.35.3.).
48 Thucydides knew the tradition: for him Campania was Opicia (6.4.5).
49 Greek influence is strikingly illustrated by the *mensa ponderaria* in the forum at Pompeii on which Greek measures are given oscanized names (*P.* 109) or by a lamp (also from Pompeii) inscribed in Greek and Oscan (*P.* 120). Some Greek was even to be found at Capua: Suetonius, *Caesar* 81. See, too, Strabo 5.4.4, p. 243.
50 Bilingual inscriptions in Etruscan and Oscan have also been found in Campania (*V.* 106a). Etruscan was still spoken there after 350: B. d'Agostino in *PCIA* 2.212. But the twelve communities forming the Etruscan *dodecapolis* cannot be identified. Presumably Marcina was one (Strabo 5.4.13, p. 251), and archaeological finds indicate a strong Etruscan presence at Fratte and Pontecagnano in southern Campania.
51 For the Sabelli in Campania, see Salmon [26], 37f.
52 The Capuan league included Casilinum, Atella, Calatia and apparently the community of the Sabatini. Acerrae, Cumae and Suessula may also have belonged to it at one time. The Alfaternan league is often called a *pentapolis* and it probably included Pompeii, Stabiae and perhaps Surrentum. Hyria, known only from its coins, may have been closely associated with Nola and Abella.
53 Livy (7.30.10; cf. 7.38.10; Dion. Hal. 15.3.2) implies that the Romans were prepared to defend all of Campania.
54 The silver coins of Allifae date from the days when that community formed part of Campania rather than of Samnium.
55 *V.* 147. This document lists a number of gods with strange names and unidentifiable functions, of whom Kerres (=? Ceres) is the most prominent. A recent suggestion is that it belongs to a Greek-type mystery cult deep inside Samnium: A. Prosdocimi in *PCIA* 6. 830f., 1073f.
56 G. Barker in *Antiquity* 51 (1977), 20f. *Pagi* and *vici* are Roman names for small settlements: the native words for them are unknown. The Romans later subdivided the *territoria* of their *municipia* into *pagi* which had to perform services (*munera*) and provide revenue (for their officials see Festus p. 502L. and cf. *ILLRP* 57, 621; *ILS* 5545, 5575). These Roman *pagi* did not necessarily correspond to, and should be distinguished from earlier native *pagi*, these latter being administrative entities and not mere territorial subdivisions: see M. W. Frederiksen in Zanker [16], 341f. and cf. H. Rudolph, *Stadt und Staat im römischen Italien* (Liepzig, 1935), 50f.
57 Some of the Samnite strongpoints have been carefully investigated: see G. De Benedittis, *Bovianum ed il suo territorio* (Rome, 1977), *passim*.
58 For the higher cultural level of the Caudini see B. d'Agostino [49], 195f., 206f; C. G. Franciosi in *Convegno Magna Grecia* 15 (1975), 469. Epigraphy authorizes the spelling Carricini: A. La Regina in *ArchClass* 25/26 (1973/74), 331–40.
59 Livy 10.38.5f.; A. La Regina in P. Zanker [16] 226; *V.* 149.
60 For possible specimens of the Oenotrian language see M. Lejeune in *REA* 72 (1970), 271f.; 74 (1972), 5f.; 75

(1973), 1f.; *V.* 186.

61 The name Lucani is said to mean 'wolf men', after the animal that led their original sacred spring band.

62 6.1.2, p. 254.

63 For the Lucanian tribal state see Diodorus 20.104. For the generalissimo see Heraclides (*FHG* 2.218,20); Strabo 6.1.3, p. 254; M. Cristofani in *PCIA* 7. 97 (for a recent find confirming such an appointment).

64 For Rossano di Vaglio see *P.* 154–83; M. P. Marchese in *PCIA* 6.897f. It is once again a shrine of sorts, since every 21 May it celebrates the day of Constantine and Helen with wine and kitchen spits. Minor shrines existed at Acquarossa, Garaguso and elsewhere.

65 In antiquity the name Calabria was given, not to the 'toe', but to the 'heel' of Italy. The 'toe' was called Ager Bruttius; but Bruttium is so convenient a term that modern scholars use it even though it lacks ancient authority (unless *Greek* Brettion is regarded as a variant of it).

66 It is unlikely that the name Bruttii derives from an eponymous hero, from a princess, or from a local word meaning 'runaway slave': more probably it comes from a prehistoric tongue (cf. *V.* 186).

67 Cf. Livy 25.1.2; but *see* A. J. Toynbee, *Hannibal's Legacy* (London, 1965), 1.107.

68 The most celebrated is Scoglio del Tonno near the harbour entrance at Tarentum.

69 Ephorus' assertion (quoted by Strabo 6.2.2, p. 267), that piracy and the savagery of the natives kept Greek traders out of the west for hundreds of years, is an absurdity.

70 The coming of colonies did not mean the end of trading posts. One was established at Graviscae on the coast of Etruria in the sixth century: M. Torelli in *PP* (1971), 4–67.

71 The Italiotes of Locri are said to have intermarried with the natives and, according to Polybius (12.5.10), adopted some native usages. The coins of Rhegium seem to be based on the native Italic pound. But it is significant that no Greeks ever wrote in Oscan.

72 Even Tarentum, founded by the martial Spartans, had difficulty in getting established: its defeat in 473 was the worst ever suffered up to that time by any Greek state (Hedt. 7.170) and forced it to change its constitution (Aristotle, *Pol.* 5.1303a3).

73 The colonies also attracted notable visitors from mainland Greece, such as Aeschylus, Plato and Lysippus.

74 By the fourth century their decline was very evident (Athenaeus 14.p.632, citing the contemporary Aristoxenus). For the effects of the Pyrrhic War on Croton see Livy 24.3.2. Even Tarentum, which could field over 20,000 men in the fourth century (Diod. 20.104), had become semi-Greek by the third (Florus 1.13.6).

75 The river is named only by Pliny (*NH* 3.103), and the MSS vary between Fertur and Frento. Today it is called the Fortore.

76 R. Whitehouse in *Proc. Prehist. Soc.* 40 (1974), 203f. The Oenotri, also known as Itali, were subdivided into Chones, Morgetes, and Siculi.

77 Iapyx himself is said to have come from Crete, but the Iapyges were regarded as Illyrians. Uria may have been the centre from which they spread over southeastern Italy (cf. Strabo 6.3.6, p. 282). The *Tapuzkum nomen* mentioned in the Iguvine Tables (1b17), however, were probably a separate group that had immigrated from Illyria into Picenum.

78 They range in date from the late sixth to the first century and include an *abecedarium* (*PID* 2.555). Latin *panis* ('bread') may be a Messapic word: A. von Blumenthal in *Glotta* 18 (1929), 150.

79 G. Daniel in *CAH*[3] 2.2.723.

80 The frontiers between the tribes were not firm. Gnathia is usually reckoned Peucetian (not Calabrian), and Canusium was Daunian (although south of the Aufidus). The basic element in the Peucetii and Daunii cannot be identified: D. Briquel in *MEFR* 86 (1974), 7–40.

81 Their presence may account for the later popularity of gladiatorial games in the region: P. Sabbatini Tumolesi in *RAL* 26 (1971), 735; 27 (1972), 485; 29

(1974), 283.

82 Horace (*Sat.* 1.10.30) says that Canusium was bilingual, but fails to name its two languages.

83 Strabo (6.3.8, p. 283) seems to say that the Apuli was Sabelli. It is to be noted that today the 'heel' uses a different dialect (Salento) from the tableland (Pugliese).

84 Plautus (*Miles Glor.* 648) indicates that many residents of the region knew Greek; but Greek inscriptions are very rare there, only two from the entire 'heel', both from Brundisium (*IG* 14.672,674).

85 Greek legends on coins are not evidence that Apulia was Greek-speaking: cf. Latin legends on English coins.

86 J. Whatmough in *PID* 2.p.417.

87 The names of some of the kinglets are known: Opis (Paus. 10.13.10); Artas who supplied the Athenians with javelin-men against Syracuse (Thuc. 7.33), Malemnius who founded Lupiae (SHA *M. Aur.*1.6). Ennius allegedly descended from king Messapus himself (Sil. Ital. 12.393).

88 Spelled Zis. But Latin names were also used: they had a goddess called Venas (i.e. Venus).

89 *Pol.* 7.9.1329b.

90 Not all the coins have Greek letters: e.g. some from Teanum Apulum use the Latin Alphabet.

91 The path-finding animal may have been a stag: note Steph. Byz. s.v. 'Brentesion'. (Names beginning with 'Frent-' were, however, common in central and southern Italy).

92 In 1972 an Oscan *abecedarium* was found on Frentanian territory (*P.* 101).

93 Larinum was no doubt not as unsavoury as Cicero's *Pro Cluentio* suggests (but note that Strabo found another Frentanian community 'beastly': 5.4.2, p. 241). It issued its own coins, pursued its own policy, and ended up in a different Roman Tribe from other Frentani. Another Frentanian community (called Luca or something similar: *V.* 173; *ILS* 1; Livy 8.25.3; 8.27.6; 10.11.11) may also have been independent of the main tribe: it was situated somewhere near the Samnite Carricini.

94 The form *kenzsur* is used for both singular and plural.

95 They adopted the Latin alphabet early both for coins and inscriptions (*P.* 105).

96 It is uncertain whether the river Alento or the Foro served as the boundary.

97 V. Cianfarani in *PCIA* 5. 38f.

98 5.4.2, p. 241.

99 The name of the goddess is unknown.

100 *V.* 219 names two officials; presumably *meddices*.

101 Its town plan can be traced: it looks very Roman.

102 Festus, p. 248L; Ovid, *Fasti* 3.95. The story may have arisen from a fancied connection between the names Paeligni and Pelasgi.

103 The river Salinus was their northern boundary apparently.

104 Pliny, *NH* 3.107 uses the expression *cismontani*. The two groups were joined by a road from transmontane Pinna, via Forca di Penne and Aufinum, to cismontane Peltuinum: A. La Regina in *MAL*[8] 13 (1968), 359–446.

105 The drovers' trails can still be seen on the southern slopes (Campo Imperatore) of the Gran Sasso not far from Peltuinum. *ILS* 5542 probably refers to transhumance.

106 The heavy bronze coins, inscribed V E S, date from the early third century and resemble those of the nearby Latin Colony Hadria in type and weight: R. Thomsen, *Early Roman Coinage* (Copenhagen, 1957–61), 1.161, 191; 3.249.

107 Only three specimens survive: *V.* 220, 227 and *P.* 207, all from the cismontane region. The language resembles Oscan rather than Umbrian.

108 Forca Caruso (*Latin* Mons Imeus) is over 1,100 metres high: it is the saddle between Monte Vestrino (1508m.) north of it and Montagna della Selva (1387m.) south of it.

109 *V.* 223–25, 228a; *P.* 218–24. *CIL* 1. 393 may also be Marsic. The Umbrian onomastic formula occurs in these documents. Moreover Pliny (NH 17.171) preserves a gloss common to Umbrian and Marsic. Marsi, Sabini and Hernici were all related: Festus p. 89L and the scholia on Hor. Epod. 17,29 and Odes 1.1.28 and on Virg., Aen. 7.684.

110 ILLRP 7, 44.44a. But that the cetur of V.223 is a censor and indicative of Roman influence seems questionable.

111 Letta [27], 66; Strabo 5.4.2., p. 242.

112 Their worship of Çerfus (or Çerfi) caused them to give names like Cerfennia and Corfinium to their settlements.

113 The Vestini, who stood somewhat apart from the others (Polyb. 2.24.12), may have signed separately in 302 (Livy, 10.3.1).

114 Fasti Triumph. ad an. 301 may record a triumph de Marseis, but it is significant that no Latin Colonies were established on the territories of the league members.

115 Dion. Hal. 2.49, citing Zenodotus.

116 See J. Poucet, Recherches sur la légende sabine des origines de Rome (Louvain, 1967), passim.

117 Seventh-century Sabine chamber-tombs have now been found at Colle del Forno near Cures.

118 V. 362 (seventh century) may be in archaic Sabine. V. 227 (sometimes regarded as Sabine) is more probably Vestinian.

119 Varro was probably descended from a Roman colonus.

120 Cato knew the story: Malcovati, ORF Cato fr. 78. For their life in villages see Strabo 5.3.1, p. 228; Front. Strat. 1.8.4. Their pre-Roman constitutional arrangements are unknown: at one time they may have had meddices (cf. the Sabine name Mettius). The octoviri found in Sabine praefecturae under the Romans may be a survival from pre-Roman days.

121 Hostilities are recorded for 296: ILS 54.

122 Capena preferred inhumation, whereas Falerii cremated; and its language may have been a form of Umbrian. No Faliscan inscriptions have been found at Nepete, and nearby Narce

spoke Etruscan (but see G. Colonna in SE 40 (1972), 444f.). Fidenae may have been a Faliscan bridgehead across the Tiber (cf. Livy 4.17.1; 5.8.6).

123 Strabo 5.2.9, p. 226. Inscriptions range in date from the seventh to the second century. The alphabet used is Etruscan in type and shows occasional resemblances to south Picentine writing.

124 There were at least two notable Faliscan pottery artists: the Aurora and the Nazzano painters: J. D. Beazley, Etruscan Vase Painting (Oxford, 1947), 84f.

125 For that reason they are called Etruscans, not Etrusci or Tusci, in the present study. Books about them are legion: for up-to-date bibliographies see A. J. Pfiffig, Einführung in die Etruskologie (Darmstadt, 1972), 94f.; M. Grant, The Etruscans (London, 1980), 295f.

126 Apparently there was comparatively little stock breeding, but Etruria exported much wine, cereals and the bronze and bucchero products of its artisans. The Greeks were very interested in Etruscan metals (Diod. 5.13), the bronze being shipped in ingots shaped like ox-hides, specimens of which have been found in the sea near Ischia.

127 They founded Capua perhaps in the eighth century: see J. Heurgon, Capoue préromaine (Paris, 1970), 485–95.

128 According to Plutarch, Cam. 16, there were eighteen Etruscan cities in upper Italy. They were probably not very large and many are unidentifiable (S. P. Uggeri in SE 47 (1979), 93f.). For Etruscan Mantua see Servius ad Aen. 10.200; for Etruscan Spina, Ps. Scylax, 17.

129 As with the Greeks, more than one state might supply the settlers for a new foundation. Clusium seems to have been a very active colonizer, especially in upper Italy (G. B. Pellegrini in PCIA 6.116).

130 The league was revived by the emperor Claudius (possibly with fifteen members) and its head was then called praetor Etruriae (in Etruscan zilath mechl rasnal). Possibly the tradition was that centuries earlier the zilath occasionally served as generalissimo of the league's forces (M. Torelli, *Elogia Tarquiniensia* (Florence, 1975), 68f.).

131 Sometimes there apparently was some economic cooperation. In the third century Populonia, Vetulonia and a third state (Rusellae? Vulci?) formed a currency union that issued bronze coins for them all.

132 They never really recovered from their naval defeat by the Syracusans in 474 near Cumae.

133 Oddly enough no record of these treaties survives; but that there were such treaties is beyond dispute: W. V. Harris, *Rome in Etruria and Umbria* (Oxford, 1971), 85f.

134 Note the seventh-century *tholos* near Quinto Fiorentino, the largest pre-Roman specimen in Italy: M. Pallottino, *The Etruscans* (London, 1975), pl. 50.

135 They knew how to write by the eighth century, to judge from a proto-Corinthian *kotyle* found at Tarquinii. They had probably learned the art from the Italiotes (but see H. J. Izzo, *Tuscan and Etruscan* (Toronto, 1972), 140f.); they developed more than one alphabet.

136 Roman aristocrats sent their sons to Etruria for schooling in the fourth century: Livy, 9.36.3.

137 For the luxuriousness of their upper classes, Diod. 5.40; Athenaeus 12, p. 517. For the servile condition of the lower, Dion. Hal. 9.5.4; Livy 33.36.1–5; cf. J. Heurgon in *Festschrift Altheim* (Berlin, 1965), 1.273f. and the literature there cited. For Roman borrowings, Sil. Ital. 8.483; F. Roncalli: *Le lastre dipinte da Cerveteri* (Florence, 1965), 69f.; M. Pallottino [134], 99f.

138 M. Pallottino in *PCIA* 6. 459f.

139 R. Bianchi Bandinelli and A. Giuliano, *Etruschi e Italici prima del dominio di Roma* (Milan, 1973), 256; Pallottino [134], 101.

140 The earliest Umbrian writing (fourth century) is on the Mars of Todi. The date of the Iguvine Tables is disputed, but can hardly be earlier than 200 (J. Heurgon, *Convegno Studi Umbri* 1 (1964), 115). Plautus (*Asinaria* 260), himself an Umbrian, seems to quote

Tab. Iguv. VIa 1.

141 *P.* 1 was found near Bologna but probably originates from Nuceria Umbra. Ptolemy (3.1.46, 47) seems to differentiate northern Umbri from southern.

142 Ps. Scylax, 16; G. Radke in *RE* supp. Bd. 9 s.v. Umbri, 1751f.

143 Livy 9.41.8f.; 10.18.2; *ILS* 705.

144 There was a celebrated temple of Jupiter Appenninus near Iguvium and the Scheggia Pass: (*ILS* 3073, H. Nissen, *Italische Landeskunde* (Berlin, 1883–1902), 1.218). M. Verzer in Zanker [16], 118 suggests that this was a pan-Umbrian shrine; but there is no proof, and the temple may not have existed before Roman times. According to Strabo (5.2.10, p. 227), the Umbrians lacked a common political organization.

145 *Uhtur* has the same form in singular and plural: that it is cognate with Latin *auctor* is dubious. Whether *marones* were originally Etruscan or Umbrian is a moot point. The *uhtur* are known to have been more than mere religious officials: they were in fact superior to the *marones* (E. Campanile and C. Letta, *Studi sulle magistrature indigene e municipali in area italica* (Pisa, 1979), 50–60).

146 Celts were beginning to appear there *c.*350 (Ps. Scylax 18): Auximum is said to be a Celtic name.

147 The relevant texts are: Diod. 20.35.3; Livy 9.36.7; 9.37.11; 9.41; 10.1.4; 10.27; Cic. *Pro Balbo* 20; *ILS* 432.

148 The Umbrian character of the Sarsinates (or Sassinates) has been questioned. But they clearly belonged to the Sapinian tribe which was Umbrian (Livy 31.2.6; 33.37.1); Plautus came from Sarsina, but his evidence (*Mostellaria* 770) is inconclusive. According to Strabo (5.1.7, p. 214 and elsewhere; cf. Pliny *NH* 3.115), Ravenna was also Umbrian: but its name looks Etruscan.

149 These prehistoric inhabitants of the region were probably very heterogeneous, but can be called collectively Picenes, a geographical term which has no ethnic implications. The Illyrian element is referred to in the Iguvine Tables (see n. 77) and, according to Pliny

(*NH* 3.110), at least part of it survived into the days of the Empire.

150 V. Cianfarani *Culture Adriatiche d'Italia* (Rome, 1970), 111f., 236; Bianchi Bandinelli-Giuliano [139], 98. A remarkable specimen of the art of the Picenes is the Warrior of Capestrano (*c.*500), which is very expressive of their martial spirit. The Picentine fondness for spirals is found also on the other side of the Adriatic.

151 See n. 128. Ps. Scylax ignores Picenum and its inhabitants: for him the whole coastline was either in 'Samnite' or Umbrian hands.

152 Picenum is more likely an Illyrian word: there was a Piquentum in Istria, a river Picentinus in Pannonia, a people called Picenses in Dalmatia; and an (Illyrian?) god, Piquius Martius, is mentioned in the Iguvine Tables (Vb 10).

153 Festus p. 235: *Sabini* obviously means *Sabelli*. The name Praetuttii is formed from the Oscan word *touto* (='people', 'community'). It survives in modern Italian as Abruzzi.

154 The Romans were obviously relieved to have the Picentes as allies instead of enemies in 299 (Livy 10.10.2; 10.11.7).

155 It is clear that the name Ligures was used indiscriminately: not all the tribes to which it was given were in fact Ligurian (the Stoeni, for instance, who were conquered in 117: Fasti Triumph. *ad an.*).

156 Cato fr. 31 P; cf. Cicero, *pro Sest.* 69. According to Plutarch (*Marius* 19) they were 'Ambrones', which is not very enlightening, and according to Dion. Hal. (1.11) Greeks, which is absurd.

157 Non-Indo-European elements in north Italian toponymy may be due to them.

159 Cicero, *Brutus* 255 and Livy 40.38.9, suggest that 'triumphs' over Ligures could be cheaply won: but they are exaggerating. The first 'triumph' recorded was in 236; yet many tribes were still unconquered in 154 (Polyb. 33.7; Strabo 4.6.2, p. 202).

159 Ligurian poverty was proverbial: Cicero, *De leg. agr.* 2.95; Virg. *Georg.* 2.168. But Livy mentions *principes*

Ligurum (40.34.8).

160 They are known to have worshipped Bormo (or Bormanus), a deity of hot springs.

161 For a list of the lesser known tribes see M. G. Tibiletti Bruno in *PCIA* 6. 193. Modern toponymy preserves the names of some: e.g. Frignano in the area of the Friniates.

162 L. Barfield, *Northern Italy before Rome* (London, 1971), 145; F. R. Vonwiller in *PCIA* 4.290.

163 Livy, proud of his Venetic descent, begins his *ab urbe condita* with a comparison of Antenor and his companions arriving at the head of the Adriatic with Aeneas and his Trojans reaching Latium: both made landfall at a spot called Troia. Cato evidently knew this tale: Pliny *NH* 3.130. There were people called Veneti also in Paphlagonia (Homer *Il.* 2.852), Illyria (Hedt. 1.196), Gaul (Caesar, *B G* 2.34 and often elsewhere) and central Europe (Tac. *Germ.* 46).

164 See G. B. Pellegrini and A. Prosdocimi, *La lingua venetica* (Padua, 1967). A Venetic *abecedarium* has been found at Ateste. The earliest inscription is on a bronze vase from Lozzo Atestino: D. Briquel in *MEFR* 85 (1973), 65f. The Veneti learned writing from the Etruscans before the latter had adopted the symbol 8 for the labio-dental spirant *f*, which appears as *vh* in Venetic.

165 Pliny *NH* 3.130, 133, 134. Verona is said to have been founded by Euganei.

166 The rivers Livenza and Tagliamento seem to have formed their eastern boundary. Atria, to be distinguished from the homonymous settlement in Picenum, is the town after which the Adriatic Sea is named, although it was not on the sea but only linked to it, like Spina, by canal. Its origin (Venetic? Etruscan?) is unknown; many Greek vases have been found there.

167 It is possible that the Veneti introduced cavalry into Italy; but by Augustus' day their horse-training days were over (Strabo, 5.1.9, p. 215).

168 She came to be variously identified with Juno, Lucina, Orthia and Artemis. But, as a result of their contacts with other Italian peoples, they also came to know many male divinities: e.g. Apollo, Nepture (for them a god of fresh water), the Dioscuri, Diomede, and even Geryon (Suet. *Tiberius* 14).

169 *ILLRP* 476, 477.

170 Early Venetic culture might apr opriately be called Atestine (despite the umber of Etruscan inscriptions founa at Ateste). Patavium was able to repel Cleonymus of Sparta in 302 (Livy 10.2), but that it could field 120,000 men (Strabo 5.1.7, p. 213) is absurd: in 225 the whole nation could outfit only 20,000 (Polyb. 2.24.7).

171 Baltic amber was one of their trading staples. Mars apparently was not much worshipped among them and few weapons are found in their necropoleis. They were renowned for their seriousness (Pliny *Epp.* 1.14.6; Martial 11.16).

172 The only eminences of any consequence in the plain are the Astigiana and Monferrato mountains of Piemonte and the Euganean Hills of the Veneto. The one gap in the mountains encircling the plain is near the head of the Adriatic and is controlled by Ariminum: cf. Strabo 5.1.11, p. 217.

173 For the much travelled Polybius, Cisalpina was the most fertile of all lands (2.14.7). But its marshes were notorious (P. A. Brunt, *Italian Manpower* (Oxford, 1971), 172f.) and even after reclamation most difficult to control: by 350 Spina was moribund and later its very site disappeared under silt and was not rediscovered until 1956. Flooding is still a grave menace for Rovigo and the Polesine district; and Pavia is notorious for its fogs.

174 The Gauls may have been stimulated by either their own or the Germans' over-population (cf. Livy 5.34.2). See, too, Polyb. 2.17.

175 Livy (5.34) places it two centuries earlier.

176 Pliny *NH*3.72. The site of Melpum is unknown: there is a town called Melzo between Milan and Bergamo with a La Tène necropolis nearby.

177 According to Livy (5.33) and Plutarch (*Camillus* 15), this band was

attracted into Italy by a waggon-load of wine, oil and figs offered by Arruns of Etruscan Clusium, who wanted to punish another Etruscan for seducing his wife. More seriously, the Roman cliché, *tumultus Gallicus*, is indicative of the impression made by the Celts.

178 Polyb. 2.14, 17, 19, 21.

179 Gods with strange Celtic names were still worshipped under the Empire: e.g. Bergimus, Falvennius. For human sacrifice among the Cisalpine Gauls see Barfield [162], 154.

180 But the necropolis of Carzaghetto near Mantua has yielded the best collection of Celtic material, which on the whole is surprisingly scanty in Cisalpina.

181 Celtic tribes and war bands were difficult to identify: Strabo 4.1.3, p. 187.

182 Livy (5.35.2) on the Boian entry is a bit fanciful. Pliny's statement (*NH* 3.124) that they founded the town now known as Lodi suggests that they came by one of the central Alpine passes. According to Cato (*apud* Pliny *NH* 3.116) they comprised 112 sub-tribes. (Were the Lingones one of these?)

183 G. Tibiletti, *Storie locali dell'Italia romana* (Pavia, 1978), 306 regards them as non-Celtic.

184 The river Addua, however, may have been the boundary.

185 Polyb. 2.17.4. They retained their Celtic identity longest (down to the age of Augustus, to judge from their necropoleis).

186 But Ticinum itself, originally a settlement of the Ligurian Laevi and Marici (Pliny *NH* 3.124), is not recorded before the age of Augustus. Mediolanium ('mid-plain settlement') was later called Mediolanum.

187 Livy 23.24.12; 36.40.12; cf. Diod. 5.29.3–5; Strabo 4.4.5, p. 198. The Gauls still behaved like Celts in battle in the Social War: Appian *BC* 1.50 (unless he is referring to transalpine mercenaries).

188 Earlier they seem to have been Taurisci (Polyb. 2.15.8; 3.60.8).

189 Cf. Polyb. 2.19.1; 34.10; Livy 5.34.7f.

190 Usually the ancients, however, reckoned the Taurini as Ligures in origin: Polyb. 2.15.8; Strabo 4.6.6, p. 204; Pliny *NH* 3.123. Livy calls them *semigalli* (21.38.5).

191 But Eporaedia, an important settlement of the Salassi, has an unmistakably Gallic name.

192 Examples: Anauni (Val di Non), Bergalei (Val Bregaglia), Camunni (Val Camonica), Isarci (Val d'Isarco), Lepontii (Val Leventina), Sabini (Val Sabbia), Trumplini (Val Trompia), Venostes (Val Venosta).

193 The Raeti, for instance, raided Comum in the first century: Tibiletti [183], 229–52.

194 Roman coins circulated widely among the mountain tribes in the first century.

195 Apparently they are not to be identified with the Comenses whom the Romans defeated in 196 (Livy 33.36). Whether they, the Ligures, or some other people (e.g. the Orombovii of Pliny, *NH* 3.124) are responsible for the -ASC- suffix found in certain Italian words (Comasco, Bergamasco, etc.) is a moot point.

196 An inscription recently found at Prestino looks decidedly Celtic, however: Tibiletti Bruno [161], 141f. The inscriptions are written in the so-called Lugano alphabet, which derives from an Etruscan script and was used also by some other peoples in the area. Ancient writers do not mention the language.

197 Livy 5.33.11. Polybius, too, knew of the Raeti: Strabo 4.6.12, p. 209. But the first clear reference to them belongs to 102. They are said to have invented the wheeled plough. Not only the language, but also Raetic toponymy looks non-Indo-European. The similarity of the name Reitia, the Venetic goddess, is no doubt coincidental.

198 The Camunni and the Lepontii are both sometimes called Raeti (Pliny *NH* 3.133; Strabo 4.6.8, p. 208).

199 Little attention has been paid to suppressed, and possibly enslaved substrata. There is also much linguistic simplification: some of the languages

mentioned (e.g. Celtic) were little better than bundles of dialects. A unitary view of Italy (including Cisalpina) is hard to document before Cato the censor.

200 Perhaps too there was everywhere a peculiarly Italian quality about the way people lived, the *italicità* of Prosdocimi [55], 545f.

201 According to Livy (7.11.1; 7.12.8; 8.14.9), some Latini sided with the Gauls.

202 Rome had aimed at supremacy in Latium in regal days and since (note Polyb. 3.24): in 358 she tried to make her allies dependent (Livy 7.12.7; Werner [16], 357f., 469); and in 348 the consuls allegedly prayed to the gods to increase Rome's power and majesty and to make the Latini for ever obedient: R. E. A. Palmer, *Roman Religion and Roman Empire* (Philadelphia, 1974), 102f.; W. V. Harris, *War and Imperialism in Republican Rome* (Oxford, 1979), 121, 265. This prayer, however, may be an Augustan forgery: A. D. Momigliano in *JRS* 31 (1941), 165.

203 The only Campanian state actually named is Capua. But the peace terms prove that Cumae, Suessula and Acerrae were also involved. Moreover Rome still possessed *ager publicus* near Cumae and Acerrae in the first century (Cic. *De leg. agr.* 2.66).

204 Livy (8.1–5; 8.2.3; 8.11.2) minimizes the role of the Samnites.

205 The expression Latium Adjectum is taken from Pliny *NH* 3.59.

206 Livy 8.14 (cf., too, 8.12); Velleius 1.14.2–4. They are supported by the Oxyrhynchan Chronicle (F. Jacoby, *Frag. Griech. Hist.* 2B no. 225, p. 1155).

207 Livy 8.11.3. But members of well-to-do families also participated: this ensured that the wealthy would control the eventual new Tribes, since only they could afford to go to Rome and vote in the Assemblies: L. R. Taylor, *The Voting Districts of the Roman Republic* (Rome, 1960), 67. The allotments varied from two to three *iugera*.

208 According to Livy (8.17.11; cf. 6.5.8) the new Tribes were for *novi cives* and Maecia did contain Lanuvini (cf.

Livy 6.2.8; Festus p. 121L); but generally new Tribes were for old citizens (in other words *coloni*): A. N. Sherwin White, *The Roman Citizenship*[2] (Oxford, 1973), 198. The new Tribes were created in pairs to keep the total number of Tribes odd and thus prevent a tie in the Assembly.
209 As the mutiny in the winter of 342 had demonstrated: Livy 7.38–41.
210 For the *municipium* see M. Humbert, *Municipium et civitas sine suffragio* (Rome, 1978); for the *colonia* see E. T. Salmon, *Roman Colonization under the Republic* (London, 1969).
211 The view of Galsterer [14], 42–62 that the military role of Citizen Colonies was subordinate to their real purpose, which was to romanize the nearby natives, is unconvincing: the countryside near Ostia needed no romanizing and the dates of the later Citizen Colonies on the coast of Etruria make it certain that they were intended to repel Carthaginian raiders from Sardinia.
212 Livy 27.38.3; 36.3.4–6. Three hundred was the standard number of settlers for a Citizen Colony down to 184. Traditionally Ostia was the first of them.
213 Cf. n. 16 above.
214 The Senate presumably named the communities that were to be incorporated, but only the Assembly could confer the citizenship upon them: Polyb. 6.14; Livy 8.17.12; 8.21.10; 38.36.7f.; Taylor [207], 17f.
215 Note Festus p. 126L and Aul. Gell. 16.13.6. The *municipium* could have its own local laws: but the same citizenship can encompass more than one legal system, as all Scots (and Canadians) are well aware.
216 Cicero, *Pro Caecina* 100; *Pro Balbo* 28, 29.
217 O. Gradenwitz in *SHAW* (1915), Abt. 9.38. Note how the burgesses of incorporated Capua are never called *cives Campani*.
218 For the rights, responsibilities and duties of Roman citizens see now C. Nicolet *The world of the citizen in Republican Rome* (London, 1980), *passim*. Those not registered in a Tribe had lost

their 'liberty': Livy 45.15.4.
219 Tusculum, despite its name, was Latin (Dion. Hal. 10.20): it even supplied the leader for the league of Latin states that met in the grove near Lake Nemi (Cato fr. 58P). It is improbable that the Romans would have chosen any but a Latin state for their first *municipium*.
220 Livy 6.25.26; Dion. Hal. 14.6.2; Festus p. 155L. Cicero obviously regarded Tusculum as the first *municipium* (see *Pro Balbo* 31; *Pro Plancio* 19; *De off.* 1.35).
221 Livy 6.33.6; Dion. Hal. 16.6.9. Festus p. 155L is in error in coupling the Lanuvini with the Tusculani.
222 The senate of Lanuvium is recorded even in a Greek inscription: *Ann. Épigr.* (1966), 155.
223 Local magistrates at Lanuvium could undoubtedly impose fines: *ILLRP* 130a (third century?).
224 Pliny *NH* 7.136 (who may have mistaken the man's identity). But Cicero (*Pro Plancio* 19) is eloquent on the subject of consuls from Tusculum.
225 Livy 8.14.2: Sispes may be a more accurate form of the name Sospes: Palmer [202], 18. In the case of shared cults the Roman version became the preferred one: thus Diana of the Aventine ultimately replaced Diana of Aricia: A. D. Momigliano in *RAL* 17 (1962), 387f.
226 *CIL* 10. 6554 (probably genuine: S. Panciera in *Epigraphica* 22 (1960), 9f.).
227 *V.* 222 (which may belong to the late fourth century). Notables from Velitrae who won Roman magistracies in the third century (e.g. C. Octavius Rufus, quaestor in 230) must be descendants of *coloni*.
228 Some Antiates may have contrived to live as pirates: cf. Strabo 5.3.5, p. 232 (who may, however, be referring to the period before 338).
229 But law and order were maintained: Livy 9.20.10. F. De Martino, *Storia della costituzione romana*[2] (Naples, 1973), 2.133f. argues that it was the Roman *colonia*, not the Volscian town, that needed regularizing in 318; but see Sherwin White [208], 81 and Humbert [210], 188f.

230 Colonies (both Citizen and Latin) regularly absorbed the residual natives in this way: Cicero *apud* Ascon. p. 4Cl.; Tac. *Hist.* 3.34.

231 Northern Campania was separated from southern Campania by marshlands along the river Clanis and seemed to form more of a unit with Latium Adjectum. Casilinum is not mentioned, but it must have been reckoned part of Capua (cf. Livy 23.17.7) and was incorporated with it. Cumae and Suessula were incorporated separately: they must be the *pars Samnitium* of Velleius 1.14.3.

232 Capua, in fact, is the only *municipium* of whose administration before the Social War something is known.

233 *V.* 93, 94; Livy 23.2–10; 26.16.9; 32.7.3; 38.28.36; Cicero *De leg. agr.* 1.19; cf. Heurgon [127], 231f.

234 This does not mean, however, that Capua enjoyed with Rome a subtle kind of equal relationship as maintained by Sherwin White [208], 41.51.20if., or reciprocity of the sort that Timoleon arranged between Syracuse and the Sicel states, as suggested by Toynbee [67], 1.197f. The Volsci and Campanians were not like the benighted and distant Aetolians who were ignorant of what *deditio in fidem* meant (cf. Polyb. 20.9.11). They were Rome's neighbours and fully understood that *civitas sine suffragio* was not a 'reciprocal arrangement'; after their loss of the valuable Ager Falernus the Capuani could not have mistaken their own subordination for 'equality of isopolity'.

235 It had public baths two centuries before Rome did; and to judge from the deterioration of Campanian pottery after 338, it could fairly complain that annexation by Rome had shattered its cultural compactness.

236 Livy 9.26.6.

237 The honour was *hospitium publicum* (see Appendix I), and a notable of Fundi, Vitruvius Vaccus, availed himself of it, went to Rome and set himself up in a splendid establishment on the Palatine (but later he persuaded his fellow Fundani to support Privernum against Rome, with dire consequences for himself): Livy 8.19, 20.

238 There is no positive record of misbehaviour by Formiae: but it usually behaved like Fundi and it certainly received the same treatment.

239 The relevant texts are Diod. 19.76.3; Livy 8.23.2; 9.16.2; 9.25.3; 9.43.23; 9.45.7f.; 22.13.2f.; 23.35.3; Dion. Hal. 11.7.4. It is clear that both Pyrrhus and Hannibal counted on winning their support.

240 Livy 23.7.1.

241 F. Castagnoli, *Orthogonal Town Planning in Antiquity* (Cambridge, USA, 1972), 96; J. B. Ward-Perkins, *Cities of Ancient Greece and Italy* (New York, 1974), 27.

242 *ILLRP* 665. Praetors, however, had already made their appearance in other Latin communities before 340: Circeii, Setia (Livy 8.3.9: confirmed by *ILLRP* 663), Lavinium (Livy 8.11.14).

243 Their right to vote in the Tribal Assembly is first recorded in 212, but presumably existed earlier: Livy 25.3.16; cf. Dion. Hal. 8.72.5f.; Appian *B C* 1.23; Humbert [210], 99.

244 *Ius exilii* was the right to grant asylum to those banished from Rome.

245 Livy 27.9; Asconius *In Pison.* 3; Bernardi [18], 64f.

246 Livy implies that non-Latini were always eligible for Latin Colonies and especially after 200 (3.1.7; 33.24.8f.).

247 Praeneste had incorporated eight communities and Tibur two (Livy 6.29.6; 7.18.2; 7.19.1). For their earlier treaties with Rome see Livy 2.19.2; 3.18.5; 7.19.2; Oxyrrhynchus Chron. *ad Ol* 106.3.

248 Pliny *NH* 16.237; Solinus 2.9.

249 Livy 34.57.7f.

250 *ILLRP* 512.

251 E. Badian, *Foreign Clientelae* (Oxford, 1958), 24; Sherwin White [208], 96; W. Dahlheim, *Struktur und Entwicklung des römischen Völkerrechts* (Munich, 1968), 118 n.19.

252 Polyb. 6.14.8; Livy 8.14.9f.; 23.17.8; Appian, *B C* 1.65.

253 The only Latin Colony ever recorded with *ius exilii* is Ardea, well

before 338; G. Grifò, *Ricerche sull'*
'exilium' (Milan, 1961), 1.193f., rejects
the notice.
254 *ILLRP* 60, 111, 573; *ILS* 5396,
6131; cf. Livy (26.8.11), who shows that
it was not a *municipium*.
255 Livy 8.11.3; 8.12.15. (The *de
Lavinieis* of Fasti Triumph. *ad an.* 338 is a
mistake for *de Lanuvineis*: cf. Livy
8.13.5). Brunt [173], 533, n. 4, implies
that Lavinium became a *municipium*: for
this there is no evidence. For its treaty
with Rome see *ILS* 5004, 6183;
Macrobius, *Sat.* 3.4.11; Servius *ad Aen.*
2.296; 3.12.
256 The years 338–334 were 'perhaps
the most constructive lustrum in the
whole long course of Roman constitutional history' (Toynbee [67], 1.139);
but, as Galsterer [14], 22f. points out, the
full exploitation of their novel ideas came
later, when the Romans fully developed
the urban commonwealths and acquired
a clear conception of what they themselves had devised.
257 R. Benedetto *et al.* (edd.), *Roma
medio-repubblicana* (Rome, 1973), 71
no. 46; *ILLRP* 7.
258 *Deleta Ausonum gens* (Livy 9.25.9),
which means that independent Aurunci
disappeared along with their *libertas*.
259 They annexed Satricum (mod.
Boville Ernica) (Livy 9.12.5; 9.16.2), and
made allies of Fabrateria and an
unknown Luca (Livy 8.19.1).
260 Teanum Sidicinum was soon
brought under Roman control (Livy
10.14). Livy (7.30.7) and Dion. Hal.
(15.14.1) both stress the importance of
communications with Campania.
261 At this stage peninsular Italy could
be described as *tota Italia*, although
ancient writers often apply this expression only to the Roman portions of it:
when they mean all Italy including its
non-Roman parts, they prefer the
expression *terra Italia*: Galsterer [14], 37f.
262 Latin Colonies in Umbria prove
that it also lost land. *Coloni* were
numerous on Sabine territory, and on
Samnite (around Venafrum and elsewhere): Humbert [210], 245. Thousands
of Picentes were removed, permanently,

to southern Campania (Strabo 5.4.13,
p. 251; Pliny *NH* 3.70, 110). The
reference to Paeligni depends on a
doubtful reading of Diod. 20.90.3.
263 It is assumed that the *territoria*, that
the Tribes had later, were those that they
received on their creation.
264 But native Sabini did not disappear
to judge from the many Sabine names
found there: Taylor [207], 60.
265 *Praefecti* were not needed in Latium
since court cases there could be decided
in Rome. They are first recorded in
Campania as a consequence of the
creation of the Tribe Falerna in 318 (Livy
9.20.5). The Roman system of
praefecturae has been carefully elucidated
by Humbert [210], 355–402; see, too,
Galsterer [14], 27–36.
266 The evidence for these communities is given in the *RE* entries for
each, in K. J. Beloch, *Römische Geschichte
bis zum Beginn der punischen Kriege*
(Berlin-Leipzig, 1926), 492–697, and in
the documentation meticulously provided by Humbert [210], *passim.*
Anagnia had been deprived of autonomy
on its incorporation (Livy 9.43.24), but
this was only temporary (*ILLRP* 271).
267 *ILS* 3701 (Amiternum), 6543
(Reate). Peltuinum was still called
praefectura in AD 242 (*ILS* 6110).
268 It could be a place of some size:
note Cicero's remarks on Atina (*Pro
Plancio* 21).
269 In common everyday speech it
could be used as the title for a town: so,
for instance, in Plautus, *Casina* 99, 110.
270 It has this meaning in the Lex
Mamilia Roscia (53, 55) and the Tabulae
Heracleenses (83 and often). In a
document of the second century (Lex
Agraria 32) the word *praefectura* is
avoided, for it being substituted the
periphrases *pro coloniis* (meaning
praefecturae centring on a *forum* or *conciliabulum* that were Roman by origin)
and *promunicipiis* (meaning *praefecturae*
centring on a *pagus* or *vicus* that were
Roman by incorporation).
271 Cato fr. 61P.
272 Humbert [210], 313f, 343f.
273 1.14.7. See Taylor [207], 60f.;

Poucet [116], 270, n. 22. (contra P. A. Brunt in Hommages à Marcel Renard (Brussels, 1969), 2.121f.). There was still ager publicus available in the Sabine country in the first century: Cic. De leg. agr. 2.66; Sic. Flaccus, De cond. agr., p. 136L.

274 ILLRP 143, 144, 147; V. 217, 220. The Latin is not yet completely free of oscanisms.

275 Strabo 6.1.6, p. 258. For romanizing policy under the Empire see Tacitus, Hist. 1.11; Ann. 11.19.2f.; 12.32.4 and the Tabula Banasitana 4, 5 (cited in JRS 63 (1973), 86).

276 Taylor [207], 63f. Velleius (2.20) reveals the abiding Roman worry about 'new' citizens outnumbering 'old'.

277 U. Hackl in Chiron 2 (1972), 135–70.

278 Volsci were enrolled for Antium in 338: Livy 8.14.8.

279 Autonomous communities in Italy seem to have had c.2,600 adult, free-born males on the average: Brunt [173], 126. Latin Colonies after the fourth century were regularly larger than this; and Livy (27.9.11) clearly thought that Rome supplied most of the settlers (not all of them, however: see Toynbee [67], 1.251, n. 3 on Ariminum).

280 Their role as protectors of new rustic Tribes may explain why they were usually established two at a time.

281 The townsite at Cosa was little more than thirty acres, and at Aesernia was even smaller: F. E. Brown, Cosa (Ann Arbor, 1980), 10; M. W. Frederiksen in Zanker [163], 342.

282 There are oblique references to a Latin Colony at Castrum Novum in Picenum (Livy, Per. 11; cf. Dion. Hal. 1.14; 2.49., who records, on the authority of Cato and Varro, the building of a road to it by the censor for 247). The Citizen Colony at Castrum Novum in Etruria may have caused the Picentine colony to get overlooked.

283 De leg. agr. 2.73.

284 The figure of 20,000 is actually used of Venusia (Dion. Hal. 17/18.5). For the spread of Latin note Athenaeus 14. p. 632 (Paestum ceases to be Greek-

speaking); ILLRP 504 (which may belong to the fourth century); 505, 506 (effect of the colony at Spoletium). For natives were being elected into the colony see Livy 6.10.5; 6.21.4; Brunt [173], 538f. In less than three generations natives were being elected into the highest offices at Puteoli, a Citizen Colony: ILLRP 518. Sometimes, however, the native inhabitants were driven out: Livy 9.26.1f.; Hor. Sat. 2.1.34f.

285 Except possibly at Ariminum: Badian [251], 292.

286 Pol. 3. 1280a.

287 Some mopping up operations, against the Sallentini, for instance, lasted beyond 268; the 'triumph' over the Sarsinates also came in 266 (but they were hardly in the peninsula).

288 Polyb. 2.35 suggests that against the Gauls they were ready to practise genocide. If so, it failed: Senones were to be found in the Ager Gallicus much later: L. Mercando in Zanker [16], 173f.

289 Pro Balbo 35.

290 Cic., Pro Balbo 21.46.; Livy 8.26.6; 9.36.8; 28.45.20; ILS 432 (=AD 210). 'Equal' allies that fell out with Rome were reduced to 'unequal': Samnites and Picentes are examples.

291 Taylor [207], 86f.

292 Cf. Plutarch, Caesar 11.2.

293 Livy 7.19.20; Cass. Dio 10.33, cf. Zon. 8.4; Aul. Gell. 16.13.7. See too Appendix I. Henceforth inscriptions from Caere are increasingly in Latin; and Etruscan names get latinized.

294 The ingots, that passed by weight, were called aes signatum and were in use very early: an Italian specimen of c.550 has recently been found near Gela in Sicily. Some states started imitating Roman coins early: Latin Cosa and Beneventum, for instance, issued silver coins that copied Rome's didrachms, with head of Mars (or Apollo?) on the obverse and a horse's head on the reverse. See Pliny NH, 33.44 and cf. M. H. Crawford, Roman Republican Coinage (Cambridge, 1974), 1.35f.

295 Italians might try to influence policy and Latini were sometimes

Livy 31.31.5).

312 Cic. *De div*. 1.49; Livy 21.22.6f.; Jacoby [206], 2. 175F.

313 A shrine with Ionic columns had been built there (A. La Regina in Zanker [16], 223f.): it was sacked late in the third century, probably by Hannibal, no respecter of Italian shrines (Livy 26.11.8; H. H. Scullard, *The Etruscan Cities and Rome* (London, 1967), 112).

314 The view of T. Frank, *Economic Survey of Ancient Rome* (1933–40), 1.224f., that Rome supplied the rations for allied troops on active service, is based on a mistaken interpretation of Polyb. 6.39.15.

315 See Crawford [294], 1.33f.

316 The so-called semi-libral, quadrantal, and sextantal reductions (*c*.217, 215, 211 respectively).

317 Roman coins had, of course, been circulating earlier; they are not unknown in third-century Ancona, a Greek community: L. Mercando in Zanker [16], 164f.

318 It punctiliously expiated portents, even those reported from non-Roman Italy, the rule that these were to be disregarded (see Livy 43.13.6) being waived during the Hannibalic crisis. Livy often mentions omens from Latin Colonies, Praeneste and other allies: it is unlikely that they all occurred on Roman *ager publicus*: E. Rawson in *CQ* 21 (1971), 158f. (espec. 163 n. 1).

319 Livy 22.57.6f.; Pliny *NH* 28.12f.; Plutarch *Marcellus*, 3; Oros. 4.13.

320 Livy 22.13.6; 27.28.9; 27.42.5; 28.46.16.

321 Livy (27.9.7) gives thirty as the total. He may have overlooked one (Castrum Novum in Picenum). Cicero (*de orat*. 3.43) remarks that the Latini fostered the language more than the Romans themselves.

322 Not even after the consul for 95 'ransacked the Alps with surgical probes' (Cicero, *in Pis*. 62).

323 The second volume of Toynbee [67], is devoted to this theme.

324 On the increase of transhumant pastoralism see E. Gabba-M. Pasquinucci, *Strutture agrarie e alleva-*

mento transumante nell'Italia Romana (Pisa, 1979), *passim*, and for the survival of small-scale and mixed farming see M. W. Frederiksen in *DArch* 4/5 (1970/71), 339, 357 and J. Frayn, *Subsistence Farming in Roman Italy* (London, 1979), 73–88. Cicero alludes repeatedly to the desolate state of Apulia (*Laelius* 13; *De leg. agr*. 2.71; *Ad Att*. 8.3.4; cf., too, Livy 39.29.8), but not without much rhetorical exaggeration.

325 A wealthy family in second-century Pompeii could afford a mansion (the House of the Faun) larger than the palace of the Attalids at Pergamum.

326 The consul for 196 had his Bruttian slaves flog allied magistrates for failing to care for his provisions properly (Aul. Gell. 10.3.17–19, citing the contemporary Cato). In 184 a praetor condemned 7,000 shepherds as 'brigands' (Livy 39.29.8). Note, too, the remarks of Livy 42.1.8f.

327 Festus p. 33L (who seems to confuse Boii and Insubres). Livy (36.39, 40), Strabo (5.1.6, p. 213) and Pliny (*NH* 3.116) disagree about the number of Boii driven out: it was enough to expedite romanization (Polyb. 10.15). Brixillum may be a better spelling than Brixellum.

328 The adjective 'Cispadane', unlike 'Transpadane', is not found in ancient literature. It is too convenient a term to let go unused.

329 For Copia (Thurii) Rome could not find enough *coloni* and she needed years to gather the initial quota for Aquileia (Livy 35.9.3; 39.55.5; 40.34.2). Cicero (*Pro Caec*. 98) implies that Roman criminals were acceptable as recruits. Non-Romans helped reinforce Narnia and Cosa (Livy 32.2.6f.; 33.24.8f.) and probably Venusia, too, to judge from its oscanization. *Equites* as settlers in Latin Colonies are recorded only after 200: presumably they were intended to secure a safely Roman governing élite and may have been given the equestrian status with its much larger land allotment to induce them to enrol in the colony. For Bononia see Livy 37.57.7f. and Prosdocimi [129], 88, and for the projected second colony Livy 37.47.2.

permitted to discuss military quotas: Livy 27.9; 34.56. But this is far removed from genuine consultation.

296 R. Maulding, *Memoirs* (London, 1978).

297 Didrachms of Locri *c.*282 show Rome being crowned by Fides.

298 Illustrative of this was the Via Curia, built shortly after 290, that linked two notorious enemies, Interamnia and Reate (Dion. Hal. 1.14.)

299 On Cisalpina and its development under the Romans see C. Peyre, *La Cisalpine Gauloise du IIIe au Ier siècle avant J.-C.* (Paris, 1979), 43f. On the widening of Rome's horizon see Cato fr. 85P. Nissen [144], 2.376 stresses the importance of the Appennines: for armies of those days they were as formidable an obstacle as the Alps (Livy 21.58). F. Cassola, *I gruppi politici romani nel III secolo a.C.* (Trieste, 1962), 222 and Harris [202], 199, deny that Rome was seeking an Alpine boundary.

300 *C.*225 (Polyb. 2.24). The alliance may have been imposed on the Cenomani: the Latin Colony of Cremona seems to have been on Cenomanian soil, acquired presumably by conquest.

301 Polyb. 2.24. with the notes of F. W. Walbank, *A Historical Commentary on Polybius* (Oxford, 1957–79), 1.196f. Diod. 25.13, Pliny *NH*, 3.138, and Livy's epitomators (*Per.* 20; Oros. 4.13.6; Eutrop. 3.5) also record the roster, which was not absolutely complete (it takes no account of *socii navales*).

302 The Via Flaminia replaced an earlier Rome–Sena Gallica road and provided communications with the *coloni* who since 232 had been romanizing the Ager Gallicus. It probably linked up with a *via litoranea* along the Adriatic coast.

303 Rome also found military help there: the Cenomani sent them troops for the battle of the river Trebia (Livy 21.55.4).

304 Livy (24.2.8) says that in allied communities the commons were prone to side with Hannibal, the upper classes

with Rome: but he himself give instances to the contrary. Allie[sentiments were fluid, 'shifting now thi[way, now that' (Diod. 26.12.1). Th[Bruttii were the first to rebel (Aul. Gell[10.3.19). For individual Etruscan[serving Hannibal see J. von Ungern[Sternberg, *Capua im zweiten punische[Krieg* (Munich, 1975), 57; and for like[minded Messapii see Livy 21.48.9[24.45.1f.; 26.38.6f. (all of them Dasii[the best-known Messapian *gens*). Th[coin-types of Arretium's war-time issue[indicate pro-Punic sentiment: cf. H. H[Scullard, *The Elephant in the Greek an[Roman World* (London, 1975), 173. Th[loyalty of the Pentri, often denied o[ignored by modern scholars, is explic[itly, if unemphatically, affirmed by Livy[22.61.11.

305 Livy 24.3.9f.; cf.27.35.3f.

306 Silius Italicus, in sedulou[imitation of Virgil *Aen.* 7, gives a long[list of Italian peoples who fought a[Cannae: even the Etruscans were there i[force (8.356–616); but he is scarcely [trustworthy source.

307 *Hann.* 8.

308 The *castra Claudiana* were nea[Suessula rather than in it.

309 B. L. Hallward's expression [*CAH* 8. 56 (cf., too, 34). In 265 t[Mamertini appealed for help on [ground that they were Italians (Poly[1.10); but it is to be noted that Rom[invocation of pan-Italian sentiments[on deaf ears at Capua (Livy 23.5.11f.[

310 Livy 27.9.7f. All of the fait[twelve had been founded before [That they were bled very white s[highly probable: Brunt [173], 57.

311 Casilinum, probably part o[*municipium* of Capua down to 216[to stay loyal and became a se[*praefectura* after the war (Festus p. [The Capuani retained *ius commerci[26.34.9f.), but lost *ius conubii* ur[(Livy 38.36.5f.). Nevertheless [population remained at Capua in[notables who were prominen[affairs: M. W. Frederiksen in *I[(1959), 20f. Some of its building[warehouses (Cic. *De leg. agr.* [

330 Livy 40.38, 41; Pliny *NH* 3.105; *ILS* 6509. Over 40,000 Apuani had to move. But part of the tribe remained in Liguria.

331 Archaeological evidence seems to confirm Livy (40.43.1) and Velleius (1.15.2) for a *colonia* at Luca: P. Sommella–C. F. Giuliani, *La pianta di Lucca romana* (Rome, 1974), *passim*. As it became a *municipium* after 90 (Cic. *Ad fam.* 13.13), it must have been a *colonia Latina*. For the land allotments at Luna see Livy 41.13.5 (emending LIS to VIS); cf. 45.13.10. The two colonies effectively bracketed the Apuani who remained in Liguria.

332 Despite reclamation flooding was still a problem: see Strabo 5.1.11, p. 217; Virg. *Aen.* 11.458; Lucan *Pharsalia* 4.134. As late as AD 603 Brixellum was covered with mud two metres deep.

333 They are listed in E. Ruoff-Väänanen, *Studies on the Italian Fora* (Wiesbaden, 1978).

334 Livy 42.4.3f. Veientes, Capenates and Falisci had participated in a viritane distribution in the early fourth century (Livy 6.4.4), but they had been given Roman citizenship to make them eligible.

335 *ILLRP* 476, 477 (with Degrassi's notes); cf.517; Livy 41.5.5; 41.27.3f.; Cic. *Pro Balbo* 32.

336 Livy 39.22.6; 39.45.6f.; 39.54; 40.34.3; *ILLRP* 324; Strabo 5.1.8, p. 214. For Aquileia as a Gallic name see Pellegrini [129], 88. One of its wards was named after the Celtic god Belenus. For its *territorium*: A. Degrassi, *Il confine nord-orientale dell'Italia romana* (Bern, 1954), 18f.

337 Livy 42.22.6; Pliny *NH* 3.46.

338 See Crawford [294], 266f. 624f. Roman coins circulated even in the 'heel' (Whatmough [86], 325, 339) and are mentioned in the Iguvine Tables (Va, Vb). Greek Velia, however, preferred to use its own coins: A. Greco Pontrandolfo in *AIIN* 18/19 (1971/72), 91–111. The *victoriati* in circulation were actually *quinarii*. Livy throughout Book 45 reflects the growing habit of reckoning sums in *sestertii*.

339 On the roads see *ILLRP* 451–65; *ILS* 5806. No Cassius who could have built the Via Cassia is known earlier than C. Cassius Longinus, the commissioner for the great Cispadane distribution of 173.

340 Forum Lepidi controlled the Cerreto pass across the Appennines. It was also known as Regium Lepidum, probably because its founder had once been tutor to a king (Ptolemy V).

341 How and when the Romans got to Dertona is unknown. Velleius (1.15.5) hesitantly records a post-Gracchan *colonia* there without being able to give its date.

342 *Brutus* 254; cf. G. Gualandi in *PCIA*, 7. 357.

343 Artists had long been attracted to Rome; Novios Plautios, for instance, produced the Ficoroni *cista* there; and the visit of the Greek philosophers Carneades, Critolaus, and Diogenes the Stoic in the second century is famous.

344 For construction in second-century Italy see P. Coarelli in Zanker [16], 21f.

345 A shrine normally belonged to a single *pagus* (*CIL*1². p. 518), but the shrine at Pietrabbondante was clearly supported by many *pagi* (note *V.* 149). The three-*cella* temple temple there was built *c.*100 by a certain Statius, probably to be identified with the man mentioned by Appian *BC* 4.25: see A. La Regina in *PP* (1975), 163f.; Prosdocimi in [55], 1068f. The Messapii also had a non-Capitoline triad: *ILLRP* 54 (latter half of the second century).

346 This, however, also happened elsewhere owing to the proliferation of *municipia* in the first century and the consequent disappearance of old native *pagi*.

347 Roman political practices were also imitated: e.g. the use of collegial magistrates: see C. Letta in *Athenaeum* 57 (1979), 404f.

348 Humbert [210], 347. Proof is lacking. Anagnia apparently had full rights and was registered in the Tribe Poblilia in the second century: Taylor [207], 53. It has been plausibly suggested that the non-Latin names that begin to appear in the Consular Fasti, M. Perperna *cos.* 130 being the first, are due to the upgrading of partial citizens: E. Badian in *DArch* 4/5 (1970/71), 381. Nevertheless, according to Appian (*BC* 1.10), there were still *municipia sine suffragio (isopolitides poleis)* in Gracchan times.

349 Livy 38.36.7f.

350 Taylor [207], 18f.; Humbert [210], 351f.; Plutarch, *Flamininus* 18; Livy 38.28.2; cf. 41.9.9.

351 Samnites and Paeligni moved into Fregellae (Livy 39.3.4f.; 41.8.6f.) and other Samnites into Aesernia (A. La Regina in *DArch* 4/5 (1970/71), 452). Immigration into Rome was on a scale to necessitate additional aqueducts.

352 Statistics about the forces and casualties have been assembled by A. Afzelius, *Die römische Kriegsmacht* (Copenhagen, 1944), 74f.

353 Lucilius 490M. suggests that a Latin might have to serve eighteen years on end (Romans were limited to six).

354 E. Gabba, *Republican Rome: the Army and the Allies* (Berkeley-Los Angeles, 1976), 107f.

355 The figure is reliable, coming from the contemporary Polybius (30.15), and was so huge as to fascinate (Livy 45.34.5; Strabo 7.7.3, p. 322; Plutarch *Aem. Paul.* 29). Nevertheless the daily turnover at the slave market on Delos of 10,000 confirms it. Not all these slaves came to Italy; but then Italy had slaves that did not come from overseas (M. K. Hopkins, *Conquerors and Slaves* (Cambridge, 1979), 140f.). The size of the slave population disquieted some observers (Plut. *Ti. Gracchus* 8; Appian *BC* 1.9).

356 Cicero (*pro Balbo* 31) asserts that the practice of granting the citizenship to individuals was never interrupted (cf. Cic. *Pro Balbo* 55; Livy 26.21.9f.; 27.5.6f.; *SIG* 2.585). Documented examples are comparatively few. Moreover many successfully posed as *cives* who were not (Ascon. p. 68 Cl.; *ILS* 212).

357 C. Nicolet in *JRS* 66 (1976), 20f.

358 Livy 39.3.4f.; 41.8.6f.

359 Rome set the standards of speech (note Cicero's remarks on Lollia, mother-in-law of the consul for 95: *De orat.* 3.45); yet it was Italians who made Latin literature (cf. Cic., *De orat.* 3.43; *Brutus* 169f., 258). Latin became so much the language of law and administration that other Italian tongues imitated it: e.g. Oscan in the Cippus Abellanus (*V.* 1). Outside Italy, however, and even in the ports of Italy (Festus p. 100L), Greek was used in business dealings; on Delos even Roman traders used it: E. Campanile in R. Gusmani (ed.), *La cultura italica* (Pisa, 1978), 106f.

360 Val. Max. 2.2.2: he is probably generalizing from the celebrated incident when an interpreter at Athens translated a terse speech by Cato into prolix and long-winded Greek (see Malcovati, *ORF*[3], Cato 20; Plut. *Cato* 12). But Cato was not the only Roman to insist on the use of Latin: see *SIG* 2.656.

361 Etruscan was not a contender. It was too strange and in any case by the third century was in decline.

362 Aul. Gell. 17.17.1.

363 According to Festus (p. 204L) some Volscian was still spoken in the second century. The suggestion of A. Prosdocimi (in *Conv. Magna Grecia* 15 (1975), 159f.) that Festus' *qui Obsce et Volsce fabulantur* might mean people who spoke Latin with Oscan or Volscian accents and mannerisms is unconvincing.

364 *De finibus* 1.3.7. The *S.C. de Bacchanalibus* of 196 may imply the same thing.

365 P. 34 (latter half of the second century).

366 30,000 Tarentines had been sold into slavery (Plut. *Fab. Max.* 22; cf. Livy 27.16.7). Latin inscriptions first appear at Tarentum in the second century, beginning with a dedication to Artemis-Diana (P. Perez in *Conv. Magna Grecia* 15 (1975), 358). Even Italiote coinage issues become rare after 200.

367 G. Susini, *Fonti per la storia greca e romana del Salento* (Bologna, 1962), 60, 152.

368 The Latin Colonies at Carseoli and Alba Fucens helped to eliminate Aequian and no doubt also affected Marsic. Latin replaced Faliscan on inscriptions at Falerii Novi *c*.150: *V*. 330; *ILLRP* 192, 238 (all with Faliscanisms).

369 Examples: Tomba del Tifone, Tomba dei Festoni. P. Bruun (*et al*.), *Studies in the Romanization of Etruria* (Rome, 1975) is particularly useful for the disappearance of Etruscan.

370 *V*. 240, 240a; Torelli in Zanker [16], 174 (an unpublished Latin inscription from Monterinaldo in Picenum).

371 Cic. *Brutus* 171f., *Ad Att*. 7.3.10; *In Pis*. 53; Ascon. p.4 Cl. Horace, *Sat*. 1.10.36f.; 2.5.40f. See, too, L. A. Holland, *Lucretius and the Transpadanes* (Princeton, 1979), 21f.

372 Polyb. 2.17.5; 2.35.4. Cremona was a noted educational centre.

373 J. Whatmough in *CPh* 29 (1934), 282; G. Fogolari in *PCIA* 4. 119f.

374 Formulaic sepulchral inscriptions are not trustworthy indicators of everyday language: *requiescat in pace* is common on modern tombstones.

375 On Ancona see L. Mercando in Zanker [16], 175. Sabelli readily took to Greek on Delos and to the Latin alphabet in southern Italy, and latinisms are common in Paelignian inscriptions: E. Campanile in Gusmani [359], 105, 107f., 117f. A sling bullet used at Asculum in 90 is inscribed in Venetic: Pellegrini [129], 121.

376 The upgrading of *cives sine suffragio* reinforced this, since the partial citizens had served as a sort of bridge between Romans and allies.

377 After the battle of Aquilonia in 293 some captured spoils were distributed to the *coloniae* and allied states (Livy 10.46. 8); and the so-called *tituli Mummiani* are well known (*ILLRP* 122, 321, 326–30, 332, 335, 338–40).

378 Cicero, *Pro Font*. 41. He usually calls the war, in which he himself fought, *bellum Italicum*; and it is due to this circumstance that modern scholars refer to speakers of Osco-Umbrian languages as Italici, since the *socii* who fought Rome were precisely these.

379 The expression *consortium imperii* is taken from Justin (38.4.13), who excerpted Pompeius Trogus, a contemporary of survivors of the war. Strabo (5.4.2, p. 241), Velleius (2.15; 2.17) and Appian (*BC* 1.21, 34, 39) also make it clear that the allies wanted partnership. Cf., too, E. Badian, *Roman Imperialism in the Late Republic* (Pretoria, 1967), 40f.; 60; 72f.; 84.

380 Aristocratic control of the military tribunate had already weakened: Harris [202], 13f. And in 130 an Etruscan, M. Perperna, even became consul (*MRR, ad an*.).

381 Clear evidence of this are the deliberate archaisms in the famous Herentas inscription of the Paeligni (*V*. 213): Prosdocimi [363], 159f.

382 Cispadane Ravenna, for example, was still a *populus foederatus* with *ius exilii* in 51 (Cic. *Ad fam*. 8.1.4; Taylor [207], 124, n. 19).

383 Appian *BC* 1.49; Sisenna p. 17P.

384 For Sulla's Etruscan supporters see E. Rawson in *JRS* 68 (1978) 149f. It was the lower orders in Etruria that felt his vengeance: Gran. Licin. fr.34 Fl.; Sallust *Hist*. 1.65M.

385 No definitive list of Sulla's colonies is possible: as he demobilized twenty-three legions it is tempting to argue that he founded twenty-three *coloniae*. Recently evidence has been found for a Sullan *colonia* at Privernum (M. Cancellieri in *RAL* 29 (1974), 245) and perhaps for one at the otherwise unknown Firmum Apulum (*ILLRP* 592). His colony at Urbana ended up by becoming a *pagus* of Capua (Pliny *NH* 41.62).

386 There is no reason to doubt the existence of such 'double' communities: epigraphic and archaeological evidence exists for Interamnia Praetuttiorum (*ILLRP* 617, 618; A. La Regina in *Enciclopedia d'Arte Antica* 6. 712); and for Arretium note Pliny *NH* 3.52.

387 The figure is impossibly high. Brunt [173], 305 suggests *c*.80,000.

388 Eutropius (5.9) and Orosius (5.22.4) both give the figure as 'about 200'. Cf. Appian *BC* 1.103.

389 The Statius who built the large temple at Pietrabbondante (see n. 345) may have been elevated by Sulla: R. Syme, *The Roman Revolution* (Oxford, 1939), 88. The ancient canard that Sulla put common soldiers in the Senate is absurd. Communities that lost notables to the Senate were seriously weakened.

390 Some communities were not constituted as *municipia* before his day: e.g. Veii (*municipium Augustum Veiens: ILS* 6582) or Marsic Marruvium (A. La Regina in *Convegno sulla Città* (Bologna, 1966), 193, n. 29). For the Sabine *praefecturae* see below. It was in Augustus' reign apparently that the thoroughgoing subdivision of municipal *territoria* into *pagi* occurred (Frederiksen in Zanker [16], 348f.).

391 Its romanization is revealed by the literary activity there: Catullus, the *poetae novi*, Catius Insuber, Cornelius Nepos, Masurius Sabinus, Alfenus Varus, not to mention Virgil and Livy, were all from Cisalpina.

392 *Coloni* were sent to Comum, Tergeste and Forum Julium: Comum, in fact, is said to have had 8,000 *coloni* although how its small *territorium* could accommodate that number is a mystery. These places, like *coloniae* of old, were clearly *propugnacula*: they were bastions against Raeti and others (note Strabo 5.1.6, p. 213).

393 Native coinages ceased there in 89; its first governor was M. Fonteius in 74 (Sallust *Hist.* fr. 98M.).

394 Cicero *Pro Balbo* 21.

395 W. Seston in *CRAI* (1977), 529f. The same suggestion was made much earlier by E. G. Hardy, *Six Roman Laws* (Oxford, 1911), 161, n. 23.

396 *ILS* 6468, 6469 (Petelia); *ILS* 6125 (Interamna Lirenas), 6359 (Pompeii), 6518 (Gnathia, or possibly Aesernia). There is no ancient authority for calling such enabling acts *leges datae*. From the Lex Tarenti it looks as if communities were bluntly told to institute *quattuorviri* (or in some cases *duoviri*); cf., too, Cic. *Ad Att.* 5.2.3. But to judge from Bantia (see below), they had more than a little to say about their constitutions.

397 *Pro Milone* 20, *In Pisonem* 41 (and frequently elsewhere). *ILS* 212 shows that there were still unurbanized Italians down to the reign of Tiberius.

398 Changes may also have been made in existing *municipia*: it may have been now that the *municipium* at Capena was enlarged by the addition of nearby communities (cf. *CIL* 11. p. 570).

399 There was a *municipium* near Frigento (*in Hirpinis*) whose name is unknown (*ILLRP* 598, 599). There were equally anonymous *municipia* in upper Italy (M. Corradi-Cervi in *Archivio storico per le provincie parmensi*³, 1 (1938) 117–26).

400 On constitutional variety after 90 see De Martino [229], 370 and on the flexibility of the local magistrates G. Tibiletti in *RSA* 3 (1973), 188f.

401 *ILS* 6584 (cf. Pliny *NH* 3.52) (Forum Clodii), 6110 (Peltuinum); despite *ILS* 6529 there is no certainty that Peltuinum ever became a true *municipium*: *CIL* 9, p. 324.

402 *Lib. Col.* p. 231, 233L: both places became quattuorviral *municipia*.

403 *ILLRP* 552 (Aufidena), 562a, 563 (Casinum) (all with Degrassi's comments); *V.* 2 (Bantia).

404 *Pro Plancio* 19, 20 suggest that Atina was changing from *praefectura* to *municipium c.*54; *Pro Vareno* frs. 3, 4 imply the same for Fulginiae. Caesar *BC* 1.15 shows that Labienus prepared Cingulum for municipalization shortly before 49.

405 *ILS* 6543 (Reate), 6552 (Nursia), 3701, 6545 (Amiternum). For Trebula see Humbert [210], 229f.

406 Letta [145], 45f.

407 Cicero *Pro Cluentio* 25 (Larinum); *V.* 29, 30, *ILLRP* 643, 644 (Pompeii: cf. *ILLRP* 640, the earliest Pompeian inscription in Latin); *ILLRP* 615 (Interamna Nahars). But the list of early *municipia Italiae splendidissima* in Florus (2.9.27) is unreliable.

408 Forum Novum (*CIL* 9, p. 453) and Interamnia Praetuttiorum (Front. *Corp. Agrim.* p.7f. Thulin) were respectively a *forum* and a *conciliabulum* converted into *municipia*. The celebrated Forum Appii, however, was a *forum* that did not become a *municipium*. Synoecism of *pagi* is illustrated by Aufidena (*CIL* 9, p. 259), Superaequum (*CIL* 9, p. 311) and the communities with names like Duopagi, Septempagi etc. Examples of synoecism of *vici* are Amiternum (*ILLRP* 531, 532) and Res Publica Aequiculorum (*CIL* 9, p. 388) which never acquired a true urban centre, Nersae being a mere hamlet: Nissen [144], 462. Territory was apparently taken away from Tarquinii for Blera, Tuscana and Surrina; from Capena for Lucus Feroniae and Civitas Sepernatium; and from Heraclea for Grumentum. Caudium exceptionally seems to have been allotted hardly any *territorium*.

409 *V.* 2; H. Galsterer in *Chiron* 1 (1971), 191f. Bantia had perhaps been part of Venusia and was taken from that Latin Colony when it opposed Rome in the Social War. Like Venusia it numbered *tribuni plebis* among its local magistrates and like contemporary Rome it prescribed a *cursus honorum* for the latter. That it became a duoviral *municipium* is proved by *CIL* 9, p. 418 which wrongly prints *IIIIvir* for *IIvir*: see M. Torelli in *Arch Class* 21 (1969), 2–17.

410 See, for example, *Ad fam.* 11.1; 13.4; 13.7; 13.11.

411 L. Bove in *Labeo* 13 (1967), 22–48; J. Martin in *Hermes* 98 (1970), 72–96. Apparently the municipal courts were only loosely related to the praetor's court in Rome until Augustus intensified standardization.

412 The Lex Rubria tried to do this for Cisalpine Gaul: see F. J. Bruna's edition of this law together with the Fragmentum Atestinum (Leiden, 1972). But a bronze inscription (? from Sedulia-Vadargate), found during World War II, suggests that it was not completely successful: see V. Arangio-Ruiz and A. Vogliano in *Athenaeum* 20 (1940), 1–10, with the textual corrections suggested by Degrassi [32], 1.593f. (The text can now be found in E. Malcovati (ed.), *Imp. Caes. Aug. Operum Fragmenta*[4] (Turin, 1960), XVIII–XXV, 49f.

413 *ILS* 140.

414 It remained a war theatre, however. Raeti assaulted Comum in the first century (Strabo 5.1.6, p. 213), and a proconsul was to be found at Mediolanium in 25 (Suet., *De rhet.* 6). The invasion of the Cimbri had strengthened pro-Roman sentiment.

415 *Aeneid* 12. 837.

416 M. Volponi, *Lo sfondo italico della lotta triumvirale* (Genoa, 1976), 85f., has attempted to identify them.

417 Appian *BC* 4.3. The list of victim cities was subject to change: Appian *BC* 4.86.

418 Appian, *BC* 5.12, 22, 27; Dio 47.14; 48.6; 48.9. The suggestion that Lucius Antonius' operations at Perusia (42/41) represented Italy rising against Rome for the last time (Syme [380], 208) is unconvincing: there it was a case of country dwellers, 'old' Romans as well as 'new', protesting against Octavian's confiscations. See, too, Volponi [416], 90, 123f. There is no evidence of Italian separatism, unless it be in Cicero's allusions to Italians' indifference to Rome (*Ad Att.* 7.7; 8.13; *Pro Cluentio* 56), with which contrast his asseverations about pro-Roman sentiment in the *municipia* and especially among the tribal Marrucini (*Phil.* 5.23; 7.27).

419 The fusion was particularly noticeable amongst the troops (and every year between 80 and 30 at least one tenth of all adult Italians were under arms). All the soldiers had the same outlook and the same aims: pay; booty, land and, above all, peace (note how they repeatedly sought to bring Antony and Octavian together: Appian, *BC* 5.57, 64; Dio 48.37.2). After 89 their officers were just as likely to be 'new' Romans as 'old': J. Suolahti, *The Junior Officers of the Roman Army* (Helsinki, 1955), *passim*.

420 Strabo (6.1.2, p. 254): he was a contemporary. At Bantia an augural shrine was built that conformed exactly in size and orientation to Roman prescriptions: M. Torelli *RAL* 21 (1966), 1–23; 24 (1969), 39f.

421 Tacitus, *Ann.* 15.33. Spartacus' operations had been fatal to hellenism in most of Magna Graecia (cf. Strabo 6.1.2, p. 253).

422   *PID* 2.556 may be later than AD 1. But note the remarks of C. Santoro in *PCIA* 6. 933f.

423   *V.* 236.

424   Bruun [369], especially 85f. A possibly post-Augustan inscription in Etruscan, adduced by M. Cristofani in *SE* 38 (1970), 288, is the exception to prove the rule.

425   Veneti adopted Roman *praenomina* and latinized their *gentilicia*: M. Lejeune, *Ateste à l'heure de la romanisation* (Florence, 1978), *passim*.

426   Cicero's *De oratore* (set in 91) and *Brutus* (set in 46) imply that normally upper class Italians not only knew Latin, but were fluent in it.

427   Note Cicero, *Phil.* 3.15 and cf. Velleius 2.127: lack of lineage was no barrier to political preferment.

428   *Res Gestae* 25.2. This document was first published in AD 14. It may have been composed in 2 BC.

429   Suet. *Aug.* 17 (Bononia); Tibiletti [183], 122 (Ariminum); Placentia had to cede territory to Veleia (*CIL* 11, p. 205); Nursia had strongly opposed Octavian in 42 (Suet. *Aug.* 12; Dio 48.13.14). For persecution of Antonian supporters after Actium see Dio 49.14.5; 51.2.5f.; 51.4.6; cf. T. Mommsen, *Gesammelte Schriften* 5.229.

430   The expression of J. M. Carter, *The Battle of Actium* (London, 1970), 196.

431   T. P. Wiseman in *Historia* 14 (1965), 333.

432   Cic. Ad Att. 16.11.6 reveals that in 44 Octavian found his support in country towns like Cales and Teanum.

433   Syme [389], 372f.

434   Note, too, Propertius 3.11.41 with its insistence on the pan-Italian nature of Rome's religion. Not that Propertius was very enthusiastic about Augustus.

435   *Annals* 1.1.

436   Non-Roman weights, measures and coins now begin to disappear: Dio 52.30.9. Thus the *mensa ponderosa* at Pompeii (see n. 49) was modified to this end (Prosdocimi [55], 870).

437   E. A. Judge in J. A. S. Evans (ed.)

Polis and Imperium (Toronto, 1974), 279–311.

438   Italians automatically became members of the Order if they served in their municipalities as *tribuni militum a populo* (a title that seems to have been honorary and confined to Italy): C. Nicolet, *L'ordre équestre* (Paris, 1966), 68f.

439   *ILS* 206.

440   *RG* 16, 28.2.

441   Suet. *Aug.* 46.

442   J. B. Ward-Perkins (with A. Boethius), *Etruscan and Roman Architecture* (Harmondsworth, 1970), 151f.

443   Oscan is also found on some brick stamps: P. Mingazzini in *RAL* 25 (1970), 403.

444   They must not be confused with the subdivisions that the Romans called *pagi*: see n. 56.

445   Aulus Gellius 15.7.

446   R. Syme in *SBAW* (1974), Abt. 7, 3–34; cf. the same scholar's *History in Ovid* (Oxford, 1978), 25f.

447   *RG* 35: for the day and month see J. Gagé, *Res Gestae Divi Augusti* (Paris, 1950), 147f.

448   S. Weinstock, *Divus Julius* (Oxford, 1971), 200f.

449   *Augustus* 58.

450   For the role of Messalla see Suet., *Aug.* 58.3; Tac. *Ann.* 4.34; and cf. Syme [389], 411, 512. Similarly, when Octavian was seeking the name Augustus in 27, an ex-republican, L. Munatius Plancus, was chosen to propose it.

451   As the emperor Claudius was to point out: *ILS* 212.

452   Dio 55.13.4; 55.25.5.

453   It is difficult to discover what determined the boundaries for the eleven Regions. Sometimes they seem to coincide with geographic, ethnic or historical frontiers, but by no means invariably: R. Thomsen, *The Italic Regions* (Copenhagen, 1947), *passim*. This organization, however, enabled Augustus to give the name Italia to the whole country; and Gallia as the name for its Cisalpine section disappears.

454 6.4.2, p. 188: Strabo, born perhaps in the same year as Augustus, wrote these words shortly after his death.

455 As Seneca (*Ad Helviam* 7) points out, *ubicumque vicit Romanus, habitat.*

456 Evidence for this has been found recently at Pietrabbondante: an inscribed tile of *c.*95 reveals an Oscan-speaking master with a Latin-speaking slave: *P.* 21; cf. Prosdocimi 55, 843f.

457 See for example Livy 24.3.11 (on Croton), Velleius 1.4.2 (on Neapolis). For the importance of literacy to a society see M. I. Finley, *The Ancient Greeks* (New York, 1963), 13.

458 Note Polyb. 11.19.4; Livy 23.5.11, 13; 24.3.12 (in all of which passages law is placed ahead of language). According to Humbert [210], 376, 'la juridiction était le seul facteur de romanisation.'

459 Cic. *Cato Maior* 41: the date is given as 349, probably to lend verisimilitude to a fiction.

460 H. Kohn, *The Idea of Nationalism* (New York, 1945), 6: 'Before the age of nationalism, the spoken language was in no way regarded as a political or cultural factor, still less as an object of political or cultural struggle.'

461 *ILS* 157, 212; A. Degrassi (ed.), *Inscr. Italiae* XIII. 3; Livy 10.38.6; Dion. Hal. 2.49.4; Pliny *NH* 16.237; Suet. *Aug.* 1; Censorinus, *De die nat.* 17.5; Harris [133], 29; Benedetto [257], 278f.; Torelli [130], *passim*; T. J. Cornell in *Ann. Sc. Norm. Pisa,*[3] 6 (1976) 411f.; L. Bonfante in *AJAH* 3 (1978), 136f.

462 In the Social War, for instance, the insurgents hoped for the support of the Dioscuri just as much as the Romans did.

463 R. Bianchi Bandinelli, *Rome, the Centre of Power* (London, 1970), 30.

464 Augustus himself said *simus* for *sumus*: Suet. *Aug.* 87.

465 U. von Wilamowitz Moellendorff in *RFIC* 4 (1926), 1–18.

466 R. Syme, *Colonial Elites* (London, 1958), 1–22.

467 Sherwin White [208], 58f., followed by Galsterer [14], 64f., who suggests that *oppida civium Romanorum* were at first called *municipia* in 188.

468 It could equally well mean 'one who assumes functions'.

469 Livy 8.14.2. The words of Festus p. 155L (*qui post aliquot annos cives Romani effecti sunt*) apply only to the Tusculani.

470 Livy 23.20.2.

471 They possessed neither a *civitas* of their own nor in effect that of Rome; thus they had lost *libertas.*

472 Aul. Gellius 16.13.7; Livy 8.14.10. For the *tabulae Caerites* (not *Caeritum*) see in addition Horace *Epp.* 1.6.62 (*Caerite cera*) and Strabo 5.2.3, p. 220 (*hai deltoi Kairetanon*, without a definite article before *Kairetanon*).

473 This has been well pointed out by M. Sordi, *I rapporti romanoceriti* (Rome, 1960), 110f. Conceivably many Caeretans went to Rome *c.*386 to help with the rebuilding after the Gallic sack.

474 *Année Épigraphique* (1967), 239.

475 Livy (5.50) says that Rome rewarded the Caeretans after the Gallic sack with *hospitium publicum*, for which see Polyb. 3.22.10; 3.24.12 (Carthage); Caesar, *BG* 1–31 (Aedui); Justin 43.5.10 (Massilia); Brunt [173], 516; Humbert [210], 139f. Presumably it was reciprocal.

476 Livy 8.11.6.

477 The date suggested by M. Humbert in *MEFR* 84 (1972), 231–68. E. Ruoff-Väänen In Bruun [369], suggests *c.*309, which is quite unconvincing.

478 Livy 24.18.9.

479 It is just as plausible to argue, with Brunt [173], 20, 25, 515f., that the registers were called Caerite Tables because Caere was the last community to be integrally incorporated with *civitas sine suffragio.*

480 Strabo (5.2.3, p.220) had also noted the incongruity much earlier.

481 Livy 9.6.7; 9.7.1; 23.5.1, 9 and especially 31.31.11; Diod. 19.76.4.

482 Livy 26.16.10. For the *praefecti* see also *ILS* 6127; Velleius 2.44.4; and F. Sartori, *Conv. Campi Flegrei* (1977), 149–71.

483 A. Piganiol, *La conquête romaine*[5], (Paris, 1967), 186f.; but see C. Nicolet, *Rome et la conquête du monde mediterranéen* (Paris, 1977), 275.

484 Livy 28.45.13f.; Tacitus, *Annals*

1.79 (where Nipperdey emends *sociorum* into *maiorum*).

485 Dionysius of Halicarnassus is more likely to call them *isopolitai* (15.7. 4: but see 15.13.2), which was not a synonym for *symmachi* (Appian *BC* 1.21). Polybius, well aware of the difficulty of finding the right word for a Roman technical expression (see 20.9.10–12), avoids any mention of *cives sine suffragio*.

486 Livy 9.20.5 (=318): at that stage no doubt the *praefecti* concerned themselves primarily with the *coloni* settled on the Ager Falernus.

487 J. Heurgon, *The Rise of Rome to 264 B.C.* (London, 1973), 203. Coins issued in the name of Capua appeared before 340: N. K. Rutter, *Campanian Coinages, 475–300 B.C.* (Edinburgh, 1979), 81f. The coins of 216–211 have Oscan legends (to advertise Capua's sovereign independence?), but the types and weights are Roman (with which the Capuani were familiar?). Cumae and Suessula also issued coins before 340 and, significantly, ceased to do so after that date.

488 *Ann.* 5.174 Vahlen.

489 Polyb. 1.7.7–12; 1.10.4: cf. Val. Max. 2.7.15.

490 Admittedly Marcellus' 'triumph' was of the second-class *ovatio* variety (*MRR* 1. 274).

491 In this connection the accounts of Caesar's 'triumphs' after Munda are relevant: Suet., *Jul. Caes.* 178; Plut., *Caes.* 56.

492 E.g. G. De Sanctis, *Storia dei Romani*[2] (Florence, 1960), 2.273; The suggestion that *gentes* like the Decii and Atilii were from Capua (F. Münzer, *Römische Adelsparteien und Adelsfamilien* (Stuttgart, 1920), 59f.), is not convincing.

493 That the Capuani resented their exclusion is shown by their demand for one of the two consulships in 216 (Livy 23.6.6f.).

494 Livy 23.31.10f.

495 See Livy 8.11.16; 23.4.7f.; 31.31.11.

496 Valuable recent discussion of the formula will be found in V. Ilari, *Gli*

italici nelle strutture militari romane (Milan, 1974), 57–85, and Brunt [173], 545f.

497 Livy 27.10.3.

498 Toynbee [67], 1. 427f.

499 Livy 29.15.6, 12; cf. 41.8.8.

500 Livy 34.56.6; cf. Polyb. 6.21.4.

501 The expression seems to mean the whole of Italy. The phrase *tota Italia* is avoided, presumably because of its ambiguity: more often than not it seems to have meant the whole of Roman Italy (Galsterer [14], 37f.).

502 Livy 28.45.20; Toynbee [67], 1.264.

503 The *socii navales* are searchingly examined by A. Milan in *CS* 10 (1973), 193–221. A key passage for them is Livy 36.42.2. Evidently some allies were required to provide either military or naval aid (or possibly both), as circumstances demanded (the Sallentini for instance: Polyb. 2.24.11; Livy 42.48.7).

504 The Italiotes not only did not wear it: they despised it (Appian *Hann.* 7.2).

505 Festus p. 117L.

506 T. Mommsen, *Römisches Staatsrecht* (Leipzig, 1887), 3.586f.; cf. A. Bernardi in *Athenaeum* 16 (1938), 250.

507 Cf. Polyb. 6.21.4. Capua down to 216 evidently maintained a list of its burgesses, and Caere had a *censor perpetuus* (*ILS* 6577, 6578).

508 Livy 10.26.14: *Per.* 12, 15; Dion. Hal. 20.1.5; 20.4.2. The *legio Campana* may have been composed of volunteers.

509 Polyb. 2.24.5, 14.

510 On the names Falerii Veteres and Falerii Novi see Varro *LL* 5. 111, 162; Dion. Hal. 1.21; Strabo 5.2.9, p. 226; Ptol. 3.1.150; and I. De Stefano Manzella in *RPAA* 49 (1976/77), 151–62.

511 *ILLRP* 192 with Degrassi's comments.

512 The tufa enceinte reminds one of the Servian Wall; the towers resemble those in the nearly contemporary but polygonal walls of Cosa.

513 Spoletium also helped to protect the *territorium* of the simultaneously created Tribe Velina.

514 E.g. Bernardi [506], 239–79.

515 Livy 22.1, 11; Plut. *Fab. Max.* 2; Orosius 4.15.1; *ILLRP* 47, 238, 582.

516 Polyb. 1.65.2; cf. Livy 7.38.1.

517 Note particularly Livy 43.13.6 (*in loco peregrino*).

518 *Amores* 3.13. The Romans may even have added a temple or two of their own, to Janus for example.

519 Livy 40.42.13.

520 Mommsen [506], 588.

521 Livy 38.28.1f.; 38.36.5f.

522 Livy 38.36.7f. The upgrading was opposed presumably because of apprehension that the Tribes Aemilia and Cornelia would pass under 'Volscian' control once Formiae-Fundi and Arpinum were added to them: Taylor [207], 93, 307f.: Toynbeé [67], 1. 405 n. 1.

523 Velleius 1.4.2.

524 Livy 38.36.10.

525 It was the year of the Lex Villia Annalis (defining the eligibility of magisterial candidates) and of the first pair of plebeian consuls (one of whom had had to get adopted into a patrician family to ensure his election).

526 Oscan, however, was still spoken at Cumae in 180: *V*. 3.

527 *ILLRP* 530, 532 (from Amiternum), 533 (from Anagnia) suggest that communities of partial citizenship needed no particular authorization.

528 Livy 40.51.9; cf. G. W. Botsford *The Roman Assemblies* (London-New York, 1909), 85, n. 3, 354f. Fulvius had already shown a disposition to register non-Romans by his enrolment of Ennius in a Citizen Colony (which, so far as is known, Ennius never actually joined).

529 Livy 41.8.6: cf. 39.3.4f.; 41.9.9.

530 Strongly advocated by Rudolph [56], 90f.

531 Duoviral Aceruntia and Caiatia (*ILLRP* 521, 559; cf. Humbert [210], 264) seem earlier than Caesar and quattuorviral Marruvium and Reate (*CIL* 9. 3694, 4686) certainly later.

532 F. Sartori, *Problemi di storia constituzionale italiota* (Rome, 1953), 157 (invalidated by Herculaneum which had a single *meddix tuticus* before 91 and *duoviri* after it: *V*. 107, *Année Épigr.* (1960), 277).

533 Letta [145], 49–72.

534 Aquinum and the unknown *municipium* near Frigento (*ILLRP* 544, 598), for example, both became quattuorviral.

535 Letta [145], 60; cf. 56, 59.

536 *V*. 236 (with the comments of Letta [406], 52, 60); *P*. 3 (first half of second century?).

537 The standardization may have been largely one of terminology, and even there far from total: Trebula Mutuesca and Nursia after their municipalization continued to refer to their chief magistrates as *octoviri: Année Épigr*. (1972), 153; *ILS* 6551.

538 For a list of them, probably incomplete, see Beloch 266, 508f., and Sartori [532], 157, n. 1. On this theory it is obvious why so many of the *municipia* constituted later under the Roman Empire were duoviral.

539 For the eagerness of municipal magistrates to parade the title *praetor* see Cic. *De leg. agr*. 2.92; Hor. *Sat*. 1.5.34; *ILLRP* 611; *CIL* 10, 3923, 4657, 6193.

540 Aul. Gell. 16.13.8 is eloquent on *coloniae* as extensions of Rome.

541 On the poor repute of the Citizen Colonies see Livy 8.14.8 (fourth century); 10.21.10 (third century); 39.23.3 (second century); Cic. *Pro Sulla* 61; Gran. Licin. p. 34Fl.; Pliny, *NH* 52. The colonial status after 42 of Perusia (certainly) and of Sutrium (probably) was a degradation: cf. Dio 48.14, App. *BC* 5. 31, Strabo 5.2.9, p. 226.

542 'Because of the greatness and majesty of the Roman People', according to Aul. Gell. 16.13.9.

543 Aul. Gell. 16.13.5.

544 Degrassi [32], 1. 165, 116, 112, 117.

545 *ILS* 6224 (Fidenae), 409; 5770, 6588 (Capena). On the expression *municipium foederatum* see P. Veyne in *Latomus* 19 (1960), 429f. Consider, too, the pride with which Camerinum advertised its ancient *foedus aequum* as late as the third century AD (*ILS* 432). Even titular *coloniae* sought to make their former independence obvious, Aventicum even going so far as to style itself *colonia foederata* (*CIL* 13. 5089).

546 Fidenae: *ILS* 5943 and Livy 4.34; Veii: *ILS* 6579, 6580 and Livy 5.21; Verulae: *ILS* 6268, *Lib. Col.* p. 68L, and Humbert [210], 213 n. 22; Herculaneum: *Année Épigr.* (1960), 277, Velleius 2.16 and Sisenna fr. 54.

547 *CIL* 11. 1 p. 350.

548 *Année Épigr.* (1969/70), 132; (1972), 94. The Lex Tarenti 7, 9, 12, 39 refers to the possibility of *quattuorviri* at Tarentum; but the language is formulaic, of the type to be found in any enabling act for the constitution of a *municipium*.

INDEX

Names mentioned only casually in the text are not listed. The numbers refer to pages of the text, unless preceded by either the letter N or the letter P, in which cases they refer to notes or illustrations respectively. Modern names of towns or rivers are italicized.